Trekking

in the

Jordanian
Dead Sea Rift

Itai Haviv

Desert Breeze
Press

Website: www.desertbreeze-press.com
E-mail: Info@desertbreeze-press.com

Maps © Itai Haviv
Drawings © Gali Richler-Grebler
Color photographs by
Noya Shiloni, Haim Anner, Ittai Glaich, Elik Chudi, Avi Blum, Lior Weiss, Doron Shlittner, Onn Crouvi, Avraham Izdarechet, Yehoram Doron, Itai Haviv (I. H.)
Satellite imagery © 2000 ROHR Productions Ltd. and C.N.E.S
Cover design by Noya Shiloni
Front cover: Wadi Hasa. Photograph by Noya Shiloni

ISBN 965-90315-0-5

From the author

Having watched the Jordanian Dead Sea Rift for a long time from the Israel side, I longed for the day I could get to roam through its landscapes. When peace arrived in 1994 the first thing I did was to have coffee in downtown Amman.

From that moment onwards I was captured by the beauty of this land and its people. I trekked and guided through the Rift for six years, and the more I came to know it, the keener my desire to thoroughly explore it grew. After finishing my Geology and Environmental studies I set off for one year of day-to-day exploration.

The excitement of hiking without knowing what lies behind the next bend in the canyon was addictive. Though the maps promised rugged topography, I could never have imagined so much natural beauty. Every day brought new canyons, summits, springs and waterfalls. There were fascinating encounters with Bedouin and enchanting nights of hospitality and storytelling. It is amazing that a region as spectacular as the Dead Sea Rift has remained unknown to hikers until the late years of the 20th century.

I have seen the sparkle in the eyes of those who trek through the region for the first time. I hope that the same is going to happen to you.

Thanks

Many people deserve my gratitude for helping this book to be written. Thanks are due:

To Nabih Riyal who runs a Jordanian adventure travel company and went out of his way in providing help. To Abdul-Razzaq from Dana Nature Reserve for supplying useful information. To Najdi Qasrawi for his constant support. To 'Abd el 'Aziz for his friendship, to 'Ali and Salma Libad for their hospitality, to 'Awad Abu Muhammad and Sabah Abu 'Ali who always welcomed me in their tents, to 'Ali and Muhammad Jmeidi, to Muhammad and Hassan en-Najadat, to Sabah and Suleiman Sweilem. To many other people of the desert who were kind and hospitable beyond imagination.

Special thanks to Nadav Khalifa who participated in several of the expeditions and went over all of the manuscript. To Tzvia Schweitzer, Asi Haviv, Rony Ben Ziony, Chaim Ben David, Meir Avraham, Yoav Derdikman, Dan Peri, Menachem Markus, Gidon Perlman, Ami Mazar, Eli Raz and Mimi Ron for their valuable remarks. To Yaron Avin for his support. To Dr. Amit Maliar for going over the chapter on First Aid. To Yoav Silberstein for his help. To Lior Enmar.

To all those who participated in the treks, checked the route descriptions and gave useful advice.

To Gali Richler-Grebler for her drawings.

To Danny Esquenazi for drawing the maps.

To Dr. Richard Cleave and ROHR Productions Ltd. for providing the satellite imagery via Dr. John K. Hall.

To all those who contributed their photographs.

To my editor Ithamar Perath.

And last but not least many thanks to my wife Noya for letting me get on with it. She was with me up mountains and down canyons in the Rift, as well as before the computer. To my mother Yedida for helping her son's dream come true.

Dedication

This book is dedicated to Yael Shiloni, forever curious and exploring.

Itai Haviv is a hiker and environmentalist. His extensive desert guiding experience includes Sinai, the Judean and Negev Deserts, and Jordan.

Contents

The mountains of Rajef and Humeima

Map list

Introduction

The Dead Sea Rift is a deep scar in the crust of the earth, whose Jordanian section includes some of the world's most rugged desert landscapes, as well as the lowest place on the earth's continents. Its winding canyons are only now beginning to be revealed, offering the trekker untamed desert wilderness with endless possibilities for exploration, well off the beaten track.

Over a short horizontal distance the altitudes range from 1,700 m above sea level to 400 m below, with numerous deep canyons carving their way from the elevated highlands to the deep bottom of the Rift. Sculptured in many varieties of rock, the landscape offers a richness of hues and shapes.

Although most of the region is arid desert, it is blessed with year-round streams, pools and waterfalls: nothing is more precious than water in the desert! Lush vegetation adorns the canyons with hanging gardens of palm trees, maidenhair ferns and orchids clinging to their vertical walls. The flora of the region is a rare combination of desert, tropical and Mediterranean vegetation. Wildlife on the whole is very shy and mostly nocturnal, but birds of prey, as well as other bird species, are a common sight.

During a single dayhike you can choose to descend the red sandstone gorge of Wadi Ghuweir, trek through the gushing thermal stream of Wadi Zarqa Ma'in, abseil the black waterfalls of Wadi Feid, or float down the gorge of Wadi Mujib — the Grand Canyon of Jordan. Alternatively you can scramble to the peak of Jabel Baqer for an unequalled view of the Gulf of 'Aqaba, lose yourself in a labyrinth of white domes at Jabel el Quseir, wander through the open juniper woodlands of Dana Nature Reserve, or scale the summit of Jabel Rum to gain awe-inspiring desert vistas. On longer treks you can walk from Petra to Humeima in the footsteps of the Nabataeans, hike the full length of Wadi Hasa's canyon among thousands of wild palms, or walk along the highland of northern Moab while viewing the Dead Sea deep below.

With the exception of villages along the King's Highway, there are almost no permanent settlements in the Rift Valley region. The area is home to nomadic Bedouin, herding their flocks and often still living in traditional goat-hair tents. Spending the night by their campfire or being invited for tea is an opportunity to get to know these desert people and their folklore.

The Nabataean kingdom flourished in this region and has bequeathed to posterity the rock-carved city of Petra. Like the Bedouin, the Nabataeans relied for their livelihood on a thorough acquaintance with the desert. There is no better way to appreciate and understand their legacy than by trekking through the environment in which they lived. Edomites, Moabites and other peoples of antiquity also left their mark along the Rift Valley. The Israelites traversed this land on their way from Egypt to Cana'an. Moses saw Cana'an from one of the summits overlooking the Dead Sea and there he died. John the Baptist was incarcerated and eventually put to death in the desert fortress of Machaerus, and the first battle between the Muslim and

Byzantine armies took place near Karak, the historical capital of Moab.

This book describes treks through eight regions, from the northern tip of the Dead Sea to the Gulf of 'Aqaba in the south. Among the 68 routes offered, 57 are dayhikes and 11 are longer treks, ranging from two to six days. On 12 canyoning routes, abseiling skills and equipment are required. Among the routes are easy walks suitable for all, as well as challenging expeditions through remote areas, only rarely visited by either Bedouin or trekker.

Wherever you are, bear in mind that the desert ecosystem is very fragile and any damage to it may be permanent, or take years to recover.

The Jordanian Dead Sea Rift is a pristine wilderness. *Tlaqi kheir!* ("may you find good").

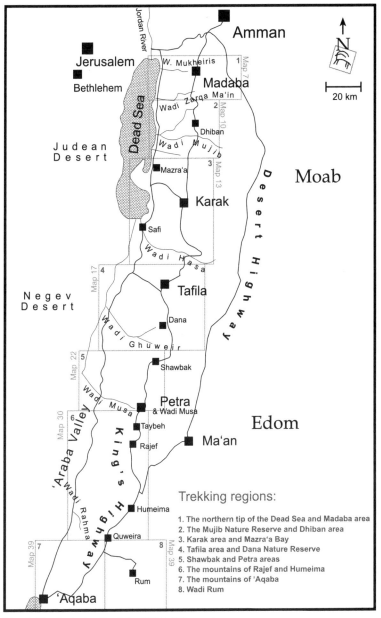

Trekking regions:

1. The northern tip of the Dead Sea and Madaba area
2. The Mujib Nature Reserve and Dhiban area
3. Karak area and Mazra'a Bay
4. Tafila area and Dana Nature Reserve
5. Shawbak and Petra areas
6. The mountains of Rajef and Humeima
7. The mountains of 'Aqaba
8. Wadi Rum

Map 1: The Jordanian Dead Sea Rift trekking regions

About the Region

Geography

The Dead Sea Rift is an elongate depression, stretching along more than 1,000 km from northern Syria to the Red Sea in the south. The Jordanian section along this depression includes the Gulf of 'Aqaba, the 'Araba Valley, the Dead Sea and the Jordan Valley. The eastern boundary of the Hashemite Kingdom of Jordan runs along the centerline of the Rift

The Gulf of 'Aqaba is part of the Red Sea, which is a northern extension of the Indian Ocean. Between the Gulf of 'Aqaba and the Dead Sea stretches the 'Araba Valley, divided by a rather indistinct mid-valley watershed into a northern section, which drains toward the Dead Sea, and a southern section, which consists largely of mud flats and salinas. The lowest part of the Rift is the Dead Sea, whose present shores lie at 410 m below sea level.

The Rift's flank east of the 'Araba Valley and the Dead Sea forms a steep slope whose peaks reach 800–1,700 m above sea level. These peaks constitute the edge of a wide plateau, which slopes gently eastward, towards the interior of Jordan. West of the Dead Sea and the 'Araba Valley the western flank of the Rift rises to 500–1,000 m, forming the Judean Mountains and the Negev ranges. The great difference in altitude between the bottom of the Rift and the plateau to the east is responsible for a rugged terrain incised by numerous deep canyons. Many of the canyons carry year-round streams forming a sharp contrast to the arid environment.

Two geographical regions can be distinguished in Jordan between the northern part of the Dead Sea and the Gulf of 'Aqaba. The northern region corresponds to biblical Moab and the southern to biblical Edom. The transition between these two regions is marked by Wadi Hasa, which was the border between the kingdoms of Moab and Edom (12–6th centuries BCE).

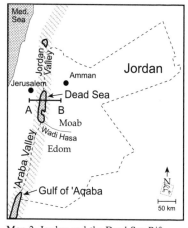

Map 2: Jordan and the Dead Sea Rift

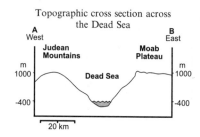

The highest peaks of Moab rise to 1,300 m, while those of Edom reach 1,700 m. The plateau of Moab was noted for its wheat and barley fields,

12

The Dead Sea

The surface level of the Dead Sea stands today at 410 m below sea level — the lowest place on earth. The lake consists of two distinct basins which were once connected through the Strait of Lynch. The bottom of the north basin lies at 730 m below sea level, whereas the south basin is only a few metres deep. Today, the south basin consists of industrial salt ponds flooded artificially by pumping.

The natural inflow from the north basin to the south basin stopped due to a constant drop in the water level, which reaches almost 1 m per year. This rapid drop is due to evaporation, which is not compensated by inflow from the Jordan River and seasonal floods. Increasing evaporation by enlarging the surface area of the salt ponds is an obvious interest of the Dead Sea potash industries since it enables it to produce more potash.

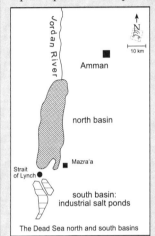

The Dead Sea north and south basins

The salt concentration in the Dead Sea water is about ten times that of ocean water (300 g salt per liter!). Its high specific gravity enables swimmers to float on the water without any effort. The Dead Sea salts did not come from the Jordan River or from other streams that flow into it, but are the accumulated residue of ancient seawater that has undergone extensive evaporation in the geological past.

The source of the seawater was the Mediterranean Sea, which invaded the Dead Sea Valley (through the Valley of Yizre'el) some 3 million years ago, and through long periods of evaporation deposited thousands of metres of salt. In time, the Rift Valley became disconnected from the Mediterranean but the thick salt deposits remained in the deeper parts of the erstwhile bay. Today many saline springs still feed the Dead Sea along its shores and through its bottom.

Bathing in the Dead Sea is considered to be therapeutic, especially for skin diseases. The lake's medical characteristics draw many cure seekers and its minerals are used in beauty and health lotions.

In the past, the Dead Sea owed its economic importance to salt and asphalt. Salt was used in the ancient world mainly to preserve food, and people were willing to pay high prices for it. Asphalt was used for medical purposes, for mummifying and for waterproofing, such as caulking of ships. Fissures in the Dead Sea bottom are known to discharge asphalt, which appears as floating blocks. These were harvested by the Nabataeans and others to good profit.

The lake is variously called the Sea of Salt, the Asphalt Lake, the Sea of Lot and the Dead Sea. Although each of the names is based on prominent characteristics the lake is not completely dead! Unicellular algae (*Dunaliella*) and halophile bacteria are active in its upper water layers, while its sediments host several bacteria species.

whereas Edom was more of a pastureland. Today, the municipal districts of southern Jordan are no longer called Moab and Edom. The region of Moab includes the districts of Amman and Karak and the region of Edom includes the districts of Tafila and Ma'an. Because of their geographical significance, the names Moab and Edom will be used throughout this guidebook. The major cities in Moab today are Karak and Madaba, while those in Edom are Tafila, Wadi Musa, Ma'an, and 'Aqaba.

The topography of the Rift dictates a steep east-west climatic gradient. Clouds, which form over the Mediterranean Sea, are blown by prevailing westerlies towards the Judean mountain ridge. As they move over the rising land, they cool and eventually precipitate, dropping most of their load (450–700 mm) over the ridge of Jerusalem, Bethlehem and Hebron. Moving further eastwards, the clouds descend towards the bottom of the Rift, warm up and hardly yield a drop of rain (20–90 mm per year). When the eastwards drifting clouds are driven up the edge of the Jordanian plateau, they precipitate once more (300–500 mm in the vicinity of Madaba and Karak) before fading away over the desert to the east. Due to the north-to-south regional aridity gradient most of Edom receives less rainfall than Moab.

This pattern of rainfall leaves Jordan with an arid desert covering more than three-quarters of the country. Only a narrow stretch along the peaks of the plateau receives an adequate amount of seasonal rainfall. Consequently, there are very few permanent settlements along the Dead Sea and the 'Araba, and none along the steep slopes of the Rift.

The climate of Jordan is a mixture of desert and Mediterranean climates. Winter is cold and rainy and summer is hot and dry. However, the east-west climatic gradient makes it possible to enjoy comfortable weather conditions in the bottom of the Rift during the winter as well as in the elevated areas during midsummer (see 'When to go' for further details).

Three main roads run the length of Jordan from north to south. The lowest road runs along the Dead Sea shore and the 'Araba Valley. High up, on the upper reaches of the steep slope, lies the historic King's Highway. Transverse roads and tracks connecting these two meridional routes are few, and their grades are very steep. On the plateau to the east is the Desert Highway — the fastest way to travel the length of Jordan.

Geology

The Syrian-African rift system
The topography and morphology of the region, and consequently its flora and fauna and human activity, are strongly related to one of the most powerful geological processes known: continental drift. The Dead Sea Rift is part of the Syrian-African rift system, which stretches from Turkey in the north to Mozambique in the south. This immense system is divided into three distinct sections: the East African Rift, the Red Sea, and the Dead Sea Rift.

The East African Rift cuts through Eritrea, Ethiopia, Kenya, Tanzania and Malawi, threatening to tear the Horn of Africa from the African mainland. Here we actually witness a continental break-up, which may eventually create a new ocean. Along the East African Rift are well-known lakes such as Nakuru and Malawi. The two highest summits of the African continent, Mount Kilimanjaro (5,896 m) and Mount Kenya (5,199 m) are volcanoes that are related to the evolution of the Rift.

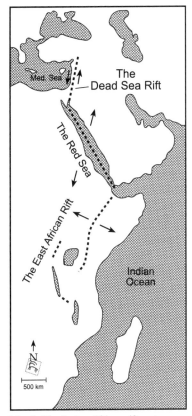

Map 3: The Syrian-African rift system

The middle part of the Syrian-African rift system is the Red Sea, which is an ocean in its infancy. It is growing wider as Arabia drifts away from Egypt and Sudan at about 1 cm a year. During the early stages of this process, about 30 million years ago, the rift of Suez was formed, and it looked as if the Mediterranean Sea was about to connect directly to the Indian Ocean. However, the divergence along the Gulf of Suez stopped, while the Red Sea continued to open. This movement was made possible by the creation of the Dead Sea Rift.

A thousand km long, the Dead Sea

Rift is a unique section of the Syrian-African rift system. The movement along its margins is not of opening but of horizontal displacement, in which Jordan and the Arabian plate are moving north in relation to Israel, Palestine and Sinai. The total movement to date amounts 105 km.

Evidence for this horizontal displacement is manifold. The most prominent is that geological features on either side of the Rift do not match. Only when the two sides are slid back 105 km, is good correspondence achieved: the Feinan copper mines in Jordan meet the Timna' copper mines

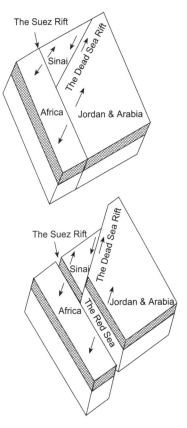

Relative movement along the Dead Sea Rift

in Israel, and igneous exposures near Eilat match up with igneous exposures near the village of Qureiqira.

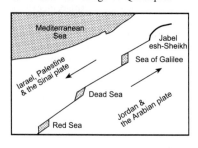

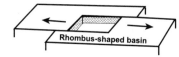

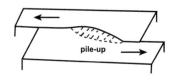

Creation of rhombus-shaped basins and pile-ups as a result of the slip movement along the Dead Sea Rift

In order to understand the variety of landscapes along the Rift, we have to take a closer look at the direction of its faults. A slip movement along a straight line is a perfect crime — leaving barely a trace on the surface. However, when the fault deviates from the straight line, two different structures can be created: a rhombus-shaped basin or a pile-up. The deep depressions of the Gulf of 'Aqaba, the Dead Sea and the Sea of Galilee are such basins, whereas Jabel esh-Sheikh (2,814 m), the highest mountain in the whole region, is a pile-up created by push-up stress.

As these deep depressions devel-

oped, canyons carved their way towards the evolving basins. The deepening was accompanied by the elevation of the Rift's margins, reaching 800 m above the northern tip of the Dead Sea and increasing southwards, where the lofty peaks of Edom attain over 1,700 m.

Rock formations

Wadis which drain westwards into the Rift Valley often descend more than 1,200 m over a short distance. Plunging steeply, they cut spectacular canyons and expose colorful rock formations. Since vegetation cover is scarce, bare rocks are a dominant feature in the landscape.

The rock sequence of Jordan can be looked upon as a three-storey building. Each storey is marked by rocks of distinctive character and age. The lowest storey is the oldest, consisting of igneous and metamorphic rocks. The second storey consists of sandstone, deposited on land, in rivers and deltas. The third storey consists mainly of marine sedimentary rocks such as limestone, chalk, clay and chert (flint). Often there is also a fourth storey consisting mainly of volcanic rock (basalt).

The rocks of the lower storey were formed more than 540 million years ago, when ancient continents collided. Great tectonic forces then lifted the rocks into mountain chains. When the collision subsided, erosional processes became dominant, eventually planing down the mountains and leaving an immense flat plain known as "the Peneplain".

Upon this ancient plain, sands were deposited. While trekking and especially while scaling summits, remnants of the now-dissected Peneplain are seen as a conspicuous border separating different morphologies.

Of the sandstone layers overlying the Peneplain, Edward Robinson (1838) wrote:

"Not the least remarkable... is the color of the rocks. They present not a dead mass of dull monotonous red: but an endless variety of bright and living hues, from the deepest crimson to the softest pink, verging also sometimes to orange and yellow."

The transition from the sandstone layers to the third storey represents a dramatic change, when a vast sea covered the ancient land. Fossils of snails, seashells and sea urchins abound in the limestone rocks of the third storey, attesting to their marine origin.

When the sea withdrew, some 35 million years ago, it was still long before the Dead Sea Rift was born. The land was flat and monotonous. Rivers flowed all the way from Jordan's eastern highlands to the Mediterranean Sea. Only 4 million years ago the Dead Sea Rift began to acquire its present form. Its dramatic relief slowly evolved intercepting the seaward flowing rivers and creating a new drainage pattern into the Rift.

Volcanic eruptions also left their mark on the landscape. Early basalt flows covered parts of the plateau with basalt. Later eruptions poured lava into deep canyons such as Wadi el Hidan and Wadi Zarqa Ma'in, which already cut their way toward the new drainage basin. The youngest basalt that has been dated along the Rift is in Wadi Zarqa Ma'in — it is half a million years old.

Structure
Trekking through the region, it is possible to cross the entire rock sequence in several hours. In Moab and northern Edom, limestone and sandstone dominate the landscape; the igneous rocks of the first storey are buried below the ground. A dramatic change in the landscape occurs in the 'Araba Valley from Feinan southwards, as igneous rock starts to take

over. South of Wadi Rahma the sandstone and limestone disappear, leaving the landscape to the sole reign of magmatic formations.

The entire rock sequence, originally horizontal, is clearly tilted to the north. Thus the first storey is buried below the surface in Moab, while near the Gulf of 'Aqaba it looms high above sea level, denuded of all rocks of the upper storeys, which were removed by erosion.

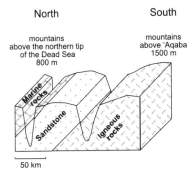

The rock sequence of Jordan consists of 3 storeys. The whole structure is clearly tilted to the north

The variety of landscapes and colors along the Dead Sea Rift is highlighted by many faults. These can create spectacular structures where rocks from all storeys are juxtaposed, and set off against each other.

Hydrology

One of the striking features of Moab and Edom is the amount of water running towards the Rift in an environment which is otherwise very arid. The contrast is emphasized when we look at the dryness of the wadis on the western side of the Dead Sea and the 'Araba Valley. The discharge of Wadi Mujib is 65 million cubic m per year, 25 times more than the flow of the 'Ein Gedi springs, the biggest water source in the Judean Desert. The discharge of Wadi Zarqa Ma'in, Wadi Hasa and other wadis descending from the Moab Plateau towards the Dead Sea, is also high. In Edom water is less abundant, but perennial streams can be found all the way south, down to Wadi Musa. Further south there are no year-round streams, but the number of springs is striking. Almost every wadi down to Wadi Rahma has at least one perennial spring.

A number of factors explain this anomaly. The high altitude of the plateaus of Moab and Edom encourages precipitation. The peaks of northern Moab receive almost 500 mm of annual rainfall, and the peaks of Edom up to 300 mm. In wintertime the latter are often covered with snow. The lower areas of Moab and Edom indeed receive less than 100 mm per year.

Another factor is the nature of the rock. Most of the rocks exposed in Moab and Edom are porous sandstone, and thus a large portion of rainfall seeps into underground reservoirs, to reappear later on in springs. The large drainage basins of some of the wadis also serve to collect large amounts of water. The Wadi Mujib drainage basin, the largest drainage basin in Jordan, encompasses over 6,500 square km, an area bigger than the drainage basin of the Jordan River itself!

Last, not of least importance, is the groundwater flow pattern. It appears that even waters that seep into the ground far from the Rift, east of the topographical watershed, eventually drain into the Rift. Thus, vast areas collect groundwater to the springs and streams that flow towards the Rift.

Ruins of ancient water collection systems are found on the Rift bottom at the outlet of many streams, often next to modern systems which utilize the water mostly for agriculture.

About one-sixth (120 million cubic m) of Jordan's annual water consumption are the waters that flow in the Riftward streams of Moab and Edom. In view of the serious water shortage in Jordan, the growing pressure to utilize this water efficiently can be understood. Lately, construction of three big dams has begun on the upper reaches of Wadi Hasa, Wadi el Hidan (Wadi Wala) and Wadi Mujib. Fortunately, a plan to build a dam in the middle of the Mujib gorge was abandoned. Water is precious in Jordan. Precious for the people, but just as precious for the preservation of the Rift's unique environment.

History

Jordan is situated on the crossroads between Africa and Asia. The Arabian Desert, Mesopotamia and the Mediterranean shores all played a role in its history, as did Islam, Christianity and Judaism. Most of the time it was a remote province of faraway empires. However, for short periods, it was also a center of indigenous cultures and kingdoms. These were born in its deserts and left a spectacular heritage.

Prehistory

The Dead Sea Rift provides some of the earliest evidence of hominid presence outside Africa. As early as 1.5 million years ago, hominids were living on the shores of a lake not far south of the Sea of Galilee ('Ubeidiya site). The Rift, with its abundant wildlife and vegetation, provided favorable conditions for their hunting and gathering.

A dramatic change in the lifestyle of Stone Age people occurred during the Neolithic period (8,300–4,500 BCE). Goats and sheep were domesticated and edible plants were cultivated.

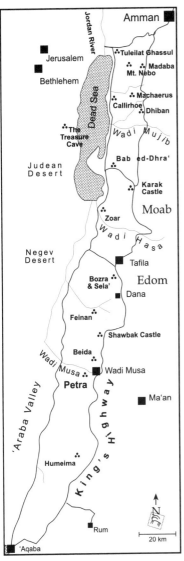

Map 4: Archeological sites along the
Jordanian Dead Sea Rift

veloped Neolithic village which was excavated near Petra, with over 60 stone-built structures.

An important prehistoric site is Tuleilat Ghassul, at the northeastern tip of the Dead Sea. The site, which is dated to the Chalcolithic period (4,500–3,400 BCE), gave its name to the characteristic culture of this period. Among its finds are unusual wall paintings, not found at other Chalcolithic sites. Another Ghassulian site yielded a cache of copper artifacts, hoarded in a cave on the western side of the Dead Sea ("The Treasure Cave"). The cache includes more than 400 items, thought to be cultic, reflecting advanced and previously unknown metallurgical skills and a well-developed ritual art.

The Bronze Age (3,300–1,200 BCE)

The Bronze Age marks the beginning of urbanization in the region, as well as trade connections with Mesopotamia and the Early Kingdom of Egypt. Among the goods traded were copper and asphalt, which was used for medical purposes, caulking and mummifying. Since copper was abundant in the 'Araba Valley and asphalt in the Dead Sea, the Rift area had a considerable economic significance.

Five Early Bronze sites have been discovered along the eastern shore of the Dead Sea. The largest site, Bab ed-Dhra', is located close to the outlet of Wadi Karak. It includes a fortified town and an enormous burial field with more than ten thousand graves. Considering the small size of the city the number of graves points to a surprisingly large nomadic society inhabiting the region. Apparently, those who died while wandering were first buried in a provisional grave along the way, and later on transferred to the central burial site at Bab ed-Dhra'.

Some researchers identify the ruins

This revolution enabled the development of permanent settlements. One of the most prominent sites of this period in Jordan is Beida — a well-de-of the Bronze Age cities with the five Cities of the Plain mentioned in Genesis 14: 1-3, which included Sodom and Gomorrah. According to the Bible story, these cities were destroyed by the wrath of God. The only survivors were Abraham's nephew Lot and his family, who fled towards Zoar. A probable candidate for the Zoar mentioned in the Bible is a Bronze Age site near the outlet of Wadi Hasa and the village of Safi.

The Iron Age
(12-6th centuries BCE)

It is in the 14-12th centuries BCE that we first hear about several indigenous geo-political entities: the Edomites, the Moabites and the Ammonites. The Edomite kingdom stretched from the Gulf of 'Aqaba to Wadi Hasa (Nahal Zered), its northern border with Moab. The Moabite kingdom reached to the northern fringes of the Dead Sea, where it had an impermanent border with Ammon. Our major source of knowledge about the early Iron Age is the Bible. Most archaeological evidence from these kingdoms is no earlier than the 9th century BCE.

The Edomite Kingdom

The land of the Edomites is mentioned in the Bible in relation to the journey of the tribes of Israel from Egypt to Cana'an. Since the strong Philistines occupied the shores of the Mediterranean and the Cana'anites inhabited the central mountain range, the obvious approaches to Cana'an were blocked. Moses had to lead his people across the Rift and then northwards along its eastern side, before crossing the Jordan River. He asked the king of Edom for permission to pass along the "King's Highway" but was refused. Having no other choice, the Israelites skirted the land of Edom from the east (Numbers 19: 14-21).

According to this biblical description, at the time of the Exodus, Edom was an organized kingdom with an assertive ruler. However, archeological evidence from such an early period (12th century BCE) is not available. Most of the sites indicate that the Edomite kingdom flourished only since the 7th century BCE. Edom's capital, Bozra, was unearthed near the small village of Buseira, which still preserves the ancient name. At the Edomite site of Umm el Biyara overlooking Nabataean Petra, a seal impression of "Qosgabar king of Edom" was found. A king with a similar name is known from Assyrian chronicles dating to the 7th century BCE. The dating of all Edomite artifacts relies almost solely on the date of this seal.

Edom's political and economic power depended on its control over Feinan, one of the largest copper production centers in the Near-East (see route 38). Moreover, the Edomites' control of the Gulf of 'Aqaba was of importance, giving them access to the trade routes of the Red Sea.

Though the Edomites hardly left any written heritage, they left intriguing sites. Among those are Ba'ja, Jabel el Quseir and Umm Ala (routes 43, 50, 56), which were discovered during the last two decades, in addition to the long-known sites of Sela' and Umm el Biyara (routes 29, 47). Surrounded by vertical cliffs, the access to these well-guarded hilltop sites is along steep slopes and narrow clefts. Rock-carved stairs and grooves, bell-shaped cisterns, hewn basins and pottery sherds of giant storage jars are abundant. What impelled the Edomites to dwell in such inaccessible cliffs? Were these meant to be strongholds, or just elevated sacred places?

At all events, the Edomites were known as crag dwellers. "Though you build your nest as high as the vulture, thence I will bring you down", prophesies Jeremiah (49: 16), who knew Edom only by reputation.

The relationship between the Edomites and the neighboring Israelites was of continuous rivalry. According to the biblical narrative, King David had conquered Edom, but later the Edomites revolted against his son, King Solomon. In a later period, King Amaziah of Judah waged war against the Edomites. Rage prophecies against Edom are abundant and were probably motivated by the active part that Edom took when Jerusalem was destroyed by the Babylonians (586 BCE). These prophecies notwithstanding, scripture attributes the origin of Edom to Esau, the twin brother of Jacob (Genesis 25: 21–34).

The Edomite kingdom vanished mysteriously during the 6th century BCE. There is no direct evidence as to what happened. However, there are reasons to believe that the Babylonians were involved in its decline. An amazing Babylonian rock relief was discovered in 1995, perched on a sheer rock face at the stronghold of Sela' (see route 29). The relief is the only archeological evidence for the Babylonian presence in Edom. When the kingdom collapsed, some Edomites probably moved to southern Judah, which was known in later times as Idumea. Others probably stayed in their homeland and intermixed later on with the Nabataeans.

The Moabite Kingdom
According to the Bible, on their way to Cana'an, the people of Israel conquered the northern part of Moab from Wadi Mujib (Nahal Arnon) to Wadi Zarqa (Nahal Yabok) (Numbers 21: 24). Thereafter, the tribes of Reuben and Gad asked Moses to settle in northern Moab and were granted permission.

In the plains of Moab, at the northern tip of the Dead Sea, Moses was told that he would not be allowed to enter the land of Cana'an. "The same day the Lord spoke to Moses and said: go up this mount Abarim, Mount Nebo in Moab, to the east of Jericho, and look out over the land of Cana'an... On this mountain you shall die and be gathered to your father's kin" (Deuteronomy 32: 49–50). After forty years of leading his people in the desert, Moses died. His successor, Joshua, was to lead the Israelites over the Jordan River and into Cana'an. Mount Nebo, the traditional site where Moses died, is held by the Franciscan fathers and still offers superb views westwards.

The Bible also specifies that the Moabites and the Ammonites are the descendants of Moab and Ben-'Ammi, sons of Abraham's nephew, Lot. Their mothers were Lot's daughters, who seduced their father after getting him drunk (Genesis 19, 30–38). Despite the alleged kinship, the relationship between the Moabites and the Israelites was of continuous struggle. During the reign of King David (a maternal descendant of Ruth the Moabite) and King Solomon, Moab was ruled by the Israelites. Later on, Mesha' king of Moab rebelled against the son of 'Omri, king of Israel (II Kings 3: 5–6). This event is also described in the stele of Mesha', one of the most important Iron Age inscription ever found.

In 1868 this stone stele was discovered in the fields of Dhiban, but shortly after its discovery it was smashed by Bedouin, who thought it might contain hidden treasure. Fortunately, before the damage, the French scholar Clermont Ganneau had produced a copy of the inscription. The partly mended stele is exhibited today in the Louvre Museum of Paris. The inscription opens with "I am Mesha', son of Chemosh, king of Moab the Dibonite... As for 'Omri king of Israel, he humbled Moab for many years, for Chemosh (the Moabite deity) was angry at his land. His son followed him... but I have triumphed over him and over his house, and Israel perished for ever". The text then describes Mesha's victory over Israel and mentions his glorious deeds. Among other things Mesha' boasts "I made the highway at the Arnon". Wadi Mujib, the biblical Arnon, intersects the King's Highway. The winding road which crosses it is an engineering feat even today.

One of the major cities of Moab was known to have stood in Karak, where another short inscription of Mesha' was found, carved upon a statue. Unfortunately, impressive Moabite ruins did not survive in Karak, or anywhere else in Moab. The kingdom of Moab, like the kingdom of Edom, declined in the 6th century BCE.

The Ammonite Kingdom

'Ammon was a small kingdom whose capital, Rabat 'Ammon, was located in present-day Amman. The well-defended city relied on a vast agricultural periphery as well as on its position on the trade route of the King's Highway.

The Hellenistic, Roman and Byzantine periods (4th century BCE to the 7th century CE)

The Iron Age kingdoms faded away in the 6th century BCE as the region fell to the Babylonians and subsequently entered the mist of the Persian Period (6–4th centuries BCE). Alexander the Great's journey of conquest to the east (333 BCE) brought the entire region under Hellenic rule. Greek-speaking populations settled in the northern parts of Jordan and their language and culture started to spread. The continuous interaction between the local and the Greek population created a new Hellenistic, local culture, which adopted many religious and cultural customs from

the Greeks. Hellenistic cities were established in the *Decapolis* region (Deca — ten, Polis — cities) in northern Jordan. The southernmost of these was Philadelphia, today's Amman. Among the other cites of this region were Jarash, Gadara, Pella, Skythopolis and Damascus.

The regional entities included the *Decapolis* cities in the north and the Nabataeans in the south and east. An area with Jewish communities extended west of Philadelphia towards the Jordan Valley and Judea.

The new rising power in Edom and Moab was that of the Nabataeans. Though their kingdom was probably only established around 167 BCE, they had considerable power long before and even confronted Alexander's successors — the Ptolemaic rulers of Egypt and the Seleucid rulers of Syria. The mutual strife of these two realms enabled the Nabataeans as well as the Hasmonaean dynasty of Judea to establish their own independent kingdoms. The Nabataeans and the Hasmonaeans first cooperated, but later on became bitter rivals, as the Hasmonaean kingdom expanded into the western parts of Moab and northern Edom. Among the Hasmonaean strongholds in the Jordanian Rift is the desert fortress of Machaerus where, at a later time, John the Baptist was incarcerated and beheaded.

The Romans became masters of the region in 63 BCE with the invasion of Pompey, which boded the end of the independent Hasmonaean kingdom. The Nabataean kingdom maintained limited independence until 106 CE when it was annexed to the Roman Empire.

During the Byzantine period, from 324 to 635 CE, Jordan flourished and its population grew bigger. Churches were built throughout the country and architectural and mosaic arts thrived. One of the major mosaic centers was in Madaba in northern Moab, where the famous 6th-century mosaic map of the Holy Land was found. Though geographically inaccurate, it is still the most realistic map of the region until the 19th century. Many localities that appear on the map were not known from any other source. The Dead Sea is depicted with Wadi Zarqa Ma'in, Wadi Mujib and Wadi Hasa flowing into it. On its shores are the thermal springs of Callirhoe (Hammam ez-Zara') and further to the south, on the outlet of Wadi Hasa, is the city of Zoar. Overlooking Zoar is a Byzantine site known today as Lot's Cave Monastery.

The Nabataean Kingdom

The Nabataeans, originally a nomadic people from the Arabian Peninsula, were lords of the desert, leaving the most glorious indigenous heritage that the Dead Sea Rift ever saw. Petra, their capital city, exhibits awe-inspiring rock-carved monuments while Humeima is a masterpiece of water collection systems. Nabataean temples, caravanserais and cisterns are found in many places along the Rift.

One of the earliest historical accounts of the Nabataeans dates back to the 4th century BCE:

"They have a rule not to sow a seed or plant a fruit tree. They do not drink wine nor do they build houses... Many Arab tribes graze their flocks in the desert, but the Nabataeans are richer than all... They carry incense and expensive spices brought from blessed Arabia towards the sea... For in this waterless region... they have dug wells at convenient intervals and have kept the knowledge of them hidden from the peoples of all other nations... This is how they keep their freedom." (Diodorus of Sicily, based on Hieronymus of Cardia. Hieronymus took part in a campaign by Antigonos, one of Alex-

ander the Great's successors, against the Nabataeans).

Controlling the major caravan routes, the Nabataeans grew rich and politically influential and established a kingdom whose capital was Petra. Their kingdom stretched from the northern part of the Arabian Peninsula in the south, to Bosra (100 km south of Damascus) in the north. In the southwest their realm reached the Mediterranean shore, expanding over the Sinai Peninsula and the Negev Desert, where five Nabataean cities were established. For a short period southern Syria and Damascus were also part of their kingdom.

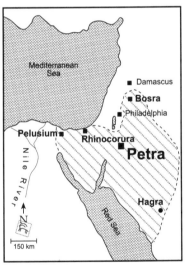

Map 5: The Nabataean Kingdom

The Roman historian, Pliny the Elder, complains:

"This land's fortune is due to people who chase luxuries even at times of death, and burn on bodies materials that were meant to be devoted to gods. Reliable sources tell us that Arabia can not produce in one year the

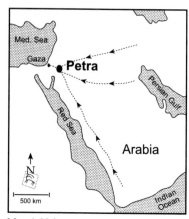

Map 6: Nabataean caravan routes

amount of incense that Emperor Nero burned at the burial ceremony of his wife Poppaea... By cautious calculation, the Arabian Peninsula takes 100 million sesterces from us each year. This is the price of our luxuries and our women."

Incense and spices were produced in southern Arabia and the Persian Gulf region, while wealthy consumers enjoyed Hellenistic lifestyles along the Mediterranean shores. A vast desert separated the valuable goods from the consumers, but the Nabataeans — knowing the routes and the water sources — knew how to cross it with heavy-laden caravans.

According to the meagre historical accounts and by comparison with 20th-century camel caravans, Nabataean caravans might have numbered hundreds of camels, each carrying about 200 kg. The average distance covered in a day was probably about 20 km, or 1,000 km in a fifty-day journey. Caravanserais included a water source and often also a built compound enclosing an inner court. Since the Nabataean goods were destined to reach the Mediterranean ports (Gaza, Rhinocorura and Pelusium) the caravans had to cross the Rift Valley. Their routes were well-planned to negotiate the steep descent and opposite ascent and to traverse the Negev Desert.

The first recorded king of the Nabataeans was Aretas I, mentioned in an inscription from 167 BCE. The kingdom reached its climax during the reigns of Obodas III (30–9 BCE) and Aretas IV (9 BCE–40 CE), during which most of Petra's temples and sepulchral monuments were built. During this period the Romans clashed several times with the Nabataeans, but gained no victories. Campaigns between the Romans and the Nabataeans came to an end in 106 CE when the Nabataean kingdom was annexed to the Roman Empire and the capital of the newly established Provincia Arabia was moved to Bosra (now in southern Syria). After the annexation new trade routes were opened, and Petra gradually declined. Though the Nabataeans lost their trade monopoly they continued to inhabit the area of their previous realm and developed sophisticated desert agriculture. An archive of papyri, lately discovered in a church in Petra, implies that during the 6th century there was still a Nabataean element amidst Petra's Byzantine culture.

The rapid rise of the Nabataean material culture is astonishing. Within a very short period and with hardly any graduality, they reached a peak of architectural achievements and ceramic skill. It is hard to understand how nomadic people without urban traditions attained such grandiosity.

Their splendid rock-carved sepulchral monuments, temples and shrines, merge eastern and western architectural styles. Their stone-carving skills doubtlessly evolved from hewing cisterns and reservoirs. The Nabataeans used Hellenistic decoration forms without following the canon of classic architecture. Assyrian, Persian, Egyptian and indigenous elements are all blended in their facades.

The Nabataean clay pottery is among the finest in the Roman world. Their eggshell pottery is thin (1–3 mm), very strong and often delicately decorated with a net of lines and palm fronds.

Little is known about the Nabataean spiritual heritage. We know the names of a few of their gods, but not much about their rites. The head of their Pantheon, Dushara, (Shara is the name of the mountains of Edom. Dushara means "the one from the Shara") was initially symbolized in the form of a stone or a conical obelisk. Following Hellenistic influences, Dushara was identified with Dionysos and then with Zeus. He was accompanied by the goddess el Uza, "the strong", also called Allat, chief goddess of the desert tribes in Arabia. Beside the Greek gods, Nabataean temples also housed gods from Syria and Babylon.

The Nabataeans who started as nomads, experienced an accelerated cultural evolution. Their booming economy and their continuous interaction with the outside world changed their old way of life. The heritage they left is an ingenious blend of a desert culture with classic-western and Semitic-eastern civilizations.

The Early Muslim period, Crusaders and Ottomans (7–20th centuries CE)

After the Prophet Muhammad strengthened his control over the Arabian Peninsula during the early decades of the 7th century, the Muslim armies were ready to invade Byzantine territories. Their forces encountered no resistance until they reached the small village of Mauta, a few kilometers south of Karak. Two close relatives of Muhammad fell in battle and the Muslims troops had to re-

treat. Thus the first confrontation of Muhammad's troops with the Byzantine army ended with a Muslim defeat. However, a few years later, by 630 CE, most of southern Jordan was under Muslim rule. The Byzantine grip over this area was weak and the local population surrendered to the Muslims before the second invasion began. Advancing northwards, the Muslim armies adhered to the desert on their east flank to avoid encircling by the Byzantine. After winning a decisive battle by the Yarmuk River their way to Damascus was opened. The most important city in the whole region fell into Muslim hands after a short siege in 635 CE.

Damascus later became the capital of the Muslim realm under the reign of the Umayyad caliphate. Magnificent Umayyad desert complexes were built at this period in Syria and Jordan's interior. Only in 750 CE was the capital moved to Baghdad as the 'Abbasid caliphate took the rule. The 'Abbasid revolution was led from the small village of Humeima, situated halfway between Petra and 'Aqaba. Its location, far away from Damascus, but on the main pilgrim route to Mecca, was ideal for plotting an overthrow. When the political and economic center was transferred to Baghdad, the settlements in Jordan went into a fast decline. The larger towns of the south (Karak, Ma'an, Shawbak and Aila (today's 'Aqaba)) managed to survive mostly due to their proximity to the pilgrim route.

The Crusaders arrived in the Holy Land in 1099 CE, and established the Latin Kingdom of Jerusalem. A few years later southern Jordan came under their rule and the first Crusader strongholds were built in Shawbak (Montreal – the royal mountain) and near 'Aqaba ('Ile de Gray – today "the Island of Salah ed-Din"). Thus, the Crusaders controlled the two main pilgrim routes to Mecca, from Egypt and North Africa, and from Damascus and the north. The most important routes of the Muslim Empire were under Christian supervision.

The largest Crusader fortress of Jordan was built in Karak in 1142 CE, giving the Crusaders control over the wheat fields of the Moab Plateau as well as the Dead Sea with its salt ponds and port toward Jerusalem. The most famous master of the castle was the notorious Reynald of Chatillon who, in defiance of an official truce, constantly attacked Muslim pilgrims. Two other citadels were built in Petra, and the local population was taxed by the Crusaders.

In 1170 CE the shrewd new leader of the Muslim troops, Salah ed-Din (Saladin), gained control over the Gulf of 'Aqaba, but his efforts to conquer the fortress of Karak failed. Only after Jerusalem fell into his hands, the fortress lost its alliance. Karak surrendered in 1188 after one year of siege. A few months later, Montreal Castle in Shawbak also fell and the Crusaders lost their last foothold in Jordan.

In 1260 the Mongols invaded the region and were confronted by the Mamluke army of Egypt. The Mamluke victory was the beginning of a long reign, whose center was in Cairo for more than 250 years, until the arrival of the Ottoman Turks.

The Ottoman Empire, whose capital was Istanbul, ruled the whole region from 1516 to 1918. Generally speaking, it did not bring the area much prosperity, and neglect and corruption prevailed. Already at the dawn of the period, tribes from the Arabian Peninsula moved into Jordan, clashing frequently with one another. The central authority was weak and public security was almost nonexistent. Travellers of the 19th century report that many villages were abandoned and struggles between nomads and farmers ("the Desert and the Sown") were

common. Farmers often had to pay protection money to the local Bedouin tribes.

Darb el Haj, the pilgrim road that crossed Jordan from north to south towards Mecca, provided the Ottoman Turks with a strategic route from Turkey to the holy cities of Arabia. By 1900 they had launched a railway project to connect Damascus with Medina. The construction of the Hejaz Railway, which stretched along 1300 km, with 48 stations, took eight years. Though the Bedouin were worried that the project would harm their income from escorting pilgrims, the railway and the telegraph line that accompanied it played an important role in the economic development of the area. From the environmental point of view, the railway caused fatal damage to forested areas, which were cut down in order to provide fuel for the steam engines. There was even a special siding near the village of Shawbak, built exclusively to serve the woodcutting.

The capital of Jordan during the last decades of the Ottoman period was es-Salt (north of Amman), whose population reached 20,000. When World War I began in 1914, the Turks sided with Germany. The Arab revolt against the Ottoman Empire broke out in Hejaz (now part of Saudi Arabia) in 1916 and the Jordanian tribes soon joined it. The revolt was led by Feisal, son of Hussein, the *Sharif* (Principal) of Mecca, accompanied by his brothers 'Abdullah, 'Ali and Zeid. It was actively supported by Britain, whose military emissary, T. E. Lawrence, aided Feisal in directing the revolt. 'Aqaba was conquered by Bedouin troops in 1917 and Petra, Shawbak and Tafila soon after. Bitter fighting took place along the railway with many victims who gave their life for Arab freedom. Jordan was a battle zone for 16 months until the Ottoman Empire collapsed in 1918.

Feisal son of Hussein,
leader of the Arab revolt

Modern history

After World War I, Arab hopes to establish an independent state from the Arabian Peninsula in the south to Damascus in the north, were crushed by the European powers. Britain and France divided the Middle East among themselves, in contradiction to early promises. France took Syria and Lebanon, and Britain took the areas of Israel, Palestine, Jordan and Iraq. In 1921 Feisal was crowned king of Iraq and in 1923 his brother 'Abdullah was appointed ruler of Transjordan under the terms of the British mandate.

'Abdullah moved the capital from es-Salt to Amman but it was only in 1946 that Transjordan gained independence, officially becoming the Hashemite Kingdom of Jordan. When the State of Israel was established in 1948, war broke out between Arabs and Jews, and Jordan was flooded with Palestinian refugees. 'Abdullah was assassinated in 1951. After the short rule of 'Abdullah's son Tallal, his grandson, Hussein, was crowned in 1953 when he was only 18 years old. When the Six-Day War broke out in 1967, Israel occupied the West Bank and more Palestinian refugees arrived in Jordan. In 1994 a historic peace agreement was signed between Jordan and Israel.

The late King Hussein was among the prominent leaders of the region. Earning the admiration of his people, he ruled Jordan for almost 50 years until his death in 1999. He was succeeded by his son, King 'Abdullah the Second.

Exploration of the Jordanian Dead Sea Rift

During most of the Ottoman period, anarchy prevailed throughout Jordan and Palestine, and security conditions were very poor. It was only in the beginning of the 19th century that a few daring explorers first ventured into the wild region east of the Jordan River and the Dead Sea, motivated by the will to discover the lands of the Bible. The charm of the Orient, as well as the spirit of adventure, soon attracted many travellers, researchers and artists. Though they carried arms and had Bedouin escorts they still faced tremendous difficulties.

"Towards sunset we reached the Samrat el Fidan, a long, low mountain ridge, on the eastern slopes of the 'Araba, where we intended to encamp. Just before entering it, we espied a company of Arabs, armed and mounted on camels and preparations were at once made in case of an attack by the strangers. Our own camels were drawn aside beneath the shelter of a rock; each of the party examined his arms and prepared to use them if necessary... there is something rather pleasant in the uncertainty and excitement of such a moment, though we were not sorry to see both parties embrace, and to find that the new comers were members of the same tribe." (E. H. Palmer, 1868)

Ulrich Jasper Seetzen, 1806-1807

The German doctor Seetzen was the first known western explorer to travel through Jordan since the Crusaders. He travelled under the name Musa el Hakim, spoke fluent Arabic and was a convert to Islam. His first journey through Jordan took him along the King's Highway to Karak and then down to the Dead Sea shore. He crossed the outlet of Wadi Hasa and skirted the southern tip of the Dead Sea. On a later journey, Seetzen walked along the entire eastern shore of the Dead Sea! He insisted on following the lake's shoreline even where his Bedouin guides declared it to be impossible.

More than 40 years after Seetzen, the traveller De Saulcy (1851) wrote about the difficulties of walking along the Dead Sea shore:

"Before starting we had held a council with the sheikhs of our escort, for the purpose of selecting the route we were to follow throughout the day. They told us that it was practicable enough to push on as far as the bank of Wadi Mujib, meaning the Arnon, but that we should not be able to ford that river, and besides, were we to succeed, we should find beyond it a beach so narrow as to be impassable."

Seetzen is the first to describe Wadi Mujib's lower gorge. Among his many discoveries were the warm springs of Wadi Zarqa Ma'in, Callirhoe (Hammam ez-Zara') and the fortress of Machaerus. Although he travelled through unknown land he did not stick to main routes. It was many years before others walked along paths that he had trod. Seetzen was murdered in Yemen in 1811.

John Louis Burckhardt, 1812

The Swiss traveller Burckhardt is renowned for discovering Petra to the western world. Disguised as a Muslim who had vowed to sacrifice a goat at the tomb of Aaron, he ventured into the ancient city and published a detailed description of the site. Burckhardt was the first to travel through Edom. After his visit to Petra it became the dream of many travellers.

John Louis Burckhardt

L. E. Laborde, 1828

A French explorer who travelled through Edom and Sinai disguised as a Bedouin. Unlike Burckhardt he travelled in style with a caravan of sixteen camels. Laborde was the first to approach Petra from 'Aqaba through the southern part of the 'Araba Valley. On his return journey from Petra to 'Aqaba, he visited Wadi Sabra and the Nabataean site Humeima. Laborde was later appointed director of the Louvre Museum in Paris. His sketches of Petra illustrated the region for many scholars and armchair travellers.

Lord Lindsay, G. H. Von Schubert, G. H. Moore and W. G. Beke, 1837

The Englishman Lindsay and the German Von Schubert travelled shortly after each other through the whole length of the 'Araba Valley.

Schubert was among the first to realize that the Dead Sea and parts of the 'Araba Valley were much lower than global sea level. At about the same time, Moore and Beke reached the same conclusion. The discovery was a scientific sensation.

D. Roberts, 1839
The artist David Roberts is renowned for his paintings of Petra as well as of many other historic sites in the region. His work reached a much wider public than the accounts of his predecessors.

W. F. Lynch, 1848
Captain Lynch headed an official exploration party of the American Navy, which negotiated the length of the Jordan River from the Sea of Galilee to the Dead Sea. The Lynch expedition produced an accurate map of the Dead Sea with many of its adjoining canyons.

During the second half of the 19th century many travellers and researchers visited Moab and Edom. These included the English clergyman and naturalist H. B. Tristram and the Czech explorer Alois Musil. The most explored route was along the King's Highway, though some travellers also visited the Dead Sea and the 'Araba Valley. Thus, we have descriptions of the upper reaches and the outlets of many canyons that flow into the Rift Valley. However, the long, jagged belt between the King's Highway and the bottom of the Rift remained only lightly explored. Transverse routes from east to west were few, steep and dangerous. Obviously, walking through canyons, which were impassable to pack animals, was out of the question. Moreover, since the main motivation for explorations was identifying biblical sites, the canyons and the rugged peaks hardly drew any attention.

For the last fifty years the access to the 'Araba Valley and the Dead Sea was limited due to their proximity to the border with Israel. There was even no tarred road along the northeastern shore of the Dead Sea until the early 90's. The 1994 peace agreement with Israel made the Rift Valley considerably more accessible. Nevertheless, even today there remains much which is still unexplored.

Flora

The rich botanic diversity of Moab and Edom is strongly related to the topography of the Dead Sea Rift. Crossing the eastern flank of the Rift east-to-west, from the plateau to the bottom of the valley, there are steep gradients of altitude, temperature and precipitation, which are responsible for a vertical succession of belts of vegetation. Along the bottom of the Rift stretches a desert belt with abundant tropical elements ('Sudanian'), above it there is a desert belt ('Saharo-Arabian'), and then a steppe belt ('Irano-Turanian'). A Semi-Mediterranean vegetation belt marks the peaks of Moab and Edom (800–1,750 m). Intermixed representatives of the different vegetation belts often form

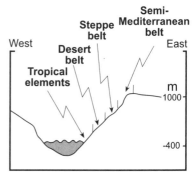

Vegetation belts across the Jordanian Dead Sea Rift

unique communities of plants of different provenance.

The high temperatures at the bottom of the Rift allow plants from tropical Africa to penetrate northwards. Among those are the Acacia (*A. raddiana* and *A. tortilis*), Sodom Apple (*Calotropis procera*), the Toothbrush tree (*Salvadora persica*) and the Jujube tree (*Ziziphus spina-christi*). It is in the Dead Sea Rift that these, and many other tropical species, reach the northernmost limit of their distribution.

The desert belt is characterized by high daytime temperatures, but its winter nights can be very cold. Among the prominent desert shrubs is the White Desert Broom (*Retama raetam*). Further up is the steppe belt with higher rainfall. Its typical representatives are the aromatic Wormwood (*Artemisia sieberi*) and the tree *Pistacia atlantica*.

The Semi-Mediterranean belt receives the highest amount of rainfall and its temperatures are the lowest. Though at this elevation rainfall decreases from north to south, Mediterranean vegetation is hardly noticeable in Moab, but thrives in parts of Edom.

Open woodlands of Red Juniper (*Juniperus phoenicea*) adorn many slopes in Edom. Other prominent Mediterranean species include the Oak (*Quercus calliprinos*) and *Pistacia palaestina*. At the beginning of this century, before the construction of the Hejaz railway, extensive woodlands were more common in Edom, but they were practically annihilated to serve as engine fuel.

It is generally accepted that Edom's Mediterranean flora is a relict of a more rainy past. During that period, a continuous cover of Mediterranean vegetation extended from the highlands of northern Jordan (the area of 'Ajlun) southwards to Edom. When the climate changed, Mediterranean vegetation survived in Edom, but was separated from the Mediterranean "mainland" of northern Jordan by the relatively arid region of southern Moab.

Still, it is hard to understand how Mediterranean species managed to survive in Edom, which on the whole is an arid region. The peaks of Edom rise to 1,700 m with rainfall up to 300 mm per year and snow almost every winter. These provide vital survival niches. Another reason has to do with the nature of the rock. Many Mediterranean species in Edom grow in sandy hollows surrounded by white sandstone domes. Runoff from the slopes of these domes drains into the closed valleys and increases the amount of water available for the plants. This sandstone morphology (Disi Formation) is found only in Edom. Moreover, Edom's forbidding topography has protected large areas from overgrazing and tree cutting.

Dalbergia sissoo

The Dead Sea Rift with its deep canyons and perennial water sources is dotted with many oases with water vegetation, which includes Tamarisk, Willow, Reed, *Ficus (F. pseudosycomorus)*, Euphrates Poplar (*Populus euphratica*) and beautifully blooming Oleanders.

"We reached the banks of the rivulet Zarqa Ma'in... It flows in a deep and

barren valley through a wood of Difle (Oleander) trees, which form a canopy over the rivulet, impenetrable to the meridian sun. The red flowers of these trees, reflected in the river, gave it the appearance of a bed of roses." (J. L. Burckhardt, 1812)

Rare species can be found in several canyons, such as the tropical tree *Dalbergia sissoo* that grows only in Wadi Hasa and can be recognized by its oval leaves. The Mediterranean Myrtle bush (*Myrtus communis*) with its pleasant fragrance survives amidst an arid desert environment in Wadi Karak, Wadi Weida'a and Wadi Ibn Hammad.

Myrtle bush (*Myrtus communis*)

Clinging to the canyons' sheer sandstone walls are spectacular hanging gardens of Palm trees, Maidenhair Fern and Sugarcane, ornamented with the white flowers of the tropical orchid *Epipactis veratrifolia*, and yellow blossoms of the *Sonchus maritimus* bush with its lanceolate leaves. The hanging gardens manage to flourish on the vertical cliffs thanks to the permeable sandstone, which is saturated with water.

Among the wildflowers of Moab and Edom are saffron, poppy, tulip, anemone, buttercup and sternbergia. Three endemic species of Iris grow here: Black Iris (*Iris nigricans*, flowering from April to May), Petra Iris (*Iris petrana*, flowering from April to May) and Edom Iris (*Iris edomensis*, flowering from December to February).

Sonchus maritimus

Prominent aromatic herbs include Wormwood (*Artemisia sieberi* and *A. judaica*), Hyssop (*Mazorana syriaca*), Lavender Cotton (*Achillea fragrantissima*), Fleabane (*Pulicaria incisa*), Stinkwort (*Asteriscus graveolens*), Origanum, Chiliadenus and Teucrium. Sorrel (*Rumex cyprius*) is abundant between February and April.

The vegetation of Moab and Edom is strongly affected by grazing. Overgrazed areas become dominated by poisonous species such as Squill (*Urginea maritima*) and *Daphne linearifolia*. The Squill, which blooms around September, creates spectacular stands of white flowering stalks. *D. linearifolia* is endemic to Jordan. Its leaves are thin and elongate and its smell is characteristic and strong.

Daphne linearifolia

Prominent trees and shrubs

Jujube (*Ziziphus spina christi*, in Arabic — Sidr)

A thorn tree of tropical origin, which can be
found in the lower reaches of most of the Rift's
canyons. Its species name means 'thorn of
Christ', since according to one tradition Jesus
was crowned with its branches. Three
prominent veins in its leaf are considered by
some as a symbol of the Holy Trinity. The
tiny apple of the jujube is edible for humans.

Palm (*Phoenix dactylifera*, in Arabic — Nakhel)

The date palm is found all over the Saharo-
Arabian region. It was probably domesticated
about 6,000 years ago in Mesopotamia or
possibly in the Rift Valley. Palm fibers are
used for ropes and basketry and its dates
can be eaten fresh or dried.

The palm groves of the Dead Sea Rift
were famous in the ancient world, especially
those of Zoar, nowadays Safi, at the outlet of
Wadi Hasa.

The abundance of feral palms in the canyons of
Moab and Edom is remarkable. Compared to
domesticated palms, their dates are very thin. Many
clusters of wild palms show fire damage. It appears
that Bedouin shepherds occasionally burn the palms to
encourage growth of fresh pasturage for their goats.

Pistacia atlantica (in Arabic — Butum)

The steppe tree *Pistacia atlantica* may grow
to great thickness (girth 1–4 m, height
3–10 m) and reach hundreds of years in age.
In the past, large trees were probably held
sacred and rituals were held beneath them.
The resin of the tree was used as incense.
Pistacia atlantica is quite common on the
upper reaches of the Rift's canyons. A
limited number survive on the
Jordanian plateau.

Red Juniper (*Juniperus phoenicea,* in Arabic — 'Ar'ar)

No other plant represents the vegetation of Edom better than the Mediterranean Red Juniper, which forms magnificent open woodlands on the slopes of Edom. Its global range of distribution includes the western Mediterranean (Morocco, Spain) as well as Crete and the Aegean Islands. Solitary stands are found on the peaks of northern Sinai. Very few junipers grow in Moab.

The red fruit of the juniper, from which medicinal decoctions were made, is responsible for its name. Beneath the juniper's bark, its branches and trunk are also red. Their distinctive smell allows easy recognition of Bedouin campfires, which burn juniper wood. In the past, strong-smelling juniper wood was used to keep hyenas from digging up dead bodies in graveyards.

Juniper used to be common building material, and beams can still be seen in the rafters of many old houses. The oldest living junipers in Edom are about 500 years old.

White Desert Broom (*Retama raetam,* in Arabic — Ratam)

The white broom, which is one of the dominant plants of the Sahara, grows in many wadi beds and is well adapted to the aridity of the desert air. During most of the year it is leafless, using its thin and elongate green stalks for photosynthesis. The exposed surface area of its stalks is small. Transpiration pores are sheltered in grooves and surrounded by tiny hairs, thus preserving humidity. Desert Broom has two webs of roots. One is shallow and collects rainwater from large areas; the other is very deep. It blooms in white around mid-winter. Since its branches and roots provide superb charcoal, it is intensely utilized by the Bedouin.

Wormwood (*Artemisia sieberi,* in Arabic — Shih)

The wormwood is a steppe bush regularly spaced over slopes and plains around the upper reaches of the Rift's canyons and on the plateau itself. Wormwood aroma spreads far and wide, attracting the goats, which have a taste for it. Its Latin name *Artemisia,* honors the hunting goddess Artemis who revealed its medicinal secrets to mortals. Tea brewed with Wormwood is used against stomach-ache. The liqueur absinthe is made of a species of wormwood and is said to increase creativity.

Fauna

The Dead Sea Rift has the most rugged relief in Jordan. Inaccessibility combined with abundant water sources, lush vegetation and sparse human population should have made it a wildlife paradise. However, intensive hunting has decreased the animal populations of the Rift, and made them extremely shy of humans. Though very fragile, a complete ecosystem has managed to survive.

The location of the Rift at the crossroads of continents, as well as its variable habitats, create a unique blend of fauna from Africa, Asia and Europe. Several Rift species, such as the Fan-Tailed Raven and the Rock Hyrax, are representatives of tropical Africa.

Among the Rift predators are Wolf, Golden Jackal (rare), Striped Hyena, Red Fox (common), Sand Fox, Blanford Fox (rare), Wild Cat (rare), Sand Cat, Jungle Cat (rare), Caracal (rare), European Badger, Honey Badger (rare) and Marbled Polecat (rare). The last Cheetah was hunted in the

Hyrax

outlet of Wadi Zarqa Ma'in in 1910. The last Syrian Brown Bear was reported in Moab in 1934. The last leopard was shot in 1973 at the outlet of Wadi Mujib.

Other mammals include the Nubian Ibex (wild mountain goat, rare) and Hyrax (rare) as well as Porcupine, Hare and Wild Boar (rare). A few

Desert Gazelles may still live in the 'Araba Valley, but the last Oryx were hunted at the beginning of this century. The Royal Jordanian Society for Conservation of Nature (RSCN) is reintroducing Ibex to the Mujib Nature Reserve and is about to reintroduce Oryx in Wadi Rum.

Freshwater fauna, which is frequently encountered in brooks flowing in the canyons, include freshwater crabs, fish that can climb cascades (*Capoeta*

Sand Cat

damascina), Tree Frog (*Hyla savignyi*), Green Toad (*Bufo viridis*), Freshwater Frog (*Rana levantina*) and the nonpoisonous Diced Water Snake (*Natrix tessellata*).

Among the reptiles are a few venomous snakes such as the Carpet Viper (*Echis coloratus*), Falsed Horned Viper (*Pseudocerastes persicus fieldi*) and Sinai Desert Cobra (*Walterinnesia aegyptia*). The Sinai Whip Snake (*Coluber sinai*) is a beautiful, nonpoisonous, striped snake.

Other reptiles of global conservation importance are the giant Desert Monitor Lizard (*Varanus griseus*) which can reach a length of 1.5 m, and the Egyptian Spiny-tailed Lizard (*Uromastix aegyptius*).

Millions of soaring birds, including storks, cranes, pelicans and birds of prey, migrate through the Dead Sea Rift. In autumn they leave their nesting areas in Europe and western Asia, heading south towards tropical Africa. There, they spend the winter before migrating back in the spring.

Since the Mediterranean Sea cannot be crossed without active flight (as opposed to soaring), most of the large birds migrate across the Strait of Gibraltar and along the Dead Sea Rift. The escarpments on both sides of the Rift, as well as its warm climate, create excellent soaring conditions with abundant thermals (rising hot air). These enable migrating birds to fly long distances without wasting precious energy.

Desert Monitor Lizard (*Varanus griseus*)

Prominent Breeding Bird Species

Little Green Bee-eater

Among the birds of prey that breed along the Dead Sea Rift are Griffon Vulture (*Gyps fulvus*), Short-toed Eagle (*Circaetus gailicus*), Golden Eagle (*Aquila chrysaetos*), Boneili's Eagle (*Hiera-aetus fasciatus*), Sooty Falcon (*Falco concolor*) and the globally threatened Lesser Kestrel (*Falco naumanni*).

Breeding species of other birds include the territorial Wheatear (*Oenanthe lugens; O. leucopyga*), conspicuous by its black and white colors; the gray Desert Lark (*Ammomanes deserti*); Blackstart (*Cercomela melanura*), which is easily recognized by its prominent black tail; Chukar (*Alectoris chukar*), a black-striped, red-beaked partridge; Sand Partridge (*Ammoperdix heyi*), which has a high and loud cry; Tristram's Grackle (*Onychognathus tristramii*), whose whistle is very distinctive and whose wings are marked with orange patches; Fan-Tailed Raven (*Corvus rhipidurus*) which breeds on steep cliffs and often displays aerobatics; Arabian Babbler (*Turdoides squamiceps*), commonly seen under acacia and tamarisk trees; Sinai Rosefinch

Tristram's Grackle

Sinai Rosefinch

(*Carpodacus synoicus*) whose rose hues blend perfectly with the reddish colors of Petra's sandstone; Yellow-Vented Bulbul (*Pycnonotus xanthopygos*) whose typical habitat is oleander thicket; the colorful Dead Sea Sparrow (*Passer moabiticus*), which wanders in flocks; the tiny Palestine Sunbird (*Nectarinia osea*), boasting a metallic-blue gloss; and Little Green Bee-eater (*Merops orientalis*), inhabiting oases and conspicuous by its beautiful bluish-green colors.

Large areas along the Rift have been used as pastureland for ages and have witnessed a relentless struggle between shepherds and predators. Every Bedouin family has a story about wolves attacking their goats. Before gunpowder, primitive leopard traps, built of stones, were set on prominent

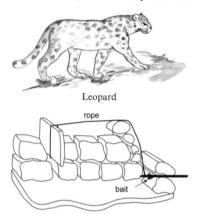

Leopard

Leopard trap

mountain saddles. Nowadays, predators are shot. Beside this ancient strife, hunting is regarded as a distinguished form of recreation. Game includes ibex, hyrax, porcupine, hare, pigeon and chukar. Hunting shelters built of stones and branches ("Kufra"

in Arabic) can be observed above water sources in many of the Rift's canyons. Since there is no need of hunting for meat, promoting the awareness to wildlife conservation may change the hunting mentality. The RSCN is currently doing so and would appreciate the help of every trekker.

"In all the wadis south of the Mujib and particularly in those of Mujib and Hasa, large herds of mountain goats, called by the Arabs Baden are met with... great numbers of them are killed by the people of Karak and Tafila, who hold their flesh in high estimation. They sell the large knotty horns to the Hebron merchants who carry them to Jerusalem, where they are worked into handles for knives and daggers." (J. L. Burckhardt, 1812)

Another conservation problem is the custom of hunting with falcons. Trained falcons are considered noble companions by wealthy sheikhs of the Arabian Peninsula, and may sell for $30,000 each. Falconry has led to a rapid decline in the numbers of the Houbara Bustard (*Chlamydotis undulata*), an impressive bird, which resembles a little ostrich.

Ibex

Nature Conservation

The Dead Sea Rift is a priceless cultural and historical possession with unequalled topographic and biotic characteristics. However, it has also been an important economic resource. Nowadays the potash companies, tourism industry, and water and irrigation projects all compete for the Rift's resources. Each of these sectors brings benefits to the region but also causes irreversible degradation of the environment. Insufficient coordination among the bordering countries adds its share of unsustainable development.

Eco-tourism itself is not always harmless, but it can be a means to prevent other, much more harmful development. It is us trekkers who carry the main obligation to keep the environment undisturbed.

Two major organizations are active in the conservation of the Jordanian part of the Dead Sea Rift:

The RSCN

The Royal Society for Conservation of Nature (RSCN) is an independent, voluntary organization devoted to the conservation of Jordan's wildlife and natural environment. It was established in 1966 under the patronage of King Hussein. The RSCN is involved in the protection and breeding of endangered species, the enforcement of conservation laws and anti-poaching measures, the prevention of environmental pollution (especially of the Gulf of 'Aqaba coastal strip) and on the whole increasing the national awareness of conservation.

Among the RSCN's achievements are the establishment of 6 nature reserves and a number of national parks. Another 6 nature reserves are in the process of being declared. Altogether the nature reserves will cover about 4% of Jordan's area.

The routes in this guidebook include the Mujib and Dana nature reserves. For further information, visit the organization's website www.rscn.org.jo or contact:
RSCN P.O. Box 6354, Amman, Jordan,
 Tel: 962–6–5337931
RSCN, Dana Visitor Center, Dana Village,
 Tel: 962–3–2270497/8

FoEME

Friends of the Earth Middle East (FoEME) is a consortium of non-governmental Jordanian, Israeli and Palestinian environmental organizations working jointly to promote sustainable development and create necessary conditions for lasting peace in the region. FoEME is promoting the registration of the Dead Sea Valley as a Biosphere Reserve and for World Heritage listing. This will be an important step towards coordinated development which will consider both man and nature.

For further details visit the organization's website www.foeme.org or contact:
FoEME P.O box 9341, Amman, Jordan,
 Tel: 962–6–5866602

People and Culture

Jordan's population is 4.7 million. The majority resides in Amman and the north, and only ten per cent in the south. Among the major cities of the south are Karak and Ma'an (with 150,000 people each), 'Aqaba (80,000), Madaba, Tafila and Wadi Musa. The population is a blend of Palestinian and Bedouin origin. Though most people of the south live in permanent settlements, a considerable number are still nomads.

The Bedouin are Arab nomads, of Muslim religion, who live throughout the Middle East, mostly in desert areas. Over the last century most of them have settled. The major Bedouin tribes which still wander in southwest

Jordan are the Howeitat, 'Amarin, Sa'idiyin, 'Azazma, Hayawat, Jahalin and Badul. In the past, clashes among the tribes were a matter of routine but since the early 20th century they have abated. The establishment of the modern state brought with it central authority, in which the Bedouin have a part. The tribes have retained their identity, but became united under one flag. Though there are no strict tribal territories any longer, there still are geographic regions in which one tribe is more prevalent than another.

The traditional Bedouin economy is based on goat herding. The goats supply milk, meat and wool and may sell for about 60 JD a head. Many Bedouin still migrate seasonally in quest of pasturage. In winter and spring, they camp in the 'Araba and the Dead Sea valleys, where it is warm and the rains usually bring early growth of grass. During summer and autumn, they prefer the coolness of the plateau. In years of drought, the Bedouin may break their usual migration pattern and travel long distances to seek pasture. Their other alternative is to stay put, and feed their flocks on bought barley and hay.

The Bedouin tent is traditionally made of woven black goat hair and can be dismantled and erected easily. The tent is supported by wooden poles and is divided into different quarters: one for the parents and the youngsters, and several others for the older members of the family, for guests and for the goats.

The Bedouin woman is responsible for raising the children as well as all the household chores such as cooking, fetching water and gathering firewood. The man is responsible for the economic and physical security of his family. Traditional Bedouin livelihood has always relied on other activities besides herding. In the past, such jobs included escorting travellers through the desert, as well as raiding other tribes, or farmers. Today, Bedouin often work in an archaeological excavation, cultivating a small field, guiding tourists or serving in the army. Among those who have forsaken the pastoral life, unemployment is widespread.

In the last decades acquiring education has become increasingly popular. Even nomadic Bedouin families send most of their children to a preliminary school. The government encourages this trend by maintaining small schools in remote areas. When a family migrates pupils might stay over with relatives.

Marriage is arranged by the families. Dating is not acceptable and the young couple usually has little say in the matchmaking. The best opportunity to get acquainted is while grazing, away from the vigilant eyes of the elders. Usually, people marry within their extended family or tribe, though inter-tribal marriages are not uncommon. Marriage celebrations are usually held in separate reception tents for males and females. Great cauldrons of goat meat and rice are cooked on an open fire while the guests enjoy camel races and honor the new couple by shooting off their rifles. Polygamy is not uncommon and you may encounter a Bedouin husband with up to four wives.

Although the pickup truck has largely taken the camel's place, camel and donkey are still the traditional pack animals of the desert. The female camels are not used as pack animals and can often be seen in herds that wander untended. Their only chore is to deliver offspring. Camels are considered precious property and may sell for more than 1,000 JD!

When a Bedouin family shifts camp, it may leave many valuable belongings behind — under a tree, inside a cave used as a hoarding place, or outside in broad daylight. Complete folded tents are sometimes left hanging on acacia trees. As a nomadic society, the Bedouin have developed moral codes that suit life in the desert. Nobody will touch another man's belonging even when it is not locked away and hidden. Another desert custom, vital in this harsh environment, is hospitality. When passing a Bedouin tent, an invitation for tea is almost inevitable. Guests are usually welcomed to sit around the fireplace where soon enough neighboring Bedouin will gather, and storytelling will commence.

Language

The Bedouin you will encounter while trekking probably speak only Arabic. Knowing a few Arabic words can definitely help you to get along. The following are basic pronunciation rules:

Q is often pronounced like **g** as in "good". Thus 'A**q**aba actually sounds like 'A**g**aba and the village **Q**urei**q**ira at the 'Araba Valley is only known as **G**ureigira. A trail — *naqb* is *nagb* and so on.

Kh is pronounced as in the Scottish "lo**ch**".

H symbolizes two different Arabic letters. One is pronounced as in "help" (Wadi el **H**idan). The other is a strong guttural h, more like the German "nacht" (the correct sound in *mar**h**aba* — welcome). The latter h is marked by an underscore (h̲) only in the list below and in the index.

Gh is a guttural r. A cave — *mg**h**ara* sounds more like *mrara*.

The sign **'** stands for a guttural consonant. Ask a Jordanian to say **'**Aqaba, or *sab**'**a* — seven, to hear what it sounds like.

Greetings

Hello	*salam 'aleikum*
Hello (in response)	*'aleikum es-salam*
Welcome	*mar̲haba*
Thank you	*shukran*
How are you	*kif h̲alak/ek? (m/f)*
I am fine	*el h̲amdulillah*
	mabsut/a (m/f)
OK	*kwayes*
Excellent	*tammam*
Good morning	*sabah̲ el kheir*
Good evening	*masa el kheir*
Good night	*tisbah̲ ala kheir*
Yes	*aiwa*
No	*la*

Sorry	*afwan*
No problem	*ma fi mushkila*
Please	*min fadlak/ek (m/f)*
Goodbye	*ma'a salameh*
Have a good journey	*tlaqi kheir (may you find good)*

Features

Mountain	*jabel*
Spur, ridge line	*'arqub*
Saddle	*raqabeh*
Cliff/s	*towr, tiran*
	sid, sudud
Gorge	*siq*
Water	*mai*
Valley, watercourse	*wadi*
Stream, flood, flow	*sill*
Waterfall	*shalal*
Pool	*birkeh*
Spring	*'ein*
Well	*bir*
Shallow well	*tmileh*
Hot spring	*h̲ammam*
Dam	*sadeh*
Stone	*h̲ajar*
Cairn	*rujum*
Big rock, boulder	*dims*
Cave	*mghara*
Ruin	*khirbeh*
Tree	*shajar*
Road, way	*tariq*
Tarmac road	*tariq asfalt*
Dirt road	*tariq tarabia*
Mountain trail	*naqb*
Tent	*kheimeh*
Bedouin tent	*beit esh-sha'ar*
Field	*mazra'a*
Garden	*bustan*
Firewood	*h̲atab*
Fire	*nar*
Village	*balad*
Reserve	*mahemiya*
House	*beit*
Shop	*dukan*
Hotel	*funduq*
Guide	*dalil*
Bread	*khubez*
Food	*akel*

Directions

Let's go	*yalla nimshi*

Now	el an		You (male)	enta
Early	bakir		You (female)	enti
Stop	waqef!		Him	huwa
Wait	istana/i! (m/f)		Her	heya
Quickly	bisari'a		Us	nihna
Slowly	shwayeh shwayeh		Them	humeh
Distance	masafeh			
Close	qarib		**Questions**	
Far	be'id		How much?	qadesh?
Here	hon		Where?	wein, fein?
There	hunak		Is there?	fi?
This	hada		What?	esh, shu?
From	min		When?	emta?
To	ila		Why?	lesh?
There isn't	ma fish		May I...?	mumkin...?
Left	yasar			
Right	yamin		**Help**	
Straight	'ala tul		Help	msa'ada
Between	bein		Ill	'ayan/e (m/f)
Up	fok		Medicine	dawa
Down	tahet		Problem	mushkila
More	kaman			
North	shimal		**Animals**	
South	janub		Camel	jamal
West	gharb		Donkey	hemar
East	sharq		Eagle	niser
			Falcon	saqer
Weather			Fox	el husayeini
Rain	matar		Goat	me'iz
Wind	hawa		Hyena	daba'
Hot	shob		Ibex	baden
Cold	bared		Mosquitoes	namus
Good	kwayes		Leopard	nimr
Bad	mish kwayes		Pigeon	hammam
			Sheep	kharuf
Adjectives			Snake	haya
Big	kbir		Wolf	dib
Small	zghir			
Easy	sahel		**Plants**	
Hard	si'heb		Acacia	sial
Tired	ta'aban/e (m/f)		Juniper	'ar'ar
Heavy	theqil		Oak	balut
Happy	mabsut/a (m/f)		Oleander	difle
Expensive	ghali		Palm tree	nakhel
Cheap	rkhis		Pistacia	butum
Hungry	ju'an/e (m/f)		Poplar	rasharish
Thirsty	'atshan/e (m/f)		Reeds	quseib
Many	ktir		Tamarisk	tarfa
			White desert broom	ratam
Pronouns			Willow	'araba
Me	ana		Wormwood	shih

Numbers

0	*sifer*
1	*wahad*
2	*tnein*
3	*talateh*
4	*arba'a*
5	*khamsa*
6	*sita*
7	*sab'a*
8	*tamaniya*
9	*tis'a*
10	*'ashara*
11	*hda-'ash*
12	*tna-'ash*
13	*talta-'ash*
14	*arba'ta-'ash*
15	*khamasta-'ash*
16	*sita-'ash*
17	*sab'ata-'ash*
18	*tamanta-'ash*
19	*tis'ata-'ash*
20	*'ishrin*
21	*wahad wa 'ishrin*
30	*talatin*
40	*arba'in*
50	*khamsin*
60	*sitin*
70	*sab'in*
80	*tamanin*
90	*tis'in*
100	*miyeh*
127	*miyeh sab'a wa 'ishrin*
200	*miten*
300	*talt-miyeh*
400	*arba'a miyeh*
1000	*alf*
¼	*rub'*
½	*nus*

Time

Hour	*sa'a*
Minute	*daqiqa*
One o'clock	*sa'a wahad*
Eleven o'clock	*sa'a hda-'ash*
Daytime	*naher*
Nighttime	*leil*
Morning	*sabah*
Evening	*masa*
Today	*el yom*
Day	*yom*
Days	*ayam*

Tomorrow	*bukra*
Yesterday	*mbareh*
Week	*usbu'*
Before	*qabel*
After	*ba'ad*
Sunday	*yom el ahed*
Monday	*yom eli-tnein*
Tuesday	*yom et-talateh*
Wednesday	*yom el arba'a*
Thursday	*yom el khamis*
Friday	*yom el juma'a*
Saturday	*yom es-sabt*

Useful verbs

I am going	*baruh*
I am walking	*bamshi*
I am climbing	*batasalaq*
I want	*bidi*

Useful phrases

Where are you going?
la wein timshi?

I am going to Wadi Mujib.
bamshi ila Wadi Mujib.

I arrived from...
jet min...

Where are you from?
min wein enta/i (m/f)?

I am from England.
ana min el Baritania.

What is your name?
shu ismak/ek (m/f)?

My name is...
ismi....

Do you speak Arabic?
btihki 'arabi?

I only speak a little.
bahki shwayeh.

Where is the way to Mount Feid?
wein tariq Jabel Feid?

This is the way!
hada el tariq!

How many hours is it to...?
kam sa'at ila...?

Where can I find a guide to...?
wein fi dalil ila...?

How is the trail to...?
kif en-naqb ila...?

How is the water?
kif el mai?

Where can I find water?
wein fi mai?
I want to walk to...
bidi amshi ila...
Is it possible to sleep here?
mumkin anam hon?

Where can I find food?
wein fi akel?
I will come back in three days.
barja' ba'ad talat-ayam.
May I take a photo?
mumkin bakhod surah?

Practical Information

When to go

Trekking and canyoning in Jordan can be undertaken throughout the year although spring and fall are considered by many as the best periods. November to March is the rainy season. It can get quite cold in the highlands, with temperatures occasionally dropping close to zero (32° F). However, along the Dead Sea and the 'Araba Valley day temperatures are usually comfortable (around 15° C, 60° F). Unless you are allergic to rain, this is a good period to explore the southern part of the Dead Sea Rift (from Wadi Musa to the Gulf of 'Aqaba) as well as to visit Jordan's better-known historical sites while they are free of crowds. The season is unsuitable for trekking in most of the northern canyons, whose waters are rather cold, and there is always a risk of flash floods. However, if the sky is clear and the forecast is unclouded, descending canyons with thermal springs can be a rare treat.

Mid-March is usually the beginning of spring in the lower valleys, but there can still be some rainy days. It is usually only in April that flowers begins to spread over the higher places. Dana Nature Reserve is then in its best attire and all the routes in this guidebook can be followed. Canyon waters, however, may still be chilly.

May is usually comfortable, allowing enjoyable hiking along most of the routes though you can expect some hot days. June, July and August are the hottest months, with day temperatures occasionally around 30–40° C (85–105° F) — an ideal period to escape into the wet, tropical shelter of several canyons north of Wadi Musa. Most of the routes in the southern regions are not recommended. Visiting historical sites when it is hot may be a tiring experience.

September and October have beautiful days, but there is always a slight risk of rain, which increases towards November. Because of flash flood hazard the Mujib Gorge is officially closed between November 1st and March 31st.

Further information about when to undertake a trek is included in the 'Trekking Information' chapter, in the introduction to each region, and in the introduction to each route.

The table below presents average annual rainfall and temperatures (courtesy of Jordan Meteorological

		Amman	Karak	Safi (Dead Sea)	'Aqaba ('Araba Valley)
Elevation		800 m	900 m	-400 m	0 m
Annual rainfall		500 mm	270 mm	70 mm	30 mm
January Mean daily temp. ⁰ C	Max.	15	16	20	20
	Min.	2	2	12	10
April Mean daily temp. ⁰ C	Max.	26	24	31	31
	Min.	8	6	19	17
August Mean daily temp. ⁰ C	Max.	32	29	37	36
	Min.	21	20	31	29

Department). Notice how the climate varies considerably from the elevated plateau to the bottom of the Rift.

Getting to Jordan

Visa: In order to enter Jordan you need a valid visa. It can be obtained in advance in Jordanian embassies throughout the world, or purchased upon arrival. The fees for the visa are 10 JD for most nationalities. The visa is valid for two weeks. It can be extended at any police station (preferably in Amman or 'Aqaba).

Via air: The national carrier is Royal Jordanian Airlines, but many other companies offer direct flights to Jordan. You may arrive either at Queen 'Alia airport, 30 minutes' drive from Amman, or 'Aqaba airport at the southern tip of the country. A bus service operates between Amman's Abdali bus station and Queen 'Alia airport.

Via land: Syria, Iraq, Saudi Arabia and Israel all have border crossings with Jordan. Entering from Syria is possible only through the er-Ramtha border crossing, northeast of Irbid. There are three border crossings with Saudi Arabia: ed-Dura on the shores of the Gulf of 'Aqaba, Mudawwara in the southeast, and el Umari south of Azraq. The only border crossing with Iraq is located east of Ruwayshid. Entering from Israel is possible through Sheikh Hussein bridge in the Jordan Valley west of Irbid, through Allenby bridge (also called Hussein bridge, open for non-Israelis with a pre-arranged visa) east of Jericho, or via the 'Araba Valley border crossing, a few km north of 'Aqaba.

Via Sea: A ferry operates between Nuweibeh in Egypt (Sinai Peninsula) and 'Aqaba

Equipment

Although daytime can be very hot, especially in the summer, the nights are usually chilly, and in the elevated places it can get very cold (in winter the temperature may drop below zero).

Long cotton trousers, a cotton shirt and a sun hat are the best outfit for the day. Carry short trousers for walking in flowing canyons. A warm jacket and a warm hat are usually enough for the night. In the rainy season, take a rainproof jacket and an extra layer of thermal underwear for the night.

Light walking boots are recommended footwear. When canyoning, sandals allow sand grains to injure your feet. Trainers are your best choice for walking in the water, but unless you don't mind carrying an arsenal of footwear with you, it is better to leave them behind. Sandals are always good to have, for instance when your boots are wet.

The recommended amount of water you need to carry is specified for each route. Bear in mind that commercial water bottles are usually too small. If you plan to camp, you will need a stock of at least 4.5 liters. Plastic beverage containers are excellent.

Water purification tablets are useful. Sunglasses, suntan lotion and a lip ointment are mandatory.

A sleeping bag and a mat are usually enough during the summer, when there is no real need for a tent. Spending the night under the star-spangled desert sky is highly recommended. During the rainy season you will need a tent and a sleeping bag which gives you a rating of at least minus 5° C.

A fuel stove or a gas cooker are both adequate, though gas cartridges are a bit hard to obtain (they are mostly available in Amman, Wadi Musa and 'Aqaba). Other necessary equipment includes a torch, a compass, a pocket-knife and a first-aid kit.

A waterproof bag can be handy on a few routes and is a must on some others.

Abseiling and special equipment

Most of the routes in this guidebook **do not require any special equipment**. However several canyons cannot be negotiated without abseiling skills and suitable abseiling equipment. A full list of these canyons is included under 'Trekking information'. None of the routes require technical climbing skills.

The introductory information for each route specifies whether or not abseiling equipment is needed, as well as the length of rope, and the number of falls (waterfalls as well as dry falls). In general, all the routes which include abseiling can be negotiated with two 50 m ropes and ordinary

abseiling gear, and most of them with shorter, 40 m ropes. The height of each fall is specified in the route description.

Bear in mind! If something goes wrong you will be far from help, as some of the canyons are only rarely visited by trekkers or Bedouin. Add to this that there are no fixed bolts and pegs, and you need to be perfectly confident in your abseiling and canyoning abilities before embarking on such a route.

Natural anchors are usually abundant. Avoid putting bolts and pegs into the rock, but take a set of chocks and cams just in case. Anchors may be several metres away from the abseiling point so carry slings and ropes to leave behind for last descent. **Do not trust abseil slings and ropes which were left by others!** Flash floods and intense sunlight degrade them rapidly.

The following table includes recommended abseiling gear.

Equipment	Quantity	Remarks
50 m rope	2	a 9 mm rope is preferable
Harness		
Carabiners	at least 10	
Friction device	at least 2	suitable for abseiling on two ropes
Slings and prusiks		
Set of chocks and cams		
Short ropes and slings for last descent		abseil points may be distant from the edge of the fall
Helmet		

Time

Jordan is two hours ahead of GMT in winter and one hour in summer.

Money

At the time of writing, the Jordanian Dinar (JD) is worth about one Eng-

lish pound. It is divided into 1,000 fils or 100 piasters (*qirsh*). A shilling coin is worth 50 fils or 5 piasters. Traveller's cheques and credit cards are accepted in the major banks. The rates and the commission vary from place to place. It is advisable always to carry some cash.

Books

A wide choice of books about Jordan is available in the bookshops of Amman and 'Aqaba. Natural history books can also be found at the souvenir shop in the Dana Nature Reserve. Among the general travel guides are:

Jordan, Syria & Lebanon Handbook, Mannheim I., Winter D., Footprint Handbooks, 1998.

Jordan, P. Greenway, D. Finlay, Lonely Planet, 2000.

Jordan, Rough Guide, Teller M., Rough Guide, 1998.

Recommended companions for your explorations are:

The Birds of the Hashemite Kingdom of Jordan, Andrews I. J., 1995.

Wild Flowers of Jordan, Al-Eisawi D. M. H., 1998.

If you are planning to trek in Wadi Rum, get hold of:

Treks and Climbs in Wadi Rum, Howard T., Cicerone Press, 1987, new edition 1997.

Walks and Scrambles in Wadi Rum, Howard T. and Taylor D., Al Kutba, 1993.

Reading the descriptions of the early explorers is fascinating, both before and after your visit. Unfortunately some of the books are hard to obtain and are only found in the larger libraries.

Travels in Syria and the Holy Land, Burckhardt J. L., London, 1822, reprinted by Darf Publishers, 1992.

Travels in Egypt and Nubia, Syria and Asia Minor, Irby C. L. and Mangles J., London, 1823, reprinted by Darf Publishers, 1985.

Letters on Egypt, Edom and the Holy Land, Lord Lindsay, London 1838.

Biblical Researches in Palestine, Mount Sinai and Arabia Petraea, Robinson E. and Smith E., London, 1838.

The United States' Expedition to the River Jordan and the Dead Sea, Lynch W. F., London, 1849.

Narrative of a Journey Round the Dead Sea and in the Bible Lands, De Saulcy F., London, 1854.

The Desert of the Exodus, Palmer E. H., New York 1872, reprinted 1940.

Seven Pillars of Wisdom, Lawrence T. E., Penguin 1962.

The following bookstores in Amman have a relatively large selection of English books:

Jordan Book Center, Queen Rania Street in front of Distour newspaper,
Tel: 06-5155882.

University Bookshop,
Garden Street near Sport City,
Tel: 06-5606271.

Amman Book Center,
3rd circle, Jordan Insurance Building,
Tel: 06-4644013.

Jordan Distribution Agency,
Tala't Jabel Amman Street,
Tel: 06-4630191.

Maps

Fine-scaled maps of Jordan and the Dead Sea Rift are very hard to obtain. The maps in this guidebook should suffice to get you through all the routes described.

Geological maps of the Rift area on a 1:50,000 scale (!), but with faint contours of 40 m intervals, can be purchased at the cost of 4 JD each at the:

National Resources Authority (NRA),
8th Circle P.O Box (7) or (2220).
Code 1118. Amman. Jordan.
Tel: 962-6-5857600.

The Royal Jordanian Geographic Center produces a fine 1:750,000 road map of Jordan which is distributed free of charge in the tourist information centers. Also available is an excellent 1:5,000 map of Petra.

Royal Jordanian Geographic Center,
P.O. Box 20214, Al Jbeha, Amman,
Tel: 962-6-534188.

A good choice for a general view of the Rift is a 1:250,000 map that was published by:

The Survey of Israel, 1 Lincoln Street,
Tel Aviv, 65220,
Tel: 972-3-6231911.

Spectacular satellite maps which include the Dead Sea Rift and its canyons are available from:

ROHR Production Ltd.
Tel: 357-2-675082
E-mail: info@rohrproductions.com

Several other general maps of Jordan are available in bookstores throughout the world.

General tourist information

The Ministry of Tourism (Amman)
Tel: 962-6-4642311
Jordan Tourism Board (Amman)
Tel: 962-6-5678294
Petra Visitors Center
Tel: 962-3-2156020

Holidays

Friday is the official weekly holiday. Institutes such as banks and post offices are closed, but many shops are open.

Dates of Islamic holidays vary, since the Islamic calendar is based on the lunar year, which is shorter than the Gregorian year. Generally, the Islamic holidays occur about 11 days earlier than last year's Gregorian date. During the Islamic holidays most of the shops are open and public transportation operates. Parks and easy-to-reach hot springs may be crowded. Approximate dates for 2000 and 2001 are given below.

Muslim New Year		
	05.04.00	26.03.00
Prophet's Birthday		
	12.06.00	02.06.01
Prophet's Nocturnal Journey		
	24.10.00	14.10.01
The fast of Ramadan (for 29–30 days)		
	27.11.00	17.11.00
'Eid el Fiter (end of Ramadan)		
	26.12.00	16.12.01
'Eid el Adha (Feast of Sacrifice)		
	03.03.01	21.02.02

Other national holidays include:

January 30	King 'Abdullah's Birthday
May 1	Labor Day
May 25	Independence Day
June 9	King 'Abdullah's accession to the throne
June 10	Army Day
November 14	Memorial of King Hussein's birthday
December 25	Christmas

Getting around

By rented car: For most of the routes described in this guidebook, renting a car is not recommended, since they start at one point and end at another.

By bus: Public transport by bus is cheap, quite efficient, and provides an excellent opportunity to get to know people. However, along the Dead Sea and the 'Araba road, their services are very limited. The buses tend to leave when they are full, so do not expect punctuality.

By taxi: Service taxis (communal taxis) are usually available between major destinations. Their prices are similar to those of local buses.

Some of the trekking routes start

The Jordanian Dead Sea Rift – Madaba, Dhiban and Karak areas.

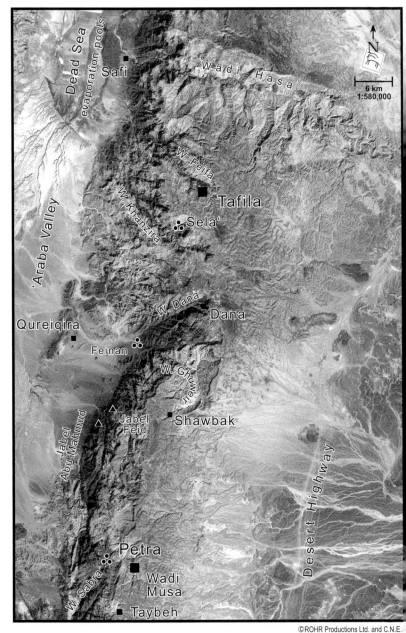

The Jordanian Dead Sea Rift – Tafila, Shawbak and Petra areas.

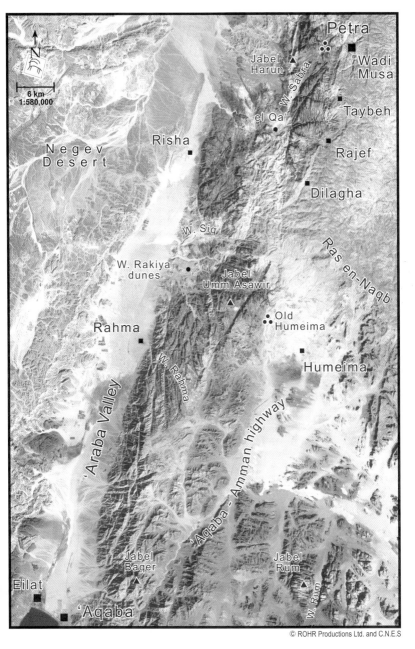

The Jordanian Dead Sea Rift – Petra, Humeima, Rum and Aqaba areas.

Top: Dana Nature Reserve. Mazes of white sandstone domes.
Left: Abseiling the upper waterfall of Wadi Karak (R.14)
Right: Swimming in the gorge of Wadi Mujib

I. H.

Noya Shiloni

I. H.

near small villages, which are best reached by regular taxi. Agree on the fare before getting on the road. An hour's drive usually costs about 5-8 JD. Hiring a taxi for the whole day costs about 50 JD.

By hitchhiking: Off the beaten track, hitchhiking is effective. It is one of the options along the Dead Sea and the 'Araba road, where many routes reach their end point. Some drivers will expect a small fee for their services.

By a local pickup truck: The approach to some of the routes is along dirt tracks, negotiable by high-clearance vehicles (4 WD is unnecessary). Since pickup trucks are the favorite Bedouin vehicle, it is possible to negotiate a ride even in very small villages. The rental cost for one day, including petrol, is around 30 JD. It can vary according to the distance you want to cover and the rules of the market. The same vehicle can pick you up at the end of your route (make sure the driver knows where!) and take you to the head of a new trail. It is appropriate to leave a tip for good service.

Women travellers

It is safer for a woman to travel on her own in Jordan than in many western countries. As a trekker you will surely surprise the local Bedouin and gain a lot of respect. Do not, however, wear shorts and sleeveless shirts in populated areas or when approaching a Bedouin encampment. The local inhabitants are not used to it, and you will probably attract undesirable attention.

Jordanian women do not frequent certain cafes and restaurants, not even with their husbands. Foreign women are generally welcome, though people will definitely stare.

Accommodation and camping

Accommodation in southern Jordan is available in Amman, Madaba, Karak, Mauta, Tafila, Dana, Wadi Musa, Ma'an and 'Aqaba. Prices for a cheap bed vary from 2 to 8 JD. A simple double room which might have a warm shower costs 6-15 JD. Higher grade hotels are not available in Tafila and Ma'an.

The only hotel accommodation along the eastern Dead Sea shore and the 'Araba Valley is close to the northern tip of the Dead Sea. Not far from the luxurious Movenpick and Dead Sea Hotel lies the Dead Sea Rest House, which is fairly cheap and might let you camp in its compound.

Official campsites operate in Dana Nature Reserve (One is located not far from the King's Highway and the other is in the 'Araba Valley, see 'Dana Nature Reserve' for details) and in Wadi Rum. Prices vary from 3 to 12 JD per person.

Camping in the wilderness is not allowed within the boundaries of the RSCN nature reserves, nor in Petra. Otherwise you may strike camp wherever, so long as you stay far from roads and settlements. Bear in mind that the local population is not yet used to self-sufficient travellers who camp on their own, and may display curiosity.

Food and drinks

There are many towns and villages along the King's Highway, where you can stock up for your trek. Recommended local groceries include:

Tehina (tahini) paste: Made from ground sesame seeds. Preparation involves mixing with an equal amount of water, adding salt, black pepper, garlic and lemon. Excellent for lunch.

Halva: A sweet pressed loaf made of sesame seeds. It can be eaten on its own or as a bread dressing.

Laban: An indestructible ball of dried goat cheese which lasts forever. To prepare it, mix with water and knead like dough. Add pieces of bread into the cheese dough. Recommended to be eaten with olive oil and hyssop (za'atar).

Burghul: Crushed wheat grains. First, prepare tomato soup. When the soup is ready, remove it from the fire, put the Burghul in, and cover the pot. Wait a few minutes until the Burghul absorbs all the fluid.

Za'atar (hyssop): A blend of thyme and two other aromatic herbs. A light spice to many dishes, or to be eaten on bread dipped in olive oil.

Tamer: Sticky hump of stoned, pressed dates. Most dates come from palm groves in Iraq, along the Euphrates River.

Apart from the above, most stores carry the usual trek foods such as rice, pasta, lentils, dehydrated soups, jam, biscuits, vegetables etc. Oatmeal and corn flakes are usually not available. Should you fancy carrying canned food, you will find a large choice. Apart from its weight it is not really environment-friendly, so why not skip it?

Simple restaurants serve mostly *hummus*, *ful* and *falafel*. Alcoholic drinks are not available in the small villages. You can get them in larger towns, in tourist cafes and restaurants.

Since the tap water in Jordan is safe, buying mineral water is not necessary. A better investment are the locally manufactured nectars of mango and guava.

Trekking information

The long treks and the routes which include abseiling are listed on the following pages. Dayhikes (as well as long treks) are listed in the introduction to each trekking region. Before choosing, check for the season and the nature of the route, then read the introduction to the route you have chosen to get further information.

The routes are rated as easy, moderate and strenuous, by taking into consideration the length of the route, the character of the trail, the altitude difference and the number of daily walking hours. The rating does not take into account abseiling skills. Where abseiling skills are required, this is clearly specified, including the length of rope you will need.

> **Easy route:** A dayhike with an obvious walking route and with hardly any demanding obstacles such as long steep ascents or exposed rock ledges. Usually takes less than 5 hours to complete.
> **Moderate route:** The trek may include short sections of bouldering, steep ascents and descents, and narrow goat trails. Walking days may last from dawn till dusk.
> **Strenuous route:** The trek may include exposed ledges, long and steep ascents and descents (sometimes upon scree with no trail at all), long bouldering sections and swimming in gorges. On the other hand, water sources may be scarce. Route-finding skills are essential.

Walking hours, in the introduction to each route, include time allotted for rest, meals, and activities such as scenic stops or dips in a pool. Thus you can expect to do the whole route within the hours specified. Net walking time, from point A to point B (without the extras mentioned), are noted under the actual route description. Abseiling time, included in the walking hours, is based on a party of three trekkers. More trekkers will increase the walking hours, and you may have to split the route over two days.

Water

The introduction to each route notes the availability of water, and a recommended amount you need to carry. Do not hesitate to carry more water on hot days. The lack or shortage of water is a major cause of trekking disasters in arid regions! When trekking for a few days you will have to rely on springs, streams, wells and sometimes stagnant water from potholes. Most of these waters are potable, though you can never be sure. Carry water purification tablets and avoid drinking from the larger streams, which carry their water from long distances. Side streams are always a safer bet, while springs which issue straight from the rock are your best choice. Hot springs can be a little salty but apart from the temperature their water is usually fine. The amount of water in potholes varies considerably according to the floods of the year and the season. Thus, canyons without year-round streams offer strings of pools but be completely dry at other periods.

Trek maps

The maps included in this guidebook combined with the route description should suffice to get you through all the routes. Their scale is 1:100,000, 1:50,000 or 1:25,000 as specified on each map. Contour interval is always 100 m. Due to the relatively large contour interval some significant terrain information cannot be shown on the map (such as low hills and cliffs).

Wherever this information is of importance it appears in the route description.

Guides and organized treks

Even the most strenuous route will look completely different if you are escorted by a Bedouin guide. Route-finding problems and worries about water are then reduced considerably. Learning about Bedouin lore is a side benefit.

Although information about the need for guides and where to look for them is given for each route, due to the language barrier finding a guide is not always so easy.

The local Bedouin know their camp environment better than anyone else. However, canyoning is not their expertise and most of them have never abseiled. Do not expect them to guide you through canyons which demand abseiling!

The cost of unprofessional guides varies, but is around 15 JD for a day. Agree on the price in advance and remember that tipping is expected.

Guides can also be contacted through a number of adventure travel companies. Since many of the routes in this guidebook are not yet known, you will have to check if they can help.

The following travel companies can organize the whole trek including guides:

Plaza Tours, Amman P.O. Box 950531,
   Amman Tel: 962-6-5651773
   E-mail: Plaza@nets.com.jo
La Beduina Tours, P.O. Box 81, Petra
   Tel: 962-3-2157099
   E-mail: beduina1@go.com.jo
Nyazi Tours, P.O. Box 1136, 'Aqaba
   Tel: 962-3-2022801
   E-mail: nyazi@index.com.jo

For routes within the nature reserves (Dana and Mujib), contact the RSCN (see 'Nature conservation').

THE LONG TREKS

Route	Days	Rating	Season	Description
4. Across northern Moab from Wadi Mukheiris to Wadi Himara	3	strenuous	spring fall	Wide canyons, abundant waterfalls, superb views towards the Dead Sea, the highest waterfalls in Jordan, impressive stalactites.
21. Wadi Hasa, the full length	2	moderate	spring fall	Boulder-studded white canyon, warm springs, spectacular red sandstone canyon, fast-flowing river, thousands of wild palms, hanging gardens.
28. From Wadi 'Aima to Wadi Khanzira	2	moderate incl. abseiling	spring summer fall	Sandstone gorges, hanging gardens, little pools, high-lying campsite with fine views.
37. From Wadi Hamra to Wadi Ghuweir	2	moderate	spring summer fall	Spectacular views, subtropical oasis, narrow sandstone gorge, lush hanging gardens, cascades.
41. The Black Mountains	4	strenuous	spring fall winter	Awe-inspiring black summits, spectacular views, canyons in igneous rocks, potholes.
42. Canyons and ancient caravan routes	5	strenuous incl. abseiling	spring	Steep and demanding trek, black canyons carved in igneous rocks, potholes, dry falls and waterfalls, rewarding views, Nabataean ruins.
51. From Petra to Taybeh	2	moderate	all-year	Intriguing archeological sites, rewarding views, narrow *siq,* mazes of white sandstone domes.
52. The Rajef Inselbergs	3	moderate	all-year	Mazes of domes, rewarding views, narrow sandstone canyons, springs.
57. Across southern Edom from Dilagha to Humeima	4	strenuous	spring fall winter	Spectacular views, impressive dune field, narrow sandstone and igneous canyons.
61. From Petra to Humeima	6	strenuous	spring fall winter	Extremely rich variety of landscapes, summits, canyons, intriguing archeological sites, sand dunes.
64. From Wadi Khubat to Wadi Rahma	3	strenuous incl. abseiling	spring	Rewarding views, dry falls, water-filled potholes.

ROUTES WITH ABSEILING

Route	Days	Rating	Season	Descript
6. Wadi Zarqa Ma'in, upper canyon (G)	1	moderate *2.2*	spring summer fall	2 waterfa pools, limestone canyon. Carry two 35 m ropes.
10. Wadi Mujib's (G) lower gorge *longest*	1	strenuous *3.1*	1st April to 31st October	Jordan's Grand Canyon. Spectacular 15 m waterfall, 200 m deep sandstone gorge, gushing water. Carry two 20 m ropes.
12. Wadi el Hidan	1	strenuous *3.4 inf* *2.5 sup*	1st April to 31st October	Majestic 50 m waterfall, basalt canyon, spectacular sandstone gorge, rich variety of colors, warm and cold springs, pools. Carry two 50 m ropes.
14. Wadi Karak (G) *ibn Hamad (G)* *Hasa longest*	1	moderate *2.9* *2.6* *2.8*	spring summer fall	2 waterfalls, narrow sandstone gorge, hanging gardens, side streams, surprising dripping waterfall. Carry two 50 m ropes.
16. Wadi 'Assal	1	moderate *2.5*	spring summer fall	6 falls (2 with water), sandstone gorge, hanging gardens. Carry two 30 m ropes.
24. Wadi Feifa and Wadi 'Aima	1	moderate	spring summer fall	4 falls (1 with water), sandstone gorge, dripping springs, hanging gardens. Carry two 20 m ropes.
28. From Wadi 'Aima to Wadi Khanzira	2	moderate	spring summer fall	As for Route 24 plus elevated campsite, rewarding views, pools and sandstone gorge in Wadi Khanzira.
40. Wadi Feid ✗	1	strenuous	spring summer fall	12 waterfalls! Awe-inspiring black canyon cutting through igneous rocks, pools, junipers. Carry two 40 m ropes.
42. Canyons and ancient caravan routes	5	strenuous	spring	Demanding trek, 10 dry falls in Wadi Qunai, 13 dry falls in Wadi Umm Hashba, 5 waterfalls in Wadi Musa,, black rocks, potholes, pools, rewarding views, Nabataean ruins. Carry two 40 m ropes.
46. Wadi Musa	1	moderate *2.0.*	spring summer fall	5 waterfalls, pools, sheer black rock faces, junipers. Carry two 30 m ropes.
63. Wadi Rahma	1	moderate	spring	3 dry falls, huge water-filled potholes, dramatic breach through a rock barrier. Carry two 50 m ropes.
64. From Wadi Khubat to Wadi Rahma	3	strenuous	spring	As for Route 63 plus a string of potholes, rewarding views. Carry two 50 m ropes.

eral code of behavior

Respect the customs and life style of local people.

Ask before you take photos.

Dress modestly (both male and female). Do not wear short trousers and sleeveless shirts in populated areas or when approaching Bedouin dwellings.

Be aware that Bedouin shepherd girls are not used to talk with male strangers and may even be frightened by their presence.

Avoid handing out candies, pens or other goodies among the local children, if there is no particular reason. It promotes begging and pestering, a habit which fortunately hardly exists in Jordan.

Leave nothing behind. Even short-lived organic waste affects the environment.

Flowers, rocks, fossils and archeological artifacts should not be collected.

Water in the desert is very precious. Do not use detergents at water sources. It kills the fauna and degrades the water quality.

Do not make large open fires. If you do make a fire, avoid blackening of stones and bury the ashes afterwards.

Burn toilet paper and bury the waste.

Leave ancient rock inscriptions to their solitude. Do not add your own graffiti!

Inside nature reserves, camping is allowed only at the appointed sites. Avoid open fires and keep to permitted hiking trails.

Avoid putting bolts and pegs into the rock when abseiling unless it is absolutely necessary. Use natural anchors instead.

Safety and First Aid

Dehydration

When trekking in an arid environment, especially during summer, you rapidly lose large amounts of water. Failure to return the amounts lost will lead to a state of dehydration (diarrhea and vomiting increase the risk). The symptoms of dehydration are dark urine or lack of urine, headaches, nausea, dry mouth, general weakness and finally prostration. Extreme dehydration is fatal.

To prevent dehydration, drink more than you feel you need. Drinking 5–7 liters during a normal summer day hike is not at all unusual. Include soup and tea in the camp menu. Wearing long cotton trousers is recommended. Head cover is a must!

Heat stroke

When putting in intensive effort in a very hot environment, you may become overheated — even if you drink enough. The result is heat stroke, the symptoms of which are high fever (sometimes above 41° C), headaches, rapid pulse, hot skin, dizziness and problems with balance and speech, fainting and possible convulsions. To avoid heat stroke, rest frequently in shady places and do not walk during the hottest hours of a summer day (11:00–15:00). Instead, use the cool hours of early morning or late afternoon.

Heat stroke should be treated as an emergency — failure to cool the body rapidly can cause death. Put the victim in a shady place and cool his body by wet clothing and fanning. Sluicing him off with water, if available, is recommended. Give the person to drink, if he can swallow. Bring him to a medical facility as soon as possible.

Flash floods

While canyoning, flash floods are a serious risk. If you get caught in a narrow gorge when the flood arrives all you can do is pray. One way of avoiding the risk is not to enter narrow canyons during the rainy season. This may be the wisest thing to do. The Mujib gorge is officially closed at this time of year and other canyons which carry streams are not so enjoyable anyway, since their water is cold.

However, some "dry" canyons, especially those of southern Edom, can be very friendly during winter. In Moab you can find canyons which flow with thermal water such as Wadi Zarqa Ma'in, Wadi 'Afra, and Wadi Ibn Hammad.

If you venture into the canyons during the rainy season, make sure that the skies are clear and check the weather forecast (any hotel with radio or television can tell you the forecast if asked for this specific attention).

Since most of the canyons draw their water from the highlands, they may flood even when the overhead sky is perfectly clear. Summer floods, though very rare, can also occur. When the sky becomes heavily clouded, or it begins to rain, get out of the canyon as quickly as you can. If stuck inside, try and reach a wide section and climb on one of the banks. Whenever canyoning, avoid camping in narrows. Even when the canyon is wide, do not camp in the actual bed, but look for elevated terraces.

Snakebite

Though several species of venomous snakes inhabit the region, cases of snakebite are very rare. To avoid bites, do not poke underneath stones and bushes. Keep your camping site clean of leftovers, which might attract rodents and their viper predators. Closed shoes are safer than sandals, but shake out shoes and clothing before putting them on.

In case of a bite, calm the victim and let him lie in complete rest. Immobilize the affected limb. Apply an elastic bandage firmly behind the bite (i.e. toward the body), but make sure you can still feel a pulse under it! Do not cut, suck, burn, or put ice on the bite. The bitten person should not eat or drink, except cold drinks, for several hours. A bitten person should not walk — carry or cart him to the nearest first-aid station. Bring the (dead!) snake for identification, or give a description of it to enable the right choice of serum.

Scorpions

Scorpions in Jordan include several species, among which the yellow scorpions are usually more dangerous than the black ones, though there are exceptions. The symptoms of a scorpion sting include severe local pain as well as redness and swelling of the affected area. Rapid pulse and breathing, cold sweat, excessive salivation and high body temperature usually evolve later.

When stung by a scorpion, follow the directions as in the case of snakebite, though the risk is smaller. Unlike snakebite it is recommended to cool the affected limb with cold water or ice. Reach a medical facility even if the victim seems fine — intoxication symptoms may appear several hours after the sting.

General

Vaccinations are not required for entering Jordan. Consult your doctor — some doctors recommend polio, typhoid, tetanus and hepatitis vaccinations. There is a very small risk of malaria. Anti-malaria tablets are usually not advised.

Rescue

Some of the treks in this guidebook go through areas where you are unlikely to see Bedouin, not to mention any other trekkers beside yourself. This, and the fact that there is no official wilderness rescue team in Jordan, and you are advised to exercise extra caution.

When in trouble and you need help, keep in mind that the King's Highway is always above you and the 'Araba and the Dead Sea road are always below. You cannot be more than 10–15 km away from the nearest help. The hazard is smaller than in many other trekking regions in the world.

The Rum tourist police has engineered several successful helicopter rescues.

If you trek south of Wadi Hasa and require assistance, you can call either of the following:

Rum Tourist Police	**03 2015661**
Petra Emergency Center	**03 2157161**

For assistance in the rest of Jordan:

Police	**192**
First Aid & Ambulance	**193**
Civil Defense	**199**

The northern tip of the Dead Sea and Madaba area
From Wadi Mukheiris to Wadi Zarqa Ma'in

Wide canyons with impressive views of the Dead Sea, high waterfalls and sparkling pools are the attractive features of this region. Its rocks are crossed by many dykes, which influence the courses of wadis and the location of falls. The highest waterfalls in Jordan, about 80 m high, are found in this region in Wadi Himara.

Descending from the 800 m high Moab Plateau, the canyons reach the Dead Sea at 400 m below sea level. Though most of the canyons carry year-round streams, their drainage basins are small and their discharge is limited. The only exception is Wadi Zarqa Ma'in. With an annual flow of 30 million cubic m, it is second only to Wadi Mujib. Wadi Zarqa Ma'in is famous for its thermal waterfalls. Descending through its canyon is worth any Jacuzzi.

The major town in the region is Madaba, an hour's drive from Amman, known for its Byzantine mosaic floor which depicts a map of the Holy Land. Madaba is a convenient base to explore this region, offering several small hotels. Northwest of Madaba is Mount Nebo, where according to tradition Moses died after seeing the Promised Land from afar.

A resort area is being developed on the Dead Sea shore near the outlet of Wadi Mukheiris. At the time of writing only three hotels operate there: the Dead Sea Hotel, the Movenpick Hotel and the Dead Sea Rest House which might let you camp in its compound. Another resort (Hammamat Ma'in) is located in the upper reaches of Wadi Zarqa Ma'in. It includes spa facilities and hotel accommodation (Hotel Ashtar).

The following routes are suggested in this region:

Route	Days	Rating	Season	Description
1. Wadi Mukheiris	1 (9 hours)	moderate	spring summer fall	Wide canyon, shallow pools, 20 m waterfall, impressive stalactites.
2. Wadi Manshala	1 (9 hours)	strenuous	spring summer fall	Six waterfalls one after the other, remarkable ravine with palm trees.
3. Wadi Himara	1 (7 hours)	strenuous	spring summer fall	The highest waterfalls in Jordan, impressive views.
4. Across northern Moab from Wadi Mukheiris to Wadi Himara	3	strenuous	spring fall	Highly rewarding views towards the Dead Sea, including Routes 1–3.
5. Wadi Zarqa Ma'in, lower gorge	1 (8 hours)	moderate	spring fall winter	Thermal stream, red sandstone gorge, abundant natural Jacuzzis.
6. Wadi Zarqa Ma'in, upper canyon	1 (7 hours)	moderate incl. abseiling	spring summer fall	Two impressive waterfalls, limestone canyon, cold water, pools.

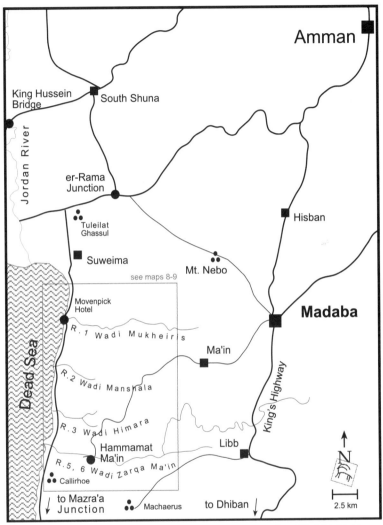

Map 7: The northern tip of the Dead Sea and Madaba area — from Wadi Mukheiris to Wadi Zarqa Ma'in

1. Wadi Mukheiris
Map 8

Wadi Mukheiris is a wide canyon with an impressive 20 m waterfall and several pools. Surprising stalactites hide behind veils of droplets and ferns in the canyon's upper reaches. The trail offers fine look-throughs towards the Dead Sea.

Type of route: One-way and back.
Altitude difference, Distance and Walking time: 500 m ascent and descent, 9 km, 9 hours.
Rating: Moderate. Expect wet shoes.
Special equipment: None.
Guides: Not really needed, but you can try the village of Suweima.
Water: A perennial stream. Those who choose not to drink from it should carry 3 liters each.
Season: Spring, summer and fall, though summer may be too hot.
Getting there and back: The trail starts and ends at the Dead Sea road, in front of the Movenpick hotel, 16 km from er-Rama junction. Make arrangements to be picked up, or you will have to hitchhike back to er-Rama or Mazra'a junctions.

Er-Rama junction offers almost constantly available taxis and local pickup trucks which can take you to the starting point of this and many other routes. To reach the junction from Amman, take the bus to the village of South Shuna. The drive takes about 30 minutes. **Mazra'a junction** is located on the Dead Sea shore beneath Karak. It is served by infrequent buses to and from Karak. The drive to Karak takes about 30 minutes.

Walking upstream through a wide canyon you arrive at a 5 m waterfall within 50 minutes. Backtrack 50 m and bypass the waterfall on the left (north). Beyond it begins a delightful series of cascades and ponds, with some tricky passages between and above huge boulders, and underneath branches of trees. A spectacular 20 m waterfall, dropping into a little pool, comes into sight within about an hour from the bypass.

To skirt this waterfall, backtrack 200 m passing two hanging gardens on the northern wall. Climb steeply northwards near a little tamarisk tree and proceed levelly above a vegetation cluster. Reaching a wide rocky ledge, continue eastwards to the head of yet another waterfall, located just above the one skirted.

Continue in the streambed for about 20 minutes until a graded waterfall and a giant boulder block the way. In order to bypass it, go right (south) into a short rocky corridor and climb over some rock slabs to the right. Following goat trails on the south bank, cross a side wadi and descend back into the main wadi, whose floor consists of a smooth rocky surface.

A beautiful surprise is reached within 20 minutes of the graded waterfall.

Inside a shallow cave are stalactites obscured by sparkling droplets. Some of the stalactites resemble elephant ears and others are more like macaroni. Maidenhair ferns adorn the mouth of the cave and at its rear end water gushes through a crevice. Just above the cave and unseen from the streambed is a water reservoir whose water is used by the local inhabitants to irrigate their fields. Leaving the cave, retrace your steps towards the Dead Sea road. The way back offers magnificent views westwards.

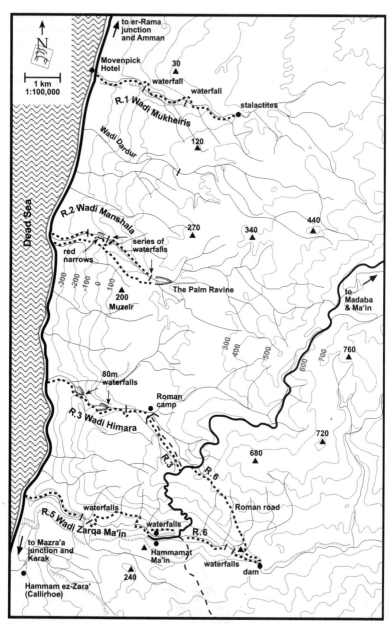

Map 8: Routes 1–6, excluding route 4

2. Wadi Manshala
Map 8

Wadi Manshala offers a beautiful series of waterfalls with abundant little pools. Travertine deposits along the wadi create draperies and chimneys in endless shapes. At its upper reaches is a little ravine crowded with palm trees.

Type of route: Circular.
Altitude difference, Distance and Walking time: 500 m ascent and descent, 8 km, 9 hours.
Rating: Strenuous. Steep with some exposed ledges. Expect wet shoes.
Special equipment: None.
Guides: Might help. Try the village of Suweima.
Water: The wadi carries a small stream with many waterfalls and ponds. The water is salty but potable. Consider carrying 3 liters each.
Season: Spring, summer and fall, though summer may be too hot.
Getting there and back: Driving south along the Dead Sea road, pass the Movenpick Hotel. Continue south for 5 km to reach the outlet of Wadi Manshala (look for a white building west of the road). The route starts and ends here. Make arrangements to be picked up, or you will have to hitchhike to er-Rama or Mazra'a junctions (see route 1).

Walking up along the dry streambed you soon encounter tamarisk, oleander and sparkling rivulets. Cross a small pool and climb over some boulders. Another little pool, hiding below a cascade, is reached within 40 minutes from the starting point. The pool is located where a volcanic dyke intrudes the sandstone.

Climb through the cascade, ascending to the right immediately beyond it, beneath a higher waterfall. Follow the streambed for 15 minutes to reach some narrows in red rock, to be bypassed along goat trails on the south bank.

The trail soon reaches a 'V'-forming pair of palm trees. In order to bypass a waterfall, which is still hidden, scramble right along loose scree towards a cluster of three palm trees. From the palm trees continue steeply up towards a higher cluster of palms.

Further on the trail contours along fine goat trails towards the head of the waterfall. Adorned by robes of travertine and plumes of palm trees the water plunges some 30 m, and gurgles through a little gorge towards a hollow surrounded by sheer cliffs. The view from the head of the waterfall includes the Dead Sea and the Judean Desert. Visibility permitting, the towers of the Mount of Olives are seen silhouetted on the far horizon.

Proceed for about 30 minutes among tall Euphrates poplars to reach another waterfall to the right of a prominent rock tower. Bypass the waterfall from the right (south) along stable scree with no trail. A string of ponds commences just above the waterfall. Cross the first pond, climb some steep rock ledges towards the others, and soon you will reach a pool encircled by Euphrates poplar, tamarisk and willow. A perfect place for a refreshing dip.

The pool is fed from a waterfall, which can be bypassed on the right. Higher up another waterfall houses a shallow travertine cave with stalactites and a giant pistacia tree growing near it. To bypass the waterfall, retrace your steps towards a well pronounced trail, climbing on the south bank.

Another waterfall lies further ahead beside a tall palm tree. Bypassing the waterfall on the right (south), you enter a ravine crowded with palm trees. After inhaling its subtropical atmosphere, head back to the waterfall and climb steeply southwards to reach faint goat trails running some 20 m below the crest of a shoulder. Proceed west for 90 minutes negotiating some rock ledges to reach the road just south of the outlet of Wadi Manshala. Along the way there are excellent views of the Dead Sea.

The Hyena in Bedouin heritage

Some Bedouin strongly believe that hyenas have bewitching powers. "The Hyena is active at nighttime. He approaches while you are asleep and starts sniffing. When you wake up he looks into your eyes and hypnotizes you. Then he starts walking and you follow. When finally enters his den, you are doomed!"

Striped Hyena

When I first heard this story I laughed. "You don't seriously believe that?" My friend looked at me and said: "How can I doubt it when I know it is true? A few years ago my cousin entered the tent with his forehead bleeding. I asked him what had happened and was told that he had encountered a hyena. The animal had looked into his eyes. He then lost all his human instincts and followed the beast. When the hyena entered its cave... Bang... his head hit the ceiling and he woke up and escaped."

The hyena is called Daba' by the Arabs and is also known as Abu el Fataias, which means "father of the carcass". When you camp in the open you will be often asked "Ma bithaf min ed-Daba'?" which means "Are you not afraid of the hyena?" Try to counter with a few good words about the merits of this impressive scavenger, and you may help it to survive.

3. Wadi Himara
Map 8

The tallest waterfalls in Jordan, about 80 m high, are located in Wadi Himara. The uppermost waterfall drops abruptly from a rocky platform, offering splendid views of the Dead Sea. The lower waterfall plunges into a deep gorge. Both falls can be bypassed. Delightful ponds glisten along the wadi.

Type of route: One-way.
Altitude difference, Distance and Walking time: 800 m descent, 5 km, 7 hours.
Rating: Strenuous, with exposed rock ledges. Expect wet shoes.
Special equipment: None.
Guides: Recommended. Try the village of Ma'in. Recommended is Abu Mansur from the Jahalin tribe, who camps in Wadi Himara (beneath the track) during fall, winter, and spring.
Water: A year-round stream with waterfalls and ponds. The water is salty but potable. Consider carrying 3 liters each.
Season: Spring, summer and fall.
Getting there and back: Leave Madaba by taxi, heading towards the spa resort of Hammamat Ma'in. About 17 km from the village of Ma'in, just before the steep switchbacks towards the resort, a dirt track branches to the right preceded by two triangular road signs. Should you miss the beginning of the track you will soon see a cluster of structures to the left.
The trail ends on the Dead Sea shore 9 km south of the Movenpick hotel. If you have no arrangement to meet a vehicle there, you will have to hitchhike to er-Rama or Mazra'a junctions (see Route 1).

Follow the track for 2 km, descending towards the oleander-packed stream of Wadi Himara. On the north bank is a stone-lined compound, remnant of a Roman camp along an ancient route connecting the Dead Sea with Zarqa Ma'in hot springs and the Moab Plateau. Walking downstream for 10 minutes you will come to the camp of a Jahalin family perched upon a wadi terrace during fall and wintertime. In an additional 10 minutes you reach two low waterfalls.

Bypass the waterfalls from the left, descending gently on the south bank for 200 m before plunging back into the wadi bed. A short walk upstream leads to the lower waterfall, which consists of a perfect travertine robe enclosing a tiny hidden pool.

Proceed downstream for 30 minutes amidst oleanders, boulders and ponds to reach a little gorge with shining pools and water slides. Above the gorge, a rocky platform leads to a majestic 80 m waterfall. This is the highest waterfall in Jordan. Looking west, the tranquil blue hues of the Dead Sea are backdrop to the green of the palm trees, sprouting from the sheer cliffs.

Bypassing the waterfall involves walking along exposed goat trails. From the head of the gorge climb south along a stable talus slope towards two tall palm trees. Once at the palm trees, look 200 m ahead (west) and a bit below you to spot another cluster of palm trees. Above the trees is a vertical cliff topped by a dark rock. To reach this rock you have to follow a very narrow goat trail contouring westwards with a sheer drop below it — **take care!**

Progress levelly towards this rock, crossing a dark igneous dyke within 50 m. From the rock proceed past an almost unnoticed shoulder to reach the head of a steep gully with stable scree. Lose about 50 m in height to spot a lone palm tree at the upper reaches of the gully. A prominent dark rock with an overhang is seen further downhill. Descend towards the rock and turn right 50 m below it, following a narrow goat trail to the base of the waterfall. Seen from the bottom, the falling water breaks into myriad droplets creating a shower that dances in the wind. Velvety green cushions of moss thrive beneath it.

Progressing downstream on the left-hand side of the streambed you pass above a little waterfall and within minutes you arrive at a small pond. Lower down are red narrows with some more pools. As you proceed, a red sandstone gate rises ahead about 30 minutes from the 80 m waterfall. The wadi passes through this gate and drops spectacularly into an 80 m deep gorge whose bottom can only be reached by abseiling.

Backtrack 100 m to reach a clear trail, which climbs on the south bank. Crossing a gravel shoulder, the trail descends into a small wadi and immediately climbs to the opposite shoulder. Descend easily along the right-hand side of the shoulder keeping giant blocks of travertine to your left. The Dead Sea road is reached within about an hour from the last waterfall. On your way there are excellent panoramas of the Dead Sea.

4. Across northern Moab
from Wadi Mukheiris to Wadi Himara
Map 9

This route links three impressive canyons, passing through a colorful arid environment, with excellent views towards the Dead Sea.

Type of route: One-way
Route:
　　Day 1: Wadi Mukheiris. Camping site at the watershed with Wadi Dardur.
　　Day 2: Wadi Manshala. Camping site at upper Wadi Manshala beneath Muzeir Hill.
　　Day 3: Wadi Himara.
Rating: Strenuous. Steep and exposed rock ledges. Expect wet shoes.
Special equipment: None.
Guides: Recommended. Try the village of Suweima.
Water: Consider carrying 4.5 liters per person for the sections between the canyons.
Season: Spring and fall.
Getting there and back: The trail starts at the Dead Sea road, in front of the Movenpick Hotel.
The trail ends on the Dead Sea shore, 9 km south of the Movenpick Hotel. If you have no arrangement to be picked up, you will have to hitchhike to er-Rama or Mazra'a junctions (see Route 1).

Day 1
Altitude difference, Distance and Walking time: 600 m ascent, 6 km, 8 hours.
Water: A perennial stream. There is no water near the proposed camping site — fill up at a spring on the way.

Follow Route 1 (carrying a full backpack your walking time may be longer than specified). To bypass the maidenhair cave, backtrack 100 m and climb steeply to the north with no obvious trail. Reaching a goat trail follow it for a short distance before descending into the wadi just above the cave. After some 100 m up the wadi, a track takes off to the right (south).

The track stretches uphill, then gently downhill and uphill again. Ignore two side tracks branching to the right. A little spring emerges to the left of the track besides a cultivated area. This is the place to fill up for the night. Within 40 minutes you reach a distinct junction, located below the crest of a shoulder. Go right (southwest), alongside a young olive grove, towards a wooden shed 200 m away. You can camp here or continue further to the south and camp closer to Wadi Manshala. There is a salty spring where the track crosses Wadi Dardur.

Day 2
Altitude difference, Distance and Walking time: 350 m descent and ascent, 8 km, 9 hours.

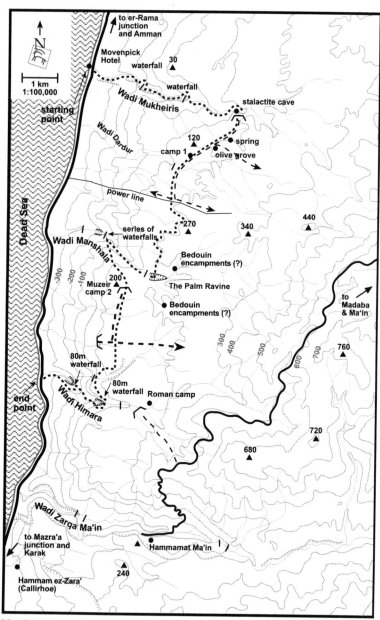

Map 9: Route 4. Across northern Moab from Wadi Mukheiris to Wadi Himara

Water: Wadi Dardur and Wadi Manshala are both perennial. Their water is salty but potable.

Following the track you cross Wadi Dardur within 15 minutes. Aim towards a high-voltage power line located due south some 800 m ahead. Once past the power line, leave the track southwards through a deserted Bedouin encampment with some rusted barrels.

The path towards Wadi Manshala is not well defined. Keep the stone-studded hills to your left, and advance southwards crossing many little wadis. Adhering more or less to the same contour, aim towards a prominent hill at the southern horizon. The hill, which is called Muzeir, is located on the south bank of Wadi Manshala above the proposed camping site of Day 2.

Wadi Manshala incises the plateau within 60 minutes from Wadi Dardur. Its deep ravine is a beautiful oasis crowded with palm trees.

The rest of the route involves a steep descent down the canyon of Wadi Manshala, and then an ascent back to the plateau along the shoulder of its south bank. Consider leaving your heavy gear behind. This will make the continuation easier and more enjoyable, but you will have to walk 1.5 km (easy-going) to get from the south bank back to your gear. If you'd rather not leave your gear unattended, you can usually find Bedouin encampments on either side of the palm ravine. To spot them, walk eastwards some 500 m above the cliffs of the ravine, until its sheer walls disappear making it possible to cross to the south bank above a dry fall. If you don't see any tents until that point, there are probably no Bedouin in the vicinity. In any case the route you have just followed is the way to return to your gear from the south bank.

The only proper descent into the ravine is from the north, about 300 m west of the crossing above the dry fall. To spot the trail, follow the goat droppings. Once in the ravine, it is well worthwhile to stroll upstream amidst a lush jungle of palms.

Backtracking downstream you soon reach the first waterfall of Wadi Manshala. Bypass it from the left to reach a second waterfall, which hosts a beautiful travertine cave and can also be bypassed from the left. Once in the streambed, walk a short distance upstream to reach the foot of this waterfall.

Not far down is the third waterfall, feeding a pool which is encircled by Euphrates poplar, tamarisk and willow. Bypass it from the left and continue **through** a string of ponds with some steep rock ledges. The fourth waterfall blocks the progress immediately afterwards. Bypass it from the left, descending steeply along a rocky slope with no trail. When the grades of the slope diminish veer east (right) to reach the streambed through a short descent.

After 30 minutes of relatively easy going, a marvellous 30 m waterfall plunges over a robe of travertine and into a tiny gorge. The best lookout point towards the waterfall is located on the south bank.

From here onwards the trail leaves the stream. Fill up with enough water for the ascent, for camping and for an hour's walk on the following day. Leaving the head of the waterfall, climb south on stable scree with no trail to reach the crest of the shoulder. Follow the crest to its head not far from the palm ravine. The whole ascent takes about 75 minutes. There are plenty of level patches suitable for camping below the hill of Muzeir (200 m).

The hill offers splendid views and dramatic sunsets over the Dead Sea. The meanders of the Jordan River as well as the city of Jericho are easily spotted. On the west side of the Dead Sea rise the escarpments of the Judean Desert. Visibility permitting, you can see the crest of the Judean Mountains dotted with the cities of Hebron, Bethlehem and Jerusalem, the latter distinguished by the Mount of Olives with its three towers.

If you left your gear on the north bank, you can backtrack and camp there, but you will have to recross to the foot of Muzeir Hill on the following day.

Day 3
Altitude difference, Distance and Walking time: 600 m descent, 6 km, 7 hours.
Water: Perennial stream in Wadi Himara. The water is salty but potable.

Leaving the base of Muzeir Hill, proceed south along a dirt track, which forks after about 20 minutes. Here you leave the track and go southwards, crossing a few shallow wadis before bearing southwest upon a flat shoulder towards a tributary of Wadi Himara.

Many palm trees dot the wadi, which carries a tiny stream. To cross the tributary, go west until the gentle grades of the plateau end with a steep drop. Descend steeply about 50 m to meet a well-defined trail just above a large cluster of palms. Follow the trail descending southwards to cross the gentle streambed where it ends abruptly at a steep drop. It takes about 50 minutes to reach this spot from the base of Muzeir Hill.

Proceed southwards, contouring along goat trails, which cross a gentle shoulder. Sheer cliffs bar your way as you approach Wadi Himara. Veer east above the cliffs towards the head of a spectacular 80 m waterfall. There are two sets of trails which can get you there: one directly above the vertical walls and therefore exposed, and the other some 30 m higher. Once above the waterfall continue according to Route 3 (from the upper 80 m waterfall and onwards).

5. Wadi Zarqa Ma'in, lower gorge
Map 8

Wadi Zarqa Ma'in is a spectacular sandstone canyon which carries a thermal stream with cascades. The first half of the walk is above the canyon, with views of its basalt and sandstone banks, studded with palm trees. The second half goes through a gorge with natural Jacuzzis. Unfortunately, garbage finds its way into the canyon. Visit the canyon immediately after the winter floods (March to April), to see it at its best.

Wadi Zarqa Ma'in drains large areas south of Madaba. Its discharge, reaching 30 million cubic m a year, is second only to Wadi Mujib. The stream is fed by numerous hot springs, some reaching temperatures over 60^0 C. Many Jordanians frequent its thermal baths, which are reputed to be good for health.

Wadi Zarqa Ma'in is depicted on the mosaic map of Madaba and its springs are described by 1st century CE historian Josephus Flavius.

The trail starts at the spa resort (Hammamat Ma'in), which is located in the upper reaches of the wadi. Entrance fee to the resort costs 2 JD or 3.85 JD including a swimming pool and a bathhouse (a sauna and hot pool). Other facilities include a simple cafeteria and the luxurious Hotel Ashtar. The resort may be overcrowded during holidays.

Type of route: One-way.
Altitude difference, Distance and Walking time: 300 m descent, 4 km, 8 hours.
Rating: Moderate. A long stretch of bouldering within the water. Crossing a few low waterfalls using a hiker's rope.
Special equipment: A 10 m hiker's rope. Abseiling gear is not needed.
Guides: Might help. Try the village of Ma'in.
Water: Do not drink the water of the stream. Consider carrying 3 liters each.
Season: Spring, fall and winter. During winter be especially aware of flash flood risk!
Getting there and back: Leave Madaba by taxi to the resort of Hammamat Ma'in, reached within 45 minutes. The trail starts near the first building beneath the entrance gate.
The route ends at the Dead Sea road, 13 km south of the Movenpick Hotel. If you have no arrangements to be picked up, you will have to hitchhike to er-Rama or Mazra'a junctions (see route 1).

The trail starts just above the elongate building. Proceed levelly, passing above a warm waterfall to reach the head of a second waterfall after a short walk. A film of water used to cover the wide rocky platform above the waterfall, plunging down in a veil of droplets. Over the years, layers of travertine have been deposited on the platform, forming basins and tiny pools at the foot of the falls. Nowadays the deposition has stopped since the water above the fall is tunneled.

On the opposite bank, black basalt forms a vertical wall. This basalt is the feeding pipe of an ancient volcano, which erupted about half a million years ago — the youngest eruption known in Moab and Edom. Some claim that the thermal springs are also related to the volcanic eruptions — it is deep basalt, still hot, which raises the temperature of groundwater.

Proceeding along the contour, you soon reach a fenced structure. Turn left (north) along the fence, heading towards the wadi. At the corner of the fence turn right (west) and walk 50 m before descending into the wadi along a travertine slope.

Walk downstream for a few minutes until a little side wadi joins from the right, near a clump of dense vegetation. Follow goat trails on the north slope ascending about 100 m. Proceed levelly among clusters of palm trees until a prominent wadi on the opposite bank joins the canyon from the south with a horseshoe dry fall, about 2 hours from the trailhead.

Descend toward the edge of a flat shoulder. Heading west along the edge of the shoulder, you reach a little side wadi, where a steep cairned trail drops into the canyon. The trail veers sharply eastwards immediately after it starts.

The canyon floor is reached within 20 minutes, just above a 4 m waterfall. From here onwards the route proceeds inside the canyon all the way to the Dead Sea. Descend along the right side of the waterfall using a hiker's rope. Below the waterfall there is a pleasant Jacuzzi and plenty of shade for rest. Soon, another low waterfall is reached, where rope might be handy. The canyon is carved in magnificent red sandstone and its running water is flecked with boulders. There are a few spots where you have to transfer your gear carefully if you want it to keep dry. The Dead Sea road is roughly 4 hours from the first waterfall.

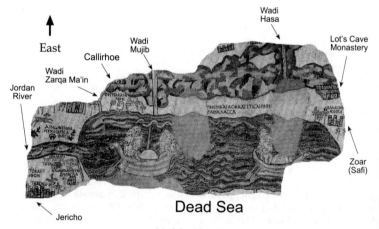

Dead Sea

Madaba Mosaic

I. H.

I. H.

I. H.

Top: Jabel Umm Asawir (R.57, 61)
Middle: The prominent cliff of Umm Ala overlooking the colorful valley of el Qaʻ.
An Edomite stronghold is located atop the cliff (R.52, 54, 56)
Bottom: Sunset from Muzeir Hill (R.4)

Saffron

Squill

Maidenhair ferns

Sternbergia

Pistacia

Red Juniper

Maidenhair ferns and orchids in Wadi Jifneh

The the tropical orchid
Epipactis veratrifolia

Haim Anner

Wadi Ibn Hammad (R.13)

I. H.

Shai Reuveni

Onn Crouvi

Top Left: Descending into the valley of Little Petra (R.44)
Top Right: Wadi Mujib's lower gorge (R.10, 11)
Bottom: Heading towards Wadi Sabra (R.51, 61)

6. Wadi Zarqa Ma'in, upper canyon
Map 8

The upper canyon of Wadi Zarqa Ma'in offers two impressive waterfalls with spectacular pools. Unlike the lower gorge, its water is of normal temperature. The approach to the upper canyon is by a Roman road, which connected the northern part of the Dead Sea with the inner regions of Moab. The trail ends at the resort of Zarqa Ma'in. (Remember — entrance fee!)

Type of route: One-way.
Altitude difference, Distance and Walking time: 500 m descent, 6 km, 7 hours (2.5 hours to first waterfall. 1 hour from the last waterfall to the end of the trail).
Rating: Moderate. **Abseiling is unavoidable.** Expect wet shoes.
Falls: Two waterfalls.
Special equipment: Two 35 m ropes and ordinary abseiling gear.
Guides: Not really needed, but you can try the village of Ma'in.
Water: A perennial stream along the second half of the route. Consider carrying 3 liters each.
Season: Spring, summer and fall.
Getting there and back: The trailhead is 200 m east from the head of the track to Wadi Himara (see Route 3). The trail ends at Zarqa Ma'in resort. Finding a taxi to Ma'in Village or Madaba should be easy.

Leaving the trailhead, go southeast towards an obvious saddle. Signs of the Roman road appear about 100 m away from the tarmac. It is about 4 m wide and its margins are lined by stones. The track descends gently and then manoeuvers steeply between nearly vertical hogbacks. Just above the final descent along the south bank of Wadi Zarqa Ma'in, a prominent knoll rises on the right. Its south slope provides excellent views towards the lower reaches of the wadi.

Return to the trail and continue eastwards for about 1 km. A series of well-designed switchbacks descends into the basalt canyon, about 90 minutes from the trailhead.

Here you leave the ancient road, which climbs up the south bank. Bypass a dam and a small water reservoir, and proceed downstream. It takes about 45 minutes among oleanders and black boulders to reach the head of a white limestone gorge. It is here that water issues from the gravel to form a small stream.

Cross a few shallow pools and slide down to the head of the first waterfall.

Fall 1: 35 m. Below the fall lies a splendid pool, girded by travertine drapes and maidenhair ferns. The second waterfall is reached in about 15 minutes.

Fall 2: 50 m. Holding on to a rope, it is possible to descend about 15 m to a lower step, which leaves 35 m to abseil. The fall drops into a pool of some 10 m diameter. Above the pool lies a giant boulder, wetted by spray.

Soon afterwards, pass a cascade on the right. This is the end of the narrow gorge and the beginning of a mild-grade wadi. It takes about 30 minutes to reach the first thermal springs, which soon raise the stream's temperature. The cafeteria of Zarqa Ma'in resort is only 15 minutes away.

The Mujib Nature Reserve and Dhiban area

From Wadi Zarqa Ma'in to Wadi Shuqeiq

The Mujib Nature Reserve stretches between Wadi Zarqa Ma'in to the north and Wadi Shuqeiq to the south, with Wadi Mujib at its center. With a 200 m deep sandstone gorge, spectacular pools, and a majestic waterfall, Wadi Mujib is the Grand Canyon of Jordan.

The wadis in the reserve descend from an elevation of 800–1,000 m of the Moab Plateau. Many of them have perennial streams, some fed by thermal springs, others by ordinary springs and a few by both. The reserve also offers unique basaltscapes, which include extinct volcanoes on the south bank of Wadi Zarqa Ma'in and the spectacular basalt gorge of Wadi el Hidan.

An important goal of the reserve is to reintroduce and protect the Nubian Ibex (wild mountain goat) which have been hunted in Jordan to near extinction. The Royal Society for Conservation of Nature (RSCN) has established a breeding center in the reserve and a group of over 30 Ibex have been successfully returned to the wild.

The major wadi in the reserve is Wadi Mujib. Its drainage basin, about 6,500 square km, is the largest in Jordan — its northern tributaries reaching the capital Amman. Owing to this great drainage area the base flow of Wadi Mujib reaches 65 million cubic m a year. This is the biggest discharge in Moab and Edom, twice as big as the discharge of Wadi Zarqa Ma'in. The chief tributary of

Wadi Mujib is Wadi el Hidan, which joins the main trunk some 3 km east of its outlet on the Dead Sea shore.

Wadi Mujib is the biblical Arnon River and is depicted in the mosaic map of Madaba. The Bible relates (Numbers 21: 26) how Sihon, king of Heshbon, conquered parts of the Moabite kingdom and established the Amorite kingdom, keeping the River Arnon as the border between the two kingdoms.

Wadi Mujib (the Arnon River) is also mentioned on the stele of Mesha', king of Moab in the 9th century BCE, where the king mentions among his feats: "I have made the highway at the Arnon". To cross Wadi Mujib the King's Highway has to negotiate an altitude difference of 600 m over a short horizontal distance.

The major village along the King's Highway is Dhiban, the birthplace of Mesha'. It was hereabouts that his stele was found in the 19th century. Further to the northwest, overlooking the Dead Sea, are ruins of the desert fortress of Mukawir (Machaerus), where John the Baptist was kept prisoner and eventually beheaded. The fortress was one of the last Jewish strongholds during the Great Revolt against the Romans (66–73 CE). South of the outlet of Wadi Zarqa Ma'in along the Dead Sea shore, is the thermal springs site of Hammam ez-Zara' (Callirhoe), well known for its therapeutic baths during the Roman and Byzantine period and still very popular with the Jordanians.

Wadi Mujib Campsite
Wadi Mujib Campsite is located about 2 km southeast of the wadi's outlet to the Dead Sea. The campsite includes tents for up to 25 visitors and simple toilet facilities. Drinking water is not available! Visitors must walk to and from the campsite, but transport for luggage can be organized. Reaching the camp involves a 30-minute walk from the Dead Sea road. Register at the RSCN shed underneath the Mujib Bridge before heading to the campsite. Spending the night in the campsite is especially worthwhile for those who wish to hike through Wadi Mujib's lower gorge on the following day. Camping fees including hike fees (Route 10) are 25 JD per person.

Entrance fees and regulations
Route 11 — 5 JD.
Route 10 — 20 JD.
All the other routes require special permits from the RSCN.
Entrance fees are payable at the RSCN shed underneath the Mujib Bridge.
All visits to the reserve, apart from Route 11, should be booked in advance at the RSCN office in Amman since the number of visitors is limited:
RSCN P.O. Box 6354 Amman, Jordan,
  Tel: 962–6–5337931

The reserve is open from the 1st of April to the 31st of October.

The following routes are suggested in this region:

Route	Days	Rating	Season	Description
7. Wadi Abu Khusheiba	1 (1.5 hours)	easy	all-year	Very short walk, palms and pools.
8. Wadi 'Attun	1 (3 hours)	easy	all-year	Short walk, untamed thermal stream and cascades.
9. Wadi Daba'	1 (2 hours)	easy	all-year	Short walk, untamed thermal stream and cascades.
10. Wadi Mujib's lower gorge	1 (9 hours)	strenuous incl. abseiling	1st April to 31st October	Jordan's Grand Canyon, majestic sandstone gorge, gushing water.
11. Wadi Mujib's lower gorge, a short route	1 (2-4 hours)	easy	"	Spectacular, easy way to experience the Mujib gorge.
12. Wadi el Hidan	1 (13 hours)	strenuous incl. abseiling	"	One of a kind! Basalt canyon, narrow sandstone gorge, variety of colors, hot and cold springs, pools, majestic 50 m waterfall.

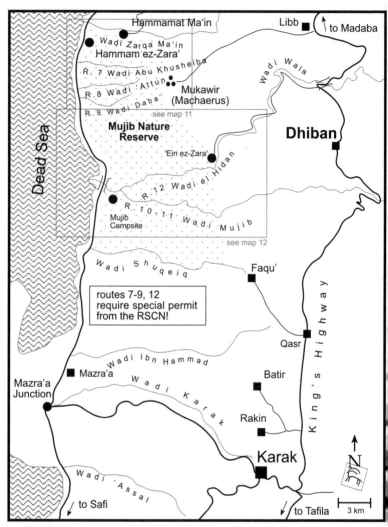

Map 10: The Mujib Nature Reserve and Dhiban area – from Wadi Zarqa Ma'in to Wadi Shuqeiq

7. Wadi Abu Khusheiba
Map 11

A pleasant short walk along a perennial stream with dripping springs, abundant water vegetation and beautiful travertine deposits. **Visiting the wadi requires a special permit from the RSCN!**

Type of route: One-way and back.
Altitude difference, Distance and Walking time: 150 m ascent and descent, 2 km, 1.5 hours.
Rating: Easy. Expect wet shoes.
Special equipment: None.
Guides: Inquire at the RSCN.
Water: Perennial stream and springs. Those who choose not to drink from them should carry 1 liter each.
Season: Year-round. Be aware of flash flood risk, especially during winter!
Getting there and back: From er-Rama junction (see Route 1), drive south along the Dead Sea road, pass Wadi Zarqa Ma'in bridge and continue for 4.5 km to reach the outlet of Wadi Abu Khusheiba. This is the first wadi south of the thermal springs of Hammam ez-Zara' (Callirhoe). Prominent on the south bank of the wadi are eucalyptus trees, a dirt track and a house. The trail starts and ends here. Make arrangements to be picked up or you will have to hitchhike back to er-Rama or Mazra'a junctions.

Walking upstream among reed and sugarcane you soon reach a 3 m waterfall plunging from the right. As you proceed, palm trees loom overhead and maidenhair fern garnishes the canyon walls. A dripping travertine overhang and a little waterfall with a pool at its foot, bar further progress within 30 minutes from the starting point. Hot springs issuing above the waterfall are responsible for its tepid temperature.

Follow the same route back to the starting point.

Griffon Vulture

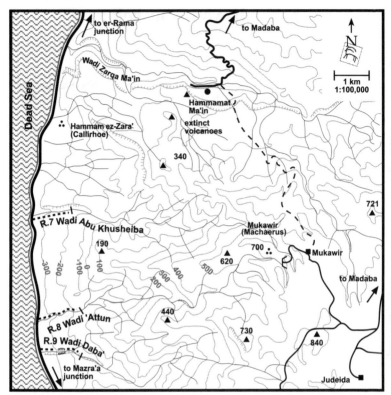

Map 11: Routes 7–9

8. Wadi 'Attun
Map 11

Wadi 'Attun is a thermal delight of hot waterfalls and springs. Thermophile microorganisms dye its water with red hues. **Visiting the wadi requires a special permit from the RSCN!**

Type of route: One-way and back.
Altitude difference, Distance and Walking time: 200 m ascent and descent, 2 km, 3 hours.
Rating: Easy. Expect wet shoes.
Special equipment: None.
Guides: Inquire at the RSCN.
Water: Thermal springs and a hot stream. Consider carrying 1.5 liters each.
Season: Year-round. Be aware of flash flood risk, especially during winter!
Getting there and back: From er-Rama junction (see Route 1), drive south along the Dead Sea road, pass Wadi Zarqa Ma'in bridge and continue south for 8 km to reach the outlet of Wadi 'Attun. The route starts and ends here. Make arrangements to be picked up or you will have to hitchhike to er-Rama or Mazra'a junctions.

Walking upstream among lush water vegetation and little cascades, the water gets hotter with every step. Within 20 minutes a little rockslide with dripping water is seen on the left. 20 minutes further ahead is a 3 m waterfall which can be climbed with a short rope, though you can probably manage without it.

Above the waterfall, steaming water bursts out of the rocks. Soon afterwards another waterfall is reached, ornamented with moss and a small travertine cave.

Bypass the waterfall by climbing on steep stable scree to the right. Progress levelly, passing above another low waterfall, before it is possible to descend back into the wadi bed. As you proceed upstream, thermal springs burst from the rocks and stalactites are abundant. About one hour from the starting point a beautiful 15 m drainpipe waterfall blocks further progress. After tasting the joys of this natural spa, retrace your steps to the starting point.

9. Wadi Daba'
Map 11

A short route through a little canyon with thermal springs and waterfalls, and a remarkable tiny limestone gorge. **Visiting the wadi requires a special permit from the RSCN!**

Type of route: One-way and back.

Altitude difference, Distance and Walking time: 150 m ascent and descent, 2 km, 2 hours.

Rating: Easy. Expect wet shoes.

Special equipment: None.

Guides: Inquire at the RSCN.

Water: Thermal springs and stream. Consider carrying 1.5 liters each.

Season: Year-round. Be aware of flash flood risk, especially during winter!

Getting there and back: From er-Rama junction (see Route 1), drive south along the Dead Sea road, pass Wadi Zarqa Ma'in bridge and continue for 9 km to reach the outlet of Wadi Daba'. The route starts and ends here. Make arrangements to be picked up, or you will have to hitchhike back to er-Rama or Mazra'a junctions.

Walking upstream for 20 minutes, you reach a steaming waterfall dropping from the north. Further up, a short limestone gorge begins with three low waterfalls one after the other. Green mosses thrive on its walls, creating a beautiful contrast to the deep gray colors of the rocks.

Skirt the gorge along goat trails on the south bank to enter a red sandstone environment, studded with green palm trees. A 3 m waterfall that bars further progress is the sign to retrace your steps towards the beginning of the trail.

10. Wadi Mujib's lower gorge
Map 12

"The view which the Mujib represents is very striking... the valley looks like a deep chasm formed by some convulsion of the earth, into which there seems no possibility of descending to the bottom." (J. L. Burckhardt, 1812)

Experiencing Jordan's Grand Canyon involves swimming, jumping, abseiling and floating. Its sheer red walls tower skyward while its entire width is filled with running water, plunging through an awe-inspiring 15 m waterfall. Beautiful pools are located near the confluence of Wadi Mujib and Wadi el Hidan, tempting the trekker to swim against the current into the majestic gorge of Wadi el Hidan.

Entrance fees to this trail are 20 JD. They are payable at the RSCN shed beneath the Mujib Bridge. It is advisable to book in advance, as the number of visitors per day is limited.

Type of route: Circular.
Altitude difference, Distance and Walking time: 200 m ascent and descent with some level stretches in between, 6 km, 9 hours.
Rating: Strenuous. **Abseiling is unavoidable.** The route includes swimming sections.
Falls: One waterfall. A few sections where hiker's rope is necessary.
Special equipment: Two 20 m ropes and ordinary abseiling gear. Unless you have a waterproof bag everything you carry will get wet.
Guides: An RSCN guide is compulsory.
Water: Gushing stream. The water is not recommended for drinking. Consider carrying 3 liters each.
Season: The Mujib gorge is open from the 1st of April to the 31st of October. Be aware of flash flood risk even during this period! The route is most enjoyable in mid-summer.
Getting there and back: From er-Rama junction (see Route 1), drive south along the Dead Sea road, cross the Mujib Bridge and proceed for another 2 km. The trail starts where a little wadi descends towards the road, near a clump of tamarisk trees and a signpost of the Mujib Nature Reserve. The route ends at the Mujib Bridge. Make arrangements to be picked up, or you will have to hitchhike back to er-Rama or Mazra'a junctions.

Ascend along the right side of the little wadi, following a ruined track to reach a T-junction after about 20 minutes. Turn left, descending past the campsite of the reserve before climbing steeply once again. It takes about 50 minutes to reach the top of the ascent.

Before you descend into Wadi Mujib, climb to one of the light-colored marl mounds for a comprehensive vista. The Dead Sea expands below with the escarpment of the Judean Desert rising above its opposite shore. At the foot of the escarpment lies the settlement of 'Ein Gedi, famous as an oasis and a subtropical nature reserve.

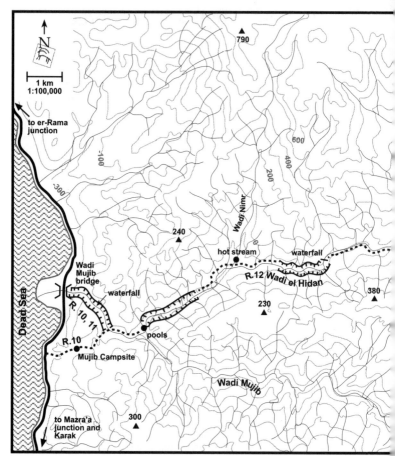

Map 12: Routes 10–12. Wadi Mujib and Wadi el Hidan

Looking east, it is easy to spot the course of Wadi Mujib, but it is almost impossible to locate its outlet. A closer look reveals that the most natural outlet is through the valley from which you ascended. The valley, however, seems to be "blocked" with light-colored marl layers, which were deposited at the bottom of the Dead Sea at a period when its level was much higher.

During the last Ice Age the water level of the Dead Sea reached 180 m below sea level, about 230 m higher

than today. The lake flooded the lower reaches of the canyons along its banks, which became bays and began to accumulate sediments. As the climatic conditions changed, about 20,000 years ago, the water level of the lake dropped, leaving the re-emergent canyons blocked with lake marl. Most canyons managed to cut through their plugged outlets and to resume their erstwhile lower courses. However, Wadi Mujib abandoned its former outlet by breaking through a cleft in the sandstone. This narrow

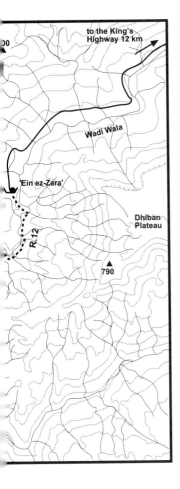

and oleanders, take left at the confluence. Advance along boulders on the left-hand side of the wadi, arriving soon at a beautiful pool. Just above the pool is a rocky platform, convenient as a base for further exploration.

Beyond the pool begins the majestic gorge of Wadi el Hidan. Its smooth sandstone walls curve upwards while sparkling water fills its whole width. Leaving your gear behind, you can swim into the gorge and even cross a few cascades before a gushing low waterfall blocks your way. It is a magical place.

Retrace your steps downstream to reach the entrance to the lower gorge of Wadi Mujib. Put valuables in a waterproof bag before progressing. Water level in the gorge may be waist-high and there are sections where you have to swim. Descending the Mujib gorge is an awe-inspiring experience. Its sheer walls are so close and so high that the sky is seen as a mere blue ribbon between the red rims. Bypassing a pile of boulders from the right, you reach the breathtaking Mujib waterfall about 40 minutes from the head of the gorge. Its gushing waters drop 15 m into a pool surrounded by vertical walls. The only way down is by abseiling.

Once beneath the waterfall, a demanding section is still ahead. Stick to the right side of the gorge, descending a vertical drop using a short rope. Soon afterwards, return to the middle of the gorge and slide down a smooth boulder. Another giant boulder lies just ahead. Hold on to a rope and slide to the edge of the boulder towards a 2 m drop into a shallow pool. A turbulent pool is a few minutes ahead — take care! The final section towards the outlet is a peaceful journey with no serious obstacles. The Mujib Bridge is reached some 90 minutes from the waterfall.

cleft became the bottleneck of an enormously large drainage basin with a huge discharge. Over the years, the cleft was scoured deeper and the gorge of Wadi Mujib was formed.

Leaving the lookout point, descend along the track to reach the wadi bed within 20 minutes. The impressive gate of the Mujib gorge can be seen to the left, but before venturing into the gorge proceed upstream for 30 minutes towards the confluence of Wadi Mujib and Wadi el Hidan. Walking in the water among reeds

11. Wadi Mujib's lower gorge, a short route
Map 12

This route enters and leaves the gorge through the wadi's outlet at the Mujib Bridge. It is suitable for everybody, provided they can swim. Though it does not follow the whole length of the gorge, it is still a spectacular way to experience its majestic beauty. Entrance fees of 5 JD are payable at the RSCN shed beneath the bridge.

Type of route: One-way and back.
Altitude difference, Distance and Walking time: About 100 m ascent and descent, 1.5 km, 2–4 hours.
Rating: Easy. The route includes swimming sections.
Special equipment: A waterproof bag can be useful if you want to carry camera and valuables.
Guides: Not really needed.
Water: Gushing stream. The water is not recommended for drinking but the gorge is shaded during most of the day. Carrying water is not necessary.
Season: The Mujib gorge is open from the 1st of April to the 31st of October. Be aware of flash flood risk even during this period! The route is most enjoyable in mid-summer.
Getting there and back: The route starts and ends at the Mujib Bridge. Reaching the bridge is possible from er-Rama junction as well as from Mazra'a junction (see Route 1).

Once past the official entrance gate, it is only minutes before you have to start swimming. The red walls of the gorge rise vertically, about 200 m above the streambed. Some of the pools are quite turbulent so take care! You can try and negotiate a few cascades before a giant boulder bars your way. Float back to the bridge, enjoying the tranquillity.

12. Wadi el Hidan
Map 12

The route starts in a magnificent basalt canyon, on the upper reaches of Wadi el Hidan. Elongate pools are abundant and you often swim more than you walk. As you descend along the canyon the black basalt gives way to red sandstone. This is where a majestic waterfall awaits you, leading into a gorge with palm trees, hot and cold springs, and a rich variety of colors. Thereafter, the canyon widens and dense vegetation makes progress difficult. Within a few hours you reach the lower gorge of Wadi el Hidan: a water amusement park with endless slides and jumps.

Descending Wadi el Hidan is a demanding adventure of at least 13 hours! Those who are willing to meet the challenge will be rewarded by one of the most beautiful localities that Jordan has to offer. **Visiting the wadi requires a special permit from the RSCN!**

Type of route: One-way.

Altitude difference, Distance and Walking time: 550 m descent, 15 km, 13 hours.

Rating: Strenuous. **Abseiling is unavoidable.** The route includes swimming sections.

Falls: One waterfall. Many low waterfalls where you have to slide or jump.

Special equipment: Two 50 m ropes and ordinary abseiling gear. Unless you have a waterproof bag everything you bring will get wet.

Guides: Inquire at the RSCN.

Water: Gushing stream and several dripping springs. The water of the stream is not recommended for drinking. Consider carrying 3 liters each.

Season: From the 1st of April to October 31st. Be aware of flash flood risk even during this period! The route is most enjoyable in mid-summer.

Getting there and back: Take a taxi from the village of Dhiban (map 10), heading north along the King's Highway to reach the bridge of Wadi Wala (Wadi el Hidan's upper reaches) after 8 km. Turn left (west) just before the bridge, and proceed along a tarred road paralleling the wadi for 11 km. Upon reaching a fork, take right and cross the wadi over a bridge. Within 3 km from the bridge is another fork. Bear left to reach the spring of 'Ein ez-Zara' after 5 km. Here the tarmac ends and a steep dirt track ascends to the right. To the left of the road is a circular pool fed by a water pipe. The trail starts here. The trail ends at the Dead Sea road, 2 km south of the Wadi Mujib Bridge. Make arrangements to be picked up, or hitchhike back to er-Rama or Mazra'a junctions (see Route 1).

From 'Ein ez-Zara' descend southeast along a basalt shoulder. Though it takes only 15 minutes to reach the wadi bed, the trail is faint and you may spend some time looking for it.

Once inside the canyon you soon reach elongate pools that must be crossed by swimming. Sliding into some of the pools may be easier with a short hiker's rope. The black basalt walls give the canyon a rugged character which keeps on for about 2.5 hours, when you arrive at a surreal sight — a 50 m waterfall topped by black basalt pillars and encircled by red sandstone cliffs and green palm trees.

The grandeur of the waterfall is revealed once you have abseiled to its foot. The basalt pillars are perched on red sandstone, which represents the old channel of the wadi at the time when it filled with lava. Since the lava flowed in an already deep canyon, the eruption must be relatively young.

Leaving the waterfall you enter a colorful gorge with hot and cold springs following each other. The hot springs are dyed red by thermophile microorganisms. It takes 50 minutes before the gorge begins to widen, though you will probably spend a few hours here.

Soon afterwards, the hot stream of Wadi Nimr joins from the north. The water gets hotter as you go up this stream, until a 10 m waterfall bars your way.

Proceeding further down the stream of Wadi el Hidan involves a continuous struggle with dense vegetation, especially during summertime. Crossing this jungle can be tiring and painful. To skip parts of it, follow a trail on the south bank just in front of Wadi Nimr. The trail climbs to about one third of the height of the slope and contours westward for less then 1 km, before descending back into the wadi.

The vegetation disappears within 2–3 hours from Wadi Nimr, where a narrow gorge with numerous low waterfalls develops. It is a 3–4 hour swimming adventure with endless surprises. You can slide through some of the waterfalls but crossing others may involve jumping into pools. Take care! Finally the gorge opens abruptly into a large pool. Above it is a rock platform, ideal for warming and resting.

Leaving the pool, 10 minutes suffice to reach the confluence of Wadi Mujib and Wadi el Hidan, and another 20 minutes to reach the head of the lower Mujib gorge. Unless you split the route into two days by spending the night at the Mujib Campsite, you will not have the time or the energy to descend this gorge. Climb south following a track to reach an elevated area with excellent views (see Route 10). Leaving this area descend westward before ascending a short distance through the Mujib Campsite to reach a junction of tracks. Turn right at the junction and continue descending to reach the Dead Sea road, 2 km south of the Mujib Bridge. The whole walk along the track takes about 70 minutes.

Karak area and Mazra'a Bay
From Wadi Shuqeiq to Wadi Hasa

Though there are no nature reserves in this region it offers superb trekking possibilities. The canyons of the region descend from the 900–1,300 m elevation of the Moab Plateau towards the Dead Sea. Most routes go through narrow gorges of reddish sandstone with the exception of upper Wadi Hasa, which offers a white limestone canyon. Year-round streams flow in most canyons, and spectacular hanging gardens cling to their walls. Thermal springs and streams are found in Wadi Hasa and in Wadi Ibn Hammad while abseiling abilities are needed to descend Wadi Karak and Wadi 'Assal.

The drive from the Dead Sea up to Karak unfolds a unique landscape as the road climbs through vertically tilted rock strata. In Wadi Weida'a the tilted layers loom over the trekker like gates to a fortress. At their foot lies the cemetery of Bab ed-Dhra', an excavated city of the Bronze Age.

Wadi Hasa, with its huge drainage basin and its deep winding canyon, is a natural barrier, which formed the historical border between the kingdoms of Moab and Edom. Descending its whole length is one of Moab's most rewarding treks.

The chief town in the region is Karak, with 150,000 inhabitants. Karak is probably the biblical Qir, the capital of Moab, but today it is more famous for its impressive Crusader-Mamluke castle (12–14th centuries CE). Karak offers tourist facilities, including hotels and restaurants. Small Nabataean temple sites are found along the King's Highway north and south of Karak (Qasr, Dhat Ras, Jabel Tannur and Khirbet Darih).

The village of Mazra'a is located beside a natural bay along the Dead Sea shore. Mazra'a Bay was a historical port, used mainly for wheat transport from Moab to Judea. South of Mazra'a is the village of Safi, located at the outlet of Wadi Hasa. The water of the wadi is used for the irrigation of extensive areas. Safi is identified with the city of Zoar mentioned in the Bible with regard to Lot, Abraham's nephew, saved from the wrath of the Lord when He destroyed Sodom and Gomorrah. Later, during the Hellenistic to Byzantine periods, the place was well known for its date plantations. Overlooking Safi are the ruins of a Byzantine monastery known as Lot's Cave Monastery. Between Safi and Mazra'a are the Dead Sea Industries, which manufacture potash by evaporating the saline water of the Dead Sea in solar salt pans.

87

The following routes are suggested in this region:

Route	Days	Rating	Season	Description
13. Wadi Ibn Hammad	1 (4 hours)	easy	all-year	Extremely colorful gorge, hanging gardens, stalactite bridge, warm spring.
14. Wadi Karak	1 (9 hours)	moderate incl. abseiling	spring summer fall	Narrow sandstone gorge, attractive waterfalls, hanging gardens, side streams, 60 m dripping waterfall.
15. Wadi Weida'a	1 (1.5 hours)	easy	all-year	Very short, on the way from the Dead Sea to Karak, palms and oleanders, narrows.
16. Wadi 'Assal	1 (10 hours)	moderate incl. abseiling	spring summer fall	Narrow sandstone gorge, six falls (2 with water), hanging gardens.
17. From Wadi Numeira to Wadi Marsad	1 (9 hours)	moderate	spring fall winter	Small canyons, spectacular views of the Dead Sea.
18. Wadi Hudeira	1 (3 hours)	easy	all-year	150 m deep red sandstone gorge, shallow stream.
19. Wadi Hasa's upper canyon to Wadi 'Afra.	1 (7 hours)	moderate	spring fall winter	Boulder-studded canyon, thermal stream with natural Jacuzzis.
20. Wadi Hasa, lower canyon	1 (12 hours)	moderate	spring fall	Spectacular red, winding sandstone canyon with thousands of wild palms.
21. Wadi Hasa, the full length	2	moderate	spring fall	If you are willing to carry a full backpack, this is the best way to see Wadi Hasa.

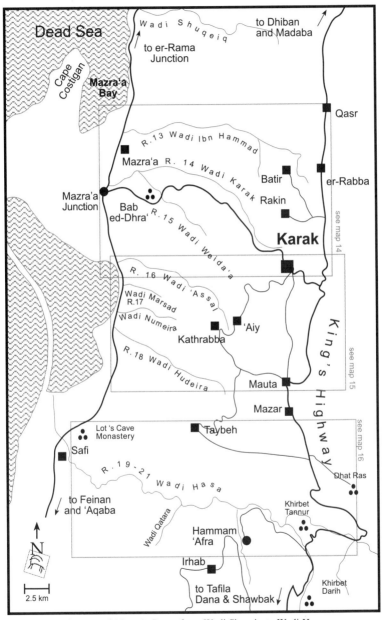

Map 13: Karak area and Mazra'a Bay — from Wadi Shuqeiq to Wadi Hasa

13. Wadi Ibn Hammad
Map 14

Almost all the features of the Jordanian canyons are represented in Wadi Ibn Hammad: a narrow sandstone gorge, abundant water and splendid hanging gardens. At the entrance to the gorge lies a pleasant hot spring called Hammam Ibn Hammad. Springs flow everywhere, supporting a variety of plants and lichens. At one point along the canyon the sky is obscured by a travertine overhang which actually connects the walls of the gorge.

If you must choose only one short route among the canyons of Jordan, do not hesitate — Wadi Ibn Hammad is it!

Type of route: One-way and back.
Altitude difference, Distance and Walking time: 100 m descent and ascent, 6 km, 4 hours.
Rating: Easy. Expect wet shoes.
Special equipment: None.
Guides: Not really needed, but you can try the village of Batir.
Water: A perennial stream, plenty of springs. Consider carrying 1 liter each.
Season: Year-round. Be aware of flash flood risk, especially during winter!
Getting there and back: Leaving Karak by a local bus or taxi, drive north along the King's Highway for less than 10 km before turning west towards the village of Batir. Here you have to arrange for a pickup truck, which will drive you about 10 km, down into the wadi, and pick you up at an agreed time (about 10 JD). A taxi driver with a good will may also negotiate this ride. From Batir, the road descends steeply towards the hamlet of Ibn Hammad. Pass the local school on your right, and just before reaching the first cluster of houses turn left to a side road which soon changes to a half-tarred track. The track is quite level for 4 km but its final section involves a steep descent into the wadi. Shortly after the track crosses the wadi it ends, about 20 minutes from its head. The hike starts and returns here.

Follow a short trail down into the wadi bed. On the south bank, a hot spring issues from an elevated terrace where its water is gathered into an artificial pool. You can enjoy the *hammam* before you enter the canyon, or leave this treat to the end of the trip.

Proceed downstream, penetrating slowly into a wonderful world with abundant springs dripping from the banks and with hanging gardens sprouting from every fissure. As you continue walking, the walls of the canyon draw closer.

About 40 minutes from the trailhead, shortly after a little side stream joins from the south, overhead daylight disappears. A travertine overhang was built up here by coalescing stalactites. The overhang actually touches the opposite wall, forming a solid bridge from one side of the gorge to the other. Below the bridge the walls are dyed with many hues of green and red. Listening carefully, you may hear the squeaking of bats above the rush of springs and water.

The gorge widens about 15 minutes beyond the travertine bridge, and the warmth of the sun is once again available. Here a pleasant waterfall plunges from the south bank. Lower down Wadi Ibn Hammad becomes quite monotonous.

Retrace your steps through the gorge. A close look at the vegetation will reveal the Mediterranean myrtle *Myrtus communis,* a rare shrub in southern Jordan, recognized by its fragrance. Sugarcane, orchid and palm trees are also abundant. Once out of the gorge, do not forget to visit the *hammam.*

Thermal springs

The canyons of the Jordanian Dead Sea Rift are blessed with a large number of thermal springs. Most of them feed streams and waterfalls, creating natural spas and Jacuzzis — a rare treat on a cold winter day!

As early as the first century BCE we first read about the thermal springs of Zarqa Ma'in and Callirhoe (Hammam ez-Zara'). The latter, whose Greek name means 'beautiful water', were visited by Herod the Great in a final attempt to alleviate his fatal disease. Those two sites are also depicted on the mosaic map of Madaba, of the Byzantine period.

Despite the popularity of therapeutic bathing resorts, many remote thermal springs remain relatively unknown and unvisited. From north to south one can count those of Wadi Abu Khusheiba, Wadi 'Attun, Wadi Daba', Wadi Nimr and Wadi el Hidan, Wadi Ibn Hammad, Wadi Weida'a, Hammam 'Afra (Wadi 'Afra), Hammam Burbeita, Wadi Hasa and Wadi Hammam Dathneh.

The highest reported water temperature is about 65° C — a temperature which makes walking in the upper waters of Wadi Zarqa Ma'in almost impossible. Surprisingly, the salinity of most of the thermal springs is low, enabling them to be used for irrigation (as in Hammam ez-Zara') and even for drinking. The low salinity is a unique property of the springs on the eastern flank of the Rift. Those of the opposite side are almost as saline as the water of the Dead Sea! The reason for this difference is not yet clear. However, it is quite obvious that the source of the water of the eastern springs is rainwater, whereas the water of the western springs are heavily admixed with fossil seawater.

It is possible that the thermal springs of Zarqa Ma'in are related to relatively young (500,000 years) volcanic activity which left some hot basaltic rocks not far below ground. If this is true, then it could be the case also in Hammam ez-Zara', Wadi Abu Khusheiba, Wadi el Hidan and Wadi Hasa.

Most of the thermal springs are characterized by the red color of their waters, due to the proliferation of thermophile microorganisms.

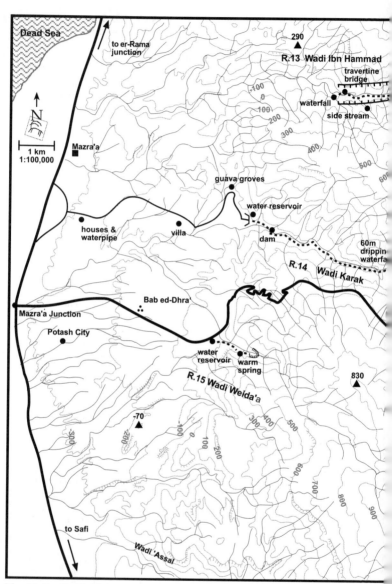

Map 14: Routes 13–15

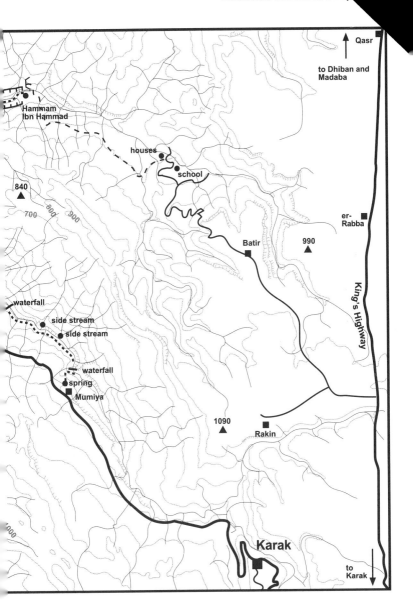

Qasr

to Dhiban and
Madaba

Hammam
Ibn Hammad

840 ▲

700 800 900

houses

school

er-
Rabba

Batir

990 ▲

King's Highway

waterfall

side stream

side stream

waterfall

spring

Mumiya

1090 ▲

Rakin

1000

Karak

to
Karak

14. Wadi Karak
Map 14

Wadi Karak offers spectacular waterfalls, a colorful sandstone gorge and impressive hanging gardens. The upper waterfall consists of three steps dropping 40 m down walls of beige sandstone. The lower waterfall gushes above two great red boulders. Several side streams flow into Wadi Karak, one of these entering as a tall dripping waterfall crowned with palm trees and stalactites. The wadi is easily accessible from the main road connecting Karak with the Dead Sea.

Type of route: One-way.
Altitude difference, Distance and Walking time: 500 m descent, 9 km, 9 hours (1 hour to the first waterfall, 4 hours from the last waterfall to the end of the trail).
Rating: Moderate. **Abseiling is unavoidable.** Expect wet shoes.
Falls: Two waterfalls.
Special equipment: Two 50 m ropes and ordinary abseiling gear.
Guides: Might help with the approach to the wadi. Try the village of Mumiya.
Water: A perennial stream with springs. It is not recommended to drink the water of the main stream. Consider carrying 3 liters each.
Season: Spring, summer and fall.
Getting there and back: Leaving Karak by a local bus or taxi, drive west towards the Dead Sea to reach the village of Mumiya after 8 km. Turn right into the village and continue shortly towards a junction at its eastern edge. Veer left, almost 180 degrees, skirting a lone house, and then descend steeply towards a little spring surrounded by olive groves. The spring is reached by a 5-minute drive from the Karak-Dead Sea road.
The trail ends near the water reservoir of Wadi Karak. To avoid the tedious 8 km walk from there to the Dead Sea road, arrange to be picked up. The pickup vehicle should descend to Mazra'a junction, drive 5 km north on the Dead Sea road and turn right to a side road, which leads to another junction within 500 m. Veer left (east), first amidst houses, and then along a water pipe towards a prominent villa. The road takes some fancy curves, passes guava groves, and eventually ends at Wadi Karak's water reservoir.

Beginning your walk at the spring, progress levelly along the road to reach a steep descent. After a series of switchbacks the road levels once again and crosses a small stream. Just before this crossing turn left down a half-tarred road. Immediately afterwards a track branches to the right leading towards a lone building. Leave the track near the building in favor of goat trails descending into the wadi. The walk from the spring to the wadi takes about 30 minutes.

Proceeding downstream, a beautiful 4 m waterfall, which can be easily bypassed from the right, is reached within 10 minutes. Below this fall lies a much higher waterfall, carved into beige sandstone with three distinct steps.

Waterfall 1: 10 m, 10 m (the only anchors are 10 m away from the edge) and 25 m (no anchors). The second and third steps should be abseiled together, as there are no anchors above the third step. Abseiling all the three steps together is also possible. Despite the water, it is usually possible to keep the gear dry while abseiling.

Leaving the waterfall the route stumbles into a boulder-studded riverbed. The first boulder barrier is negotiated through the middle of the wadi and the second from its right. As you proceed, the walls of the canyon blush red, and become adorned with palm trees, tropical orchid and maidenhair fern.

Two pleasant year-round side streams join Wadi Karak from the north. The first is some 40 minutes from the waterfall and the second an additional 30 minutes away. The gushing of a waterfall is heard within half an hour after the second side stream.

Waterfall 2: 15 m. Abseil on the left-hand side of the wadi to avoid getting wet.

A subtropical paradise of springs and luxuriant greenery commences beneath the waterfall, leading within 20 minutes to a huge boulder, stuck high above the streambed. A wooden beam that was swept by flash floods is lodged just behind the boulder. Within another 20 minutes an awe-inspiring water veil is slowly revealed, reminiscent of the Treasury of Petra between the walls of the *Siq*. A curtain of rivulets rushes 60 m down to the streambed, ornamented with palm trees and stalactites. To its right is a hidden waterfall with a small pond.

Leaving the waterfalls, it takes about two hours of leisurely progress to reach a dam, which diverts the water of the wadi into a water pipe. The road and the water reservoir are ten minutes ahead.

15. Wadi Weida'a
Map 14

Wadi Weida'a is a short and easily accessible route along a little year-round stream. Breaking through almost vertical limestone strata, the entrance to the wadi's outlet is an impressive gate of sheer rock. Along the stream are oleanders and palm trees as well as rare myrtle bushes (*Myrtus communis*) decorating a short sandstone gorge. A man-made pool, which collects the water of a warm spring, is a popular *hammam*. On holidays and fridays the place may be crowded.

Type of route: One-way and back.
Altitude difference, Distance and Walking time: 100 m ascent and descent, 3 km, 1.5 hours.
Rating: Easy. Expect wet shoes.
Special equipment: None.
Guides: Not really needed. Try the Bedouin encampment in front of the wadi's outlet.
Water: A perennial stream. The water is not recommended for drinking. Consider carrying 1 liter each.
Season: Year-round. Be aware of flash flood risk, especially during winter!
Getting there and back: From Mazra'a junction, climb east along the road to Karak. 6 km from the junction, and just before a small bridge, turn right towards a water reservoir, 100 m away from the road. If you come from Karak take the bus to Mazra'a and ask to be dropped at the entrance to the wadi. The trail starts and ends here.

Walk east along the water pipe heading towards a conspicuous gate of rock, formed by vertical strata. Reaching a dam, proceed along a well-maintained trail, crossing the little stream constantly. On the south bank, about 15 minutes from the starting point, there is an artificial pool that collects the water of a warm spring. The site is popular with the people of Karak.

Progress upstream to reach a short gorge with a clump of myrtle bushes (*Myrtus communis*) recognizable by their fragrance. This species is typical of relatively cold and humid Mediterranean environments. In southern Jordan it is rare, appearing only in Wadi Weida'a, Wadi Karak and Wadi Ibn Hammad.

At the upper end of the gorge is a 4 m waterfall. Should you pass it, you will soon reach another waterfall, which is harder to bypass.

Retrace your steps to the starting point.

16. Wadi 'Assal
Map 15

'Assal in Arabic is honey, and honey this wadi is. It offers a narrow sand-stone gorge with luxuriant vegetation and six falls, demanding abseiling skills.

Type of route: One-way.
Altitude difference, Distance and Walking time: 1100 m descent, 15 km, 10 hours (1 hour to the first waterfall, 3.5 hours from the last waterfall to the end of the trail).
Rating: Moderate. **Abseiling is unavoidable.** Expect wet shoes.
Falls: Six. 4 dry falls and two waterfalls.
Special equipment: Two 30 m ropes and ordinary abseiling gear.
Guides: Not really needed. Try the village of Kathrabba.
Water: A stream emerges only after the fourth fall. Consider carry-ing 3 liters each.
Season: Spring, summer and fall.
Getting there and back: Leave Karak by a local bus or taxi, heading southwest towards the village of Kathrabba. Once at the settlement, descend along the road to its northwestern end and cross beneath the high-voltage power line to reach a junction. One track continues parallel to the power line, the other veers to the right descending steeply towards olive groves.
The trail starts at the junction and ends at the Dead Sea road, 5 km south of Mazra'a junction and just south of a gypsum factory. If you have not arranged to be picked up, you can easily hitchhike to Mazra'a junction and take the bus back to Karak.

Take right at the junction, descending to the north along a half-tarred road on the east bank of a small wadi. Wadi 'Assal is reached in about 45 minutes. Walking down the wadi amidst beige sandstone walls, it takes 20 minutes to arrive at the first series of dry falls.

Fall 1: 20 m.
Fall 2: 10 m. A bolt is located on the right.
Fall 3: 15 m. Fall 4 is reached after about 5 minutes.
Fall 4: 15 m. The fall is created where a huge boulder is stuck in the wadi bed.

Below the fourth fall reed and tamar-isk appear for the first time. Soon water seeps out through the gravel bed, feeding a three-metre shower shortly afterwards. As you progress, the brownish sandstone turns more and more red. It takes about 30 min-utes to reach the fifth fall.

Fall 5: 7 m. A big boulder with palm trees above it. Abseil from the right-hand side to avoid getting wet. Just before the sixth fall a side stream joins from the right.
Fall 6: 15 m. Gushing water falling into a narrow sandstone gorge.

A beautiful winding gorge starts be-neath the sixth fall. It begins to widen after some 20 minutes, and soon afterwards a little stream joins from the left. It is well worthwhile to

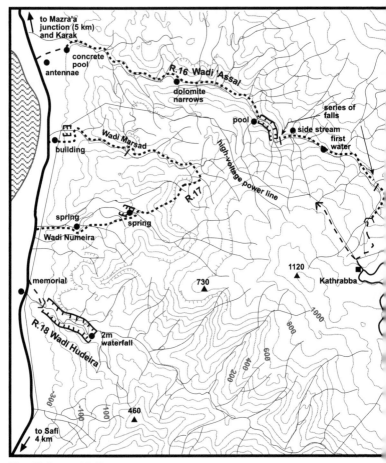

Map 15: Routes 16–18

venture into this side stream. Turn left climbing over a slippery 3 m waterfall to reach a hidden pool, shaded by fig and palm trees and fed by a waterfall.

Backtracking to the main stream, proceed down amidst hanging gardens. About 1 hour from the pool the wadi makes a tight bend to the north. Here you leave the sandstone and en-

ter narrows which are carved into dolomite rock. There is a pleasant shower at the head of the narrows and plenty of shade for an afternoon rest.

The Dead Sea comes into sight within an hour from the narrows. As you approach the outlet of the wadi, the water is diverted towards a concrete pool on the south bank. Near

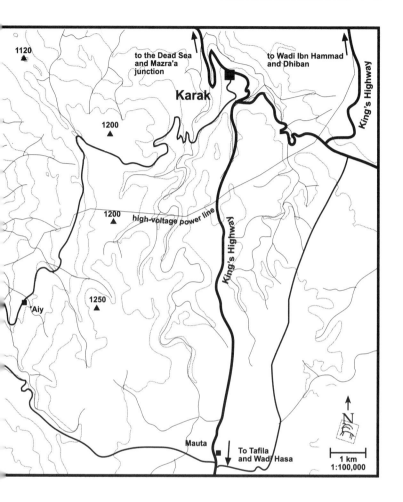

the pool are two jujube trees and close by is the ruin of an ancient water reservoir. Just south of the con-crete pool there is an excellent track, leading to the Dead Sea road in 10 minutes.

17. From Wadi Numeira to Wadi Marsad
Map 15

Wadi Numeira is a modest wadi with a tiny stream, a pleasant waterfall and a small spring. Leaving the wadi, the route ascends along an ancient trail toward a mountain plateau with fine views of the Dead Sea and the Judean Desert. Descending through Wadi Marsad you pass a 50 m dry fall and some red narrows. Be aware that the name Wadi Numeira is also used for Wadi Hudeira a few km to the south.

Type of route: Almost circular.
Altitude difference, Distance and Walking time: 700 m ascent and descent, 10 km, 9 hours.
Rating: Moderate. Expect wet shoes.
Special equipment: None.
Guides: Might help. Try the village of Safi.
Water: A tiny stream for the first 50 minutes. A little spring within 3 hours walk and another small spring within about 8 hours. Consider carrying at least 3 liters each.
Season: Spring, fall and winter. Be aware of flash flood risk, especially during winter!
Getting there and back: The starting point is at the outlet of Wadi Numeira, 12 km south of Mazra'a junction. The trail ends at the outlet of Wadi Marsad, 2.5 km north of the starting point, near a deserted building. The local bus from Mazra'a junction to Safi and from Mazra'a to Karak can be of use.

Walk along the little stream of Wadi Numeira to reach a 3 m waterfall within a few minutes. Huge boulders block the wadi about 30 minutes further, sheltering a hidden spring. Above the spring is a narrow passage between the boulders. If the passage proves difficult, retrace your steps and bypass the boulders along the south bank. Going through the boulders you arrive soon at a spring feeding a little waterfall which is surrounded by fig trees, maidenhair fern and moss. Above this point the wadi is dry.

To bypass the waterfall, backtrack 50 m and climb south along a faint trail with wooden shorings. As you go up, the trail becomes more obvious. Reaching a flat shoulder, proceed up and east, gaining glimpses of

the waterfall. A higher flat shoulder is reached 10 minutes after leaving the waterfall.

Cross a small side wadi and proceed northwest, passing through a curious cairn-strewn field. Keep walking on the flat shoulder until the dry wadi to your left and the line of cliffs to your right draw close to each other. It is here that the trail crosses the wadi, just above a wide gorge.

Leave the trail, descending over some rocky slabs to reach a tiny spring at the head of the gorge. Flat rock surfaces as well as shadowing overhangs make this spot an ideal resting place. A close look at the surrounding rocks will reveal numerous fossils. The spring is about 2 hours from the starting point.

An ancient path ascends to the

northeast from the rock platform above the spring. The beginning of the trail is somewhat hard to find on the boulder-strewn slope. Nowadays the path is not frequently used but one can imagine its past glory. Whoever built it made a conscious effort to make the ascent as easy as possible.

Climbing steeply you gain almost 400 m before reaching a flat pastureland about 90 minutes away from the spring. The view toward the Dead Sea is magnificent. The bay of Mazra'a and Cape Costigan are clearly seen to the northwest. Further to the west, on the Israel side of the border, canyons descend from the Judean Desert towards the Dead Sea. Along the western shore of the Dead Sea is a cluster of hotels and further to the north is Mount Masada. Visibility permitting, the city of Hebron can be spotted on the skyline to the northwest atop the Judean mountain crest.

Proceed northeast along the plateau and towards the cliffs. When the plateau ends continue levelly and cross a shallow side wadi. Leave the trail 100 m further, and descend to the left (north). The bottom of Wadi Marsad is reached within a 15-minute descent along an easy slope with no obvious trail.

Walking down among red sandstone banks you pass a wadi joining from the right. Within 50 minutes a 50 m dry fall suddenly appears with a little spring below it. The fall can be bypassed with care, along a steep slope on its right-hand side.

Beyond the spring the wadi widens but within about 30 minutes a short canyon develops. Though the canyon is not passable, it is worthwhile descending its upper part until a low dry fall prevents further progress (below this fall are two higher falls). Retrace your steps and climb to the south bank of the wadi. Descending along a gentle slope it takes about 15 minutes to reach the Dead Sea road.

18. Wadi Hudeira
Map 15

A short but spectacular route, easily accessible from the Dead Sea road. The wadi forms a 150 m high narrow *siq* winding through pink sandstone. The wadi is also called Wadi Judeira and Wadi Numeira.

Type of route: One-way and back.
Altitude difference, Distance and Walking time: 100 m ascent and descent, 2 km, 2.5 hours.
Rating: Easy. Expect wet shoes.
Special equipment: none.
Guides: Not really needed. Try the village of Safi.
Water: A perennial stream. Drinking its water is not recommended. Consider carrying 1 liter each.
Season: Year-round. Be aware of flash flood risk, especially during winter!
Getting there and back: Drive along the Dead Sea road 13 km south of Mazra'a junction. At the spot where a prominent white memorial is seen on the right-hand side, turn left and proceed along a dirt track for about 1 km, until it comes to a dead end. The trail starts and ends here. The local bus between Mazra'a junction and Safi and between Mazra'a and Karak can be of use.

Walking up Wadi Hudeira is like being drawn by a powerful magnet. As you enter the wadi, the walls of the canyon get higher and closer, eventually rising to more than 150 m and only a few metres apart. The narrow *siq* appears repeatedly to run into a dead end, but then changes direction abruptly. It takes about 60 minutes to reach a low waterfall at the eastern end of the *siq*. Behind the waterfall the gorge widens and the wadi continues quite monotonously. Backtrack to the starting point.

Acacia tree

19–21. Wadi Hasa
Map 16

"We ascended for a short time and then began to descend into the valley called Wadi Hasa. It had now become dark, and this was without exception, the most dangerous route I ever travelled in my life. The descent is steep and there is no regular road over the smooth rocks... We had missed our way and were obliged to alight from our horses, as many of us had suffered severe falls." (J. L. Burckhardt, 1812)

Wadi Hasa sports magnificent hanging gardens, narrow gorges and hot springs. Its upper reaches are carved into white limestone, creating a playground of giant boulders. A dramatic change of scenery is displayed along its lower course, where the wadi cuts a spectacular canyon in red sandstone.

The drainage basin of Wadi Hasa extends over 3,200 sq. km, far bigger than most of the wadis in Moab or Edom and second only to Wadi Mujib. Its discharge is about 20 million cubic m per year and the temperature of its hottest spring is about 54^0 C. A rare tropical tree (*Dalbergia sissoo*), not known elsewhere in Jordan grows in its bed.

Wadi Hasa is identified with the biblical Zered River, the traditional border between Moab and Edom. It is depicted on the mosaic map of Madaba.

At the upper reaches of Wadi Hasa, atop a prominent hill, is the ruined Nabataean temple of Khirbet Tannur. Just beneath it a new dam is being built. Though the dam is constructed above the point where the wadi's flow commences, and is meant to catch only floods, it is hard to foresee its influence on the lower reaches of the wadi.

Three trekking routes are suggested in Wadi Hasa:

19. From Wadi Hasa's upper canyon to Wadi 'Afra.
20. Wadi Hasa, lower canyon.
21. Wadi Hasa, the full length.

Dalbergia sissoo

19. From Wadi Hasa's upper canyon to Wadi 'Afra.

Map 16

The upper canyon of Wadi Hasa is carved in white limestone, with a string of cascades and hidden passages between boulders. Ascending Wadi 'Afra is a warm experience, including a hot stream and a series of low waterfalls. At the end of the route are the thermal baths of Hammam 'Afra.

> **Type of route**: Almost circular.
>
> **Altitude difference, Distance and Walking time:** 100 m descent and ascent, 4 km, 7 hours.
>
> **Rating:** Moderate. Expect wet shoes.
>
> **Special equipment:** None.
>
> **Guides:** Might help. Try the local inhabitants near Hammam Burbeita.
>
> **Water:** A perennial stream and a thermal side stream. The water of the main stream is not recommended for drinking. Consider carrying 3 liters each.
>
> **Season:** Spring, fall, winter. The water in Wadi Hasa can get quite cold in the winter but the thermal water of Wadi 'Afra will definitely compensate. Be aware of flash flood risk, especially during winter!
>
> **Getting there and back:** Driving along the King's Highway, turn west to Hammam 'Afra, at the signed junction. Avoid the first tarred road, which goes down to Hammam Burbeita near the local school, and carry on to reach another fork. Here you take right, reaching Wadi Hasa's stream after a few hundred metres. The trail starts here. The local buses from Karak to Tafila can be of use, but you will have to hitchhike from the King's Highway to the starting point. The trail ends at Hammam 'Afra. Hitchhike back to the King's Highway.

Descending along the stream of Wadi Hasa, you reach the head of a limestone gorge within a few minutes. Walk along its north bank until a rocky gully allows easy access into its bed.

Huge boulders lie along the wadi bed within an hour from the head of the gorge. Some can be bypassed but others you may have to negotiate by jumping or crawling. It takes about 3 hours to reach the confluence of Wadi 'Afra and Wadi Hasa, marked by a cluster of rare tropical trees (*Dalbergia sissoo*). The leaves of this tree are oval and their underside is hairy.

Turn left to enter Wadi 'Afra, proceeding a short distance upstream along its east (left) bank until a ruined flourmill (sugar mill?) is seen on its west bank. Cross the wadi and continue towards a string of low waterfalls, each of them a proper Jacuzzi. Soon afterwards you enter sandstone narrows. The head of the narrows is reached within about 1 hour from Wadi Hasa.

From here onwards the wadi is flat and the going easy. Hot springs erupt from its sandstone walls, which are dotted with green gardens. It takes about an hour to reach Hammam 'Afra, a spa of artificial pools (Entrance fee – 3 JD).

20. Wadi Hasa, lower canyon
Map 16

Natural gardens of palm trees adorn the spectacular sandstone canyon of Wadi Hasa as it meanders towards the Dead Sea. The tranquil atmosphere is unequaled anywhere. There are warm springs, hidden pools and countless beauty spots. No matter how early you start — at the end of the day you will probably feel you have hurried it.

Type of route: One-way.

Altitude difference, Distance and Walking time: 550 m descent (950 m descent including the walk along the dirt track), 18 km, minimum 10 hours without visiting the side streams. Otherwise, allow 12 hours or divide the route over two days.

Rating: Moderate. Expect wet shoes. Do not wear sandals if you don't want your feet to be badly scoured by sand and gravel.

Special equipment: None.

Guides: Might help. Try the village of Irhab.

Water: A perennial stream and several side streams. The water of the main stream is not recommended for drinking. Consider carrying 3 liters each.

Season: Spring and fall. The route may be too long for a hot summer day.

Getting there and back: Take a local bus or taxi from Tafila to Irhab via 'Aima. Descent to the trailhead takes 30 minutes along a steep, rough dirt track, or a 75-minute walk. If you would rather not walk you can arrange a pickup truck in Irhab (about 10 JD) or Tafila. The track branches from the road 4 km north of Irhab (100 m beyond, a rather unnoticed power line crosses the road). Ignore several side tracks until you reach a fork, whose left branch stretches levelly on a flat shoulder and reaches a dead end after 100 m. The right branch descends steeply along a very rough track. This is where the trail starts. The trail ends at the village of Safi on the Dead Sea shore. If you have arranged to be picked up, make sure the vehicle waits on the south bank of Wadi Hasa besides the aqueduct (*qanat el mai*). There is a local bus from Safi to Mazra'a junction and Karak.

Leaving the end of the left branch of the track a faint goat trail descends northwestwards. The trail soon negotiates giant limestone blocks, which seem to bar progress. Though the trail is far from clear, aim towards the obvious confluence between Wadi Hasa and a side wadi which joins from the south, and you will do fine. The descent includes short sections of loose scree. Brownish sandstone walls with abundant greenery are a colorful welcome to Wadi Hasa, reached within 30 minutes.

A warm spring, which issues on the north bank 20 minutes after reaching the streambed, creates a 2 m shower stained red by thermophile microorganisms. To round off the experience you can take a dip in the frigid stream or continue several minutes more to reach a cold waterfall coming from the south.

Within 15 minutes from the shower

The King's Highway

The King's Highway runs the length of Jordan from 'Aqaba in the south, through Amman, to the Syrian border in the north. The highway marks the caravan route used by traders and armies, and for centuries it had tremendous commercial and strategic importance. It provided access to the Arabian Peninsula, Sinai, Egypt and the Indian Ocean at one end and to Damascus and northern Mesopotamia at the other end.

The Bible mentions the King's Highway in connection with the wandering of the Israelites from Egypt to Cana'an, when Moses sent envoys to the king of Edom: "Grant us passage through your country. We will not trespass on field or vineyard, or drink from your wells. We will keep to the King's Highway" (Numbers 20: 17).

The Romans rebuilt and paved the highway after annexing the Nabataean kingdom in 106 CE. Milestones were positioned along the route, which was called 'Via Nova Traiana', or the New Road of Trajan. Besides being an important commercial route, as the eastern limit of the Roman empire it was also designed to carry a line of defence posts against invasions from the desert. Indeed, the building of the Roman border highway preceded a very long period of peace.

During the Early Muslim period the King's Highway was a major pilgrim route to Mecca. When the Crusaders arrived they built the fortresses of Karak and Shawbak along this route, and could thus supervise both the religious and commercial traffic. Reynald of Chatillon, Lord of Karak Castle, attacked several Muslim caravans. Salah ed-Din (Saladin), the shrewd Muslim leader, never forgave him, and when Reynald was captured, in the decisive battle of Hittin, near Tiberias, he is said to have personally beheaded him.

The route of the King's Highway was a compromise between proximity to water sources and convenient topography. Instead of running along the flat plateau, the road stretched along the upper reaches of the slope towards the Rift, with many ups and downs but with abundant springs.

The Ottoman Turks, who dominated the area from the 16th to the 20th century, moved the pilgrim road further to the east and onto the plateau, where it avoided the deep canyons. The new route was called "Tariq el Bint" (the Road of the Daughter, nowadays the Desert Highway), since it was a daughter of a Turkish Sultan that had found the traditional route too tiring. Fortresses and cisterns were built along the new route and the city of Ma'an thrived. Pilgrims usually travelled in organized groups headed by an "Amir el Haj", a commander of the pilgrims, who was appointed by the authorities. The local Bedouin were paid not to disrupt public order.

The Hejaz railway was built along the eastern route, in the early years of the 20th century. The railway, which stretched along 1300 km from Damascus to Madina, made the pilgrimage much shorter and easier and provided benefits to the local economy. During World War I the Arabian forces with T. E. Lawrence constantly attacked the railway, as part of the Arab revolt against the Turks. The railway is no longer active from Ma'an southwards. However, a modern branch links Ma'an with 'Aqaba, mostly for phosphate transportation.

Nowadays the Desert Highway, which parallels the railway, is the fastest route from 'Aqaba to Amman. Trucks use this route from the port of 'Aqaba to the capital and further to Iraq. The western route is still called the King's Highway or "Tariq el Muluk". Though it is a much slower means of transit, it is marked with historical sites and offers magnificent vistas towards the Rift.

the tiny stream of Wadi Qatara flows in from the south. Leaving the main stream, turn left into Wadi Qatara, arriving soon at a small pond. Climb the rock ledge on the left side of the pond to reach a hidden pool cradled in a side ravine.

Back in the main stream of Wadi Hasa, progress past a clump of the rare tropical tree *Dalbergia sissoo,* which can be identified by its oval leaves. Thereafter, an impressive gorge commences. A little waterfall flows in from the north, 40 minutes from Wadi Qatara, and soon afterwards the red walls of the wadi draw together once again. A steep rock outcrop rises on the left side of the streambed 15 minutes from the waterfall.

40 minutes ahead, a side stream which joins from the right creates the best swimming pool along Wadi Hasa. A natural sandstone sculpture, resembling a submarine, is reached after an additional 10 minutes.

Just beyond the submarine, a little stream flows in from the south. To enjoy it, turn left and climb through a smooth 4 m fall, reaching another fall immediately above it. Bypass the fall from the left and you come to a ravine with palm trees, *Ficus* and maidenhair fern growing around a waterfall with a shallow pool.

Return to Wadi Hasa and proceed downstream for 20 minutes, when another stream flows in from the south.

It is hard to realize that this is not tropical rain country — the annual rainfall here is less than 100 mm, making it an arid desert environment. If you turn left and walk upstream you will encounter more waterfalls, eventually blocking the way.

Returning to Wadi Hasa, you walk some 30 minutes before Wadi Hamarash joins from the north. This wadi is dry and can easily be missed. Up Wadi Hamarash, a few minutes walk from Wadi Hasa, you encounter an imposing dry fall with a boulder stuck in its head.

Back in Wadi Hasa, the landscape changes after about 10 minutes as the red sandstone makes way to gray dolomite with a refreshing cascade. Walking through the gray canyon, you soon re-enter a pink sandstone landscape. About one hour from the dolomite canyon is a huge boulder with a cascade beyond it. Advancing through a rose-colored gorge one hour further, another boulder totally blocks the wadi, forcing the water into a narrow, rock-overhung corridor on its left. Pass through this corridor and proceed for 30 minutes to reach a dam diverting the water into an aqueduct. Following the aqueduct you arrive at the first houses of the village of Safi, ten minutes ahead. If you have not arranged to be picked up you can find taxi or local pickup trucks at the village center. Cold beverages and *hummus* are also available.

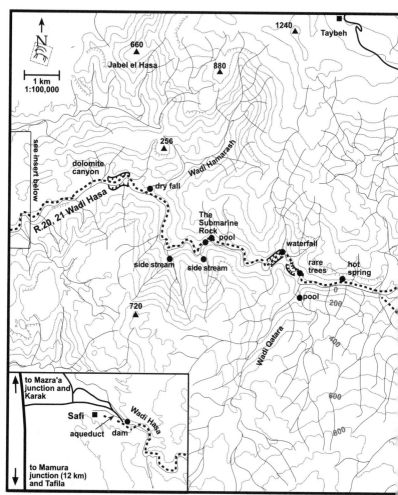

Map 16: Routes 19–21. Wadi Hasa

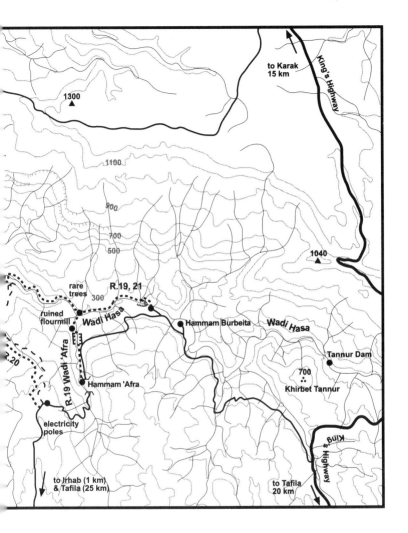

to Karak
15 km

King's Highway

▲ 1300

1100

900

700

500

1040 ▲

rare
trees

R. 19, 21

300

ruined
flourmill

Wadi Hasa

Hammam Burbeita

Wadi Hasa

Tannur Dam

R.19 Wadi 'Afra

700

Khirbet Tannur

Hammam 'Afra

electricity
poles

King's Highway

to Irhab (1 km)
& Tafila (25 km)

to Tafila
20 km

21. Wadi Hasa, the full length
Map 16

A two-day trek through a fascinating canyon. If you have the time and you are willing to carry a full backpack all along the route, this is the best way to enjoy Wadi Hasa's charms.

Type of route: One-way.
Route:
> **Day 1:** Wadi Hasa, upper canyon. Camping site at the confluence with Wadi Qatara.
> **Day 2:** Wadi Hasa, lower canyon.

Rating: Moderate. Expect wet shoes. Do not wear sandals if you don't want your feet to be badly scoured by sand and gravel.
Special equipment: None.
Guides: Might help. Try the local inhabitants in Hammam Burbeita.
Water: A perennial stream and several side streams. The water of the main stream is not recommended for drinking. Consider carrying 3 liters each.
Season: Spring and fall. The route may be too long for a hot summer day.
Getting there and back: The trailhead is close to the King's Highway near Hammam Burbeita. See Route 19 for details. The trail ends at the village of Safi, see Route 20 for details.

Day 1
Altitude difference, Distance and Walking time: 200 m descent, 9 km, 8 hours.
Water: A perennial stream not recommended for drinking. A side stream at Wadi Qatara near the suggested camping site.

Take Route 19 to reach the junction with Wadi 'Afra. Below the junction the wadi widens, the boulders disappear and progress is easy. Passing a hot spring, continue about 1.5 hours from Wadi 'Afra before a track is seen coming down on the south slope, just before a flat patch. Soon after, the stream is forced into a narrow limestone gorge with a 5 m waterfall at its head. Slide into the gorge from its left bank and backtrack to the base of the waterfall.

A boulder-strewn stretch, where the going is slow, follows the short gorge. It takes about an hour to clear this section and another 40 minutes of easy going to reach a 2 m hot shower dripping from a spring on the north bank. Wadi Qatara is 15 minutes away from the shower. This is a good camping site, with a small side stream and a nearby pond (see Route 20).

Day 2
Altitude difference, Distance and Walking time: 350 m descent, 15 km, 10 hours.
Water: A perennial stream and several side streams.

Take Route 20.

Tafila area and Dana Nature Reserve
From Wadi Hasa to Wadi Ghuweir

"It is certainly one of the most picturesque countries in the world." (E. H. Palmer, 1868, about Edom)

This region encompasses the northern part of Edom. Though the political boundaries between the now-vanished kingdoms of Moab and Edom are no longer apparent, a gradual geographical transition can be noticed. The height of the peaks increases from 1300 m near Wadi Hasa to 1650 m in the vicinity of Dana Nature Reserve, and the wadis emerge from the mountain front at increasing altitudes: from minus 400 m near Wadi Hasa, to 300 m above sea level at the outlet of Wadi Dana. All the wadis drain eventually into the Dead Sea, though some only after a long and flat journey through the northern part of the 'Araba Valley.

Near the village of es-Sela' and in Dana Nature Reserve, immediately below the rim of the plateau, a remarkable maze of rounded white sandstone hills and sandy hollows captures the eye. This landscape is not seen in Moab, since this white sandstone (Disi Formation) is missing there. Another, new type of landscape, appears at the lower reaches of Wadi Dana and Wadi Ghuweir as the sandstone gives way to savage-looking igneous rocks.

An outstanding difference between Moab and Edom is in their vegetation. Many Mediterranean species growing in Edom are rare or absent in Moab. The Red Juniper tree, for example, is an Edomite trademark. The preservation of Edom's unique vegetation was a prime reason for establish-

ing Dana Nature Reserve — the place to admire Edom's flora while trekking through labyrinths of white domes.

Northern Edom offers scenic highlands, as well as narrow sandstone gorges with year-round streams and hanging gardens, such as those of Wadi Feifa, Khanzira and Ghuweir. Abseiling abilities are needed only in Wadi 'Aima.

The chief town in the region is Tafila. Its tourist services are limited though it is possible to find here at least one budget hotel and several restaurants. Other hotel accommodation, as well as official campsites, are available in Dana Nature Reserve. Along the King's Highway there are small villages such as 'Ein el Beida, Qadisiyya and Buseira. Buseira is identified with Bozra, the historical capital of Edom. Archeological evidence attests that it was a well-planned governing center during the 8–6th centuries BCE. Near 'Ein el Beida is the half-deserted village of es-Sela' overlooking a spectacular mesa, thought to be the Edomite stronghold Sela' ("The Rock", II Kings 14: 7).

In the 'Araba Valley there is only one small settlement, the village of Qureiqira, close to the outlet of Wadi Dana. Nearby there are numerous copper mining localities, which made ancient Feinan, a notable center of copper production.

The following routes are suggested in this region:

Route	Days	Rating	Season	Description
22. Wadi Jifneh	1 (4 hours)	easy	spring fall winter	Spectacular palm ravine.
23. Jabel Muleih and Wadi Jifneh	1 (9 hours)	moderate	spring fall winter	Excellent panoramas of the Dead Sea. Including Route 22.
24. Wadi 'Aima and Wadi Feifa	1 (10 hours)	moderate incl. abseiling	spring summer fall	Sandstone gorge, 4 falls (1 with water), dripping springs, hanging gardens.
25. Wadi Umruq	1 (1 hour)	easy	all-year	Pool and waterfall, 15 minutes from the Dead Sea road.
26. Wadi Khanzira	1 (8 hours)	moderate	spring summer fall	Sandstone gorge, pools.
27. Wadi Khanzira, a short route	1 (4 hours)	easy	spring fall	Small waterfall, several dripping springs.
28. From Wadi 'Aima to Wadi Khanzira	2	moderate incl. abseiling	spring summer fall	Sandstone gorges, hanging gardens, elevated campsite with rewarding views.
29. Sela' — The Rock of Edom	1 (3 hours)	easy	all-year	Remarkable Edomite stronghold, Babylonian rock relief, impressive views.
30. The Cave trail	1 (1.5 hours)	easy	March to October	A stroll near Rummana Campsite.
31. The Campsite trail	1 (1 hour)	easy	"	A stroll near Rummana Campsite.
32. Jabel Rummana trail	1 (2.5 hours)	easy	"	A stroll near Rummana Campsite, fine views of the 'Araba Valley.
33. From Dana Village to Rummana Campsite	1 (4 hours)	easy	"	White sandstone domes, terraced groves, fine views, unique vegetation.
34. From Dana Village to Feinan Campsite	1 (5 hours)	easy	all-year	Easy way to Feinan Campsite, along a dirt track.
35. From Wadi Hamra to Hammam Dathneh	1 (9 hours)	moderate	all-year	Variety of landscapes. Highlight of Dana Reserve.
36. Wadi Ghuweir	1 (8 hours)	moderate	spring summer fall	Magnificent hanging gardens, narrow *siq* painted with iron oxides, cascades.
37. From Wadi Hamra to Wadi Ghuweir	2	moderate	spring summer fall	Wide vistas, spectacular canyons. Including routes 35-36.
38. Feinan's copper works	1 (1 hour)	easy	all-year	Ancient aqueduct, ruins of churches, heaps of copper slag.

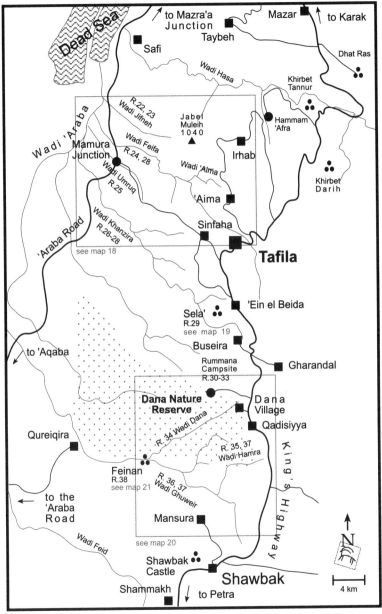

Map 17: Tafila area and Dana Nature Reserve — from Wadi Hasa to Wadi Ghuweir

22. Wadi Jifneh
Map 18

Hidden between Wadi Hasa to the north and Wadi Feifa to the south is the little ravine of Wadi Jifneh, crowded with hundreds of wild palms.

Type of route: One-way and back.
Altitude difference, Distance and Walking time: 200 m ascent and descent, 7 km, 4 hours.
Rating: Easy. Expect wet shoes.
Special equipment: None.
Guides: Not really needed. Try the village of Feifa. You may be able to contact local people in the fields opposite the outlet of the wadi.
Water: A stream and some small ponds are reached within 1.5 hours from the starting point. Consider carrying 3 liters each.
Season: Spring, fall and winter. Be aware of flash flood risk, especially during winter!
Getting there and back: Heading north along the 'Araba road, turn east into a side road, 5 km past the village of Feifa. Two km ahead is a T-junction where you should turn left (east). Leave the tarmac 500 m further and turn right (south) to a dirt track, which is negotiable with a high-clearance vehicle. The track crosses Wadi Jifneh and proceeds eastwards for 2 km along its south bank. A shed and a curious pile of stones (an ancient guard post?) mark the beginning of the trail. There is a local bus between Feifa and Safi and from Safi to Mazra'a junction. Arranging a pickup truck in Feifa should be quite easy.

Leave the track and descend into the wadi, avoiding the cliffs by walking eastward for a short while. Proceeding among tamarisk and jujube trees, you enter a wide dolomite canyon and within 50 minutes from the starting point you reach a fork of wadis. Further progress in the main (middle) streambed is almost impossible as water issues out of the gravel, supporting a dense brush of reeds. To bypass this section, climb along a good trail on north bank of the main streambed. Soon the trail levels, edging a line of cliffs.

After 30 minutes the trail descends back into the wadi near a small man-made pool. Plastic pipes lead the water from the pool towards nearby fields of watermelon and tomato.

Proceed east, towards a mass of palm trees which marks the entrance of a splendid ravine. Inside the ravine is a jungle of palms sprouting from all directions among little pools, maidenhair fern and orchid.

Return to the man-made pool, cross to the south bank of the wadi and proceed levelly westwards. After about 30 minutes the trail descends into a southern tributary of Wadi Jifneh. Another 50 minutes along the wadi bring you back to the starting point.

23. Jabel Muleih and Wadi Jifneh
Map 18

Jabel Muleih rises to 1,040 m, providing excellent panoramas towards the Dead Sea. Ascent to the summit is easy but the route into Wadi Jifneh is steep and difficult to find. Once you reach Wadi Jifneh, a little paradise of palm trees awaits you.

Type of route: One-way.
Altitude difference, Distance and Walking time: 1,350 m descent, 11 km if you arrange to be picked up, otherwise 16 km, 9 hours.
Rating: Moderate. Route-finding can be difficult.
Special equipment: None.
Guides: Might help. Try the village of 'Aima or Diba'a.
Water: Ponds and dripping springs in Wadi Jifneh 6 hours from the starting point. Consider carrying 3 liters each.
Season: Spring, fall and winter. Be aware of flash flood risk, especially during winter!
Getting there and back: Leave Tafila towards the villages of 'Aima and Diba'a, taking the local bus to Irhab or a taxi (4 JD). About 3 km beyond Diba'a, the road traverses a flat shoulder where a half-tarred track branches to the west. The trail starts here.
The trail ends at the outlet of Wadi Jifneh, 5 km east of the Dead Sea road. You can either walk to the road or arrange to be picked up by a pickup truck. From the road it is usually quite easy to hitchhike back to Tafila.
To reach the end point with a vehicle, take the scenic road descending from Tafila towards the Dead Sea. Turn right at Mamura junction and continue north towards the village of Feifa. See Route 22 for further explanations.

Go west on the half-tarred track, which takes a tight bend to the north after 2 km. Here you leave the track, heading west towards Jabel Muleih, a hillock-like peak reached within 1 hour from the starting point. From the peak (1,040 m) walk a short distance to reach a better-positioned summit (1,030 m).

Jabel Muleih offers magnificent views towards the Dead Sea and the northern part of the 'Araba Valley. To the northwest are the extensive evaporation ponds of the potash industries of Jordan and Israel. The border between the two countries is marked by an earth ramp that runs north-south across the ponds. Beyond the western ponds, just north of the industrial complex, is the elongate ridge of Mount Sodom. The mountain is a great wedge of rock salt, taking its name from the biblical city of Sodom, which tradition locates thereabouts. Further to the west and north is the Judean Desert and beyond it the Judean mountain ridge closing the horizon.

The eastern shore of the Dead Sea is dotted here with a mosaic of cultivated lands crossed by the winding course of Wadi Hasa. The copious discharge of the wadi supports a flourishing agriculture. This is the site of ancient Zoar, depicted on the 6th century mosaic map of Madaba.

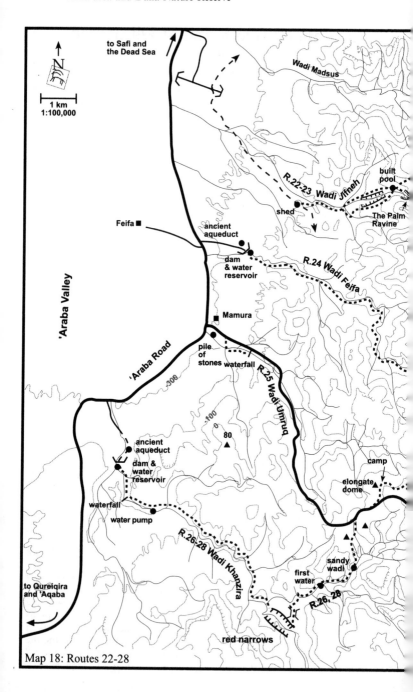

Map 18: Routes 22-28

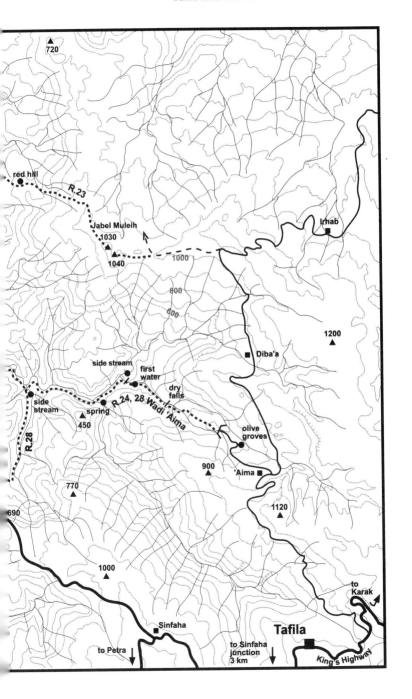

Proceed north along the crest of Jabel Muleih for about 30 minutes. Avoid the spur descending westwards about 1 km away from the peak. Instead cross a saddle and continue along the ridge looking for a faint trail branching to the west. This faint trail descends steeply along a talus slope, dropping 400 m within a short horizontal distance.

As you descend try to spot a shallow wadi running along the base of the slope from south to north. On the west bank of this wadi runs an obvious trail, reached within 1 hour from the ridge. The trail crosses a low shoulder and proceeds westwards towards a red hill. Pass the hill on its left and continue downhill towards a flat area.

A steep gully drains into Wadi Jifneh at the western rim of this flat area. Keeping the gully to your left, descend steeply almost 350 m, with no obvious trail. You reach Wadi Jifneh near a small man-made pool. From here on continue according to Route 22.

24. Wadi 'Aima and Wadi Feifa
Map 18

Wadi 'Aima is a tributary of Wadi Feifa, draining the region of Tafila towards the Dead Sea. Both wadis have deep sandstone canyons and year-round streams. Descending Wadi 'Aima involves abseiling of two dry falls leading into a red canyon with dripping springs and hanging gardens. Wadi Feifa is studded with palm trees.

Type of route: One-way.
Altitude difference, Distance and Walking time: 900 m descent, 15 km, 10 hours (1 hour to the first fall. About 8 hours from the foot of the second fall to the end of the trail).
Rating: Moderate. **Abseiling is unavoidable.** Expect wet shoes.
Falls: Four. Three dry falls and one waterfall. The first two falls require abseiling.
Special equipment: Two 20 m ropes and ordinary abseiling gear.
Guides: Not really needed. Try the village of 'Aima.
Water: A perennial stream in the lower reaches of Wadi 'Aima. Abundant dripping springs in the upper reaches of Wadi Feifa. Consider carrying 3 liters each.
Season: Spring, summer and fall.
Getting there and back: Leave Tafila by a local bus or taxi (3 JD), towards the village of 'Aima, 8 km away. Once at the village descend north towards olive groves. Do not enter the olive groves. Instead proceed northwest for about 1 km to reach the end of the road on a flat-topped shoulder.
The route ends at the 'Araba Valley near the village of Feifa. There are buses from Feifa to Safi and from there to Mazra'a junction and Karak.
To reach the end point with a vehicle, descend towards the 'Araba Valley. Turn right (north) at Mamura junction and proceed for 2–3 km until a side road branches to the east, just north of the entrance to Feifa. The side road ends after 1.5 km, at the water reservoir of Wadi Feifa.

From the end of the road, walk northwest following a stone-lined boundary between disused agricultural lands. When the stone line thins out, continue downhill, adhering to the left-hand side of the shoulder. Just before reaching the tip of the shoulder descend south into a small ravine. Wadi 'Aima is reached within a few minutes, about 40 minutes from the trailhead. The wadi is dry and its white sandstone walls are decorated by green caper bushes. A short walk leads to a series of dry falls.

Fall 1: 15 m. Limestone boulders lodged in a sandstone chimney.
Fall 2: 10 m.
Fall 3: 7 m. It is possible to descend this fall using a hiker's rope.

Soon after the third fall, tamarisk and reed appear and the walls of the wadi turn wine-red. Within an hour, water seeps make their appearance, feeding a small stream that leads to a 3 m waterfall. Beneath the waterfall lush greenery erupts from the red walls, and within a few minutes a stream flows in from the right. A short walk along this stream is worthwhile.

Leaving the junction of the streams, proceed downstream, arriving within ten minutes at a scenic spot with stalactites and palm trees. Soon afterwards, you reach the confluence of Wadi 'Aima and Wadi Feifa. Turn left walking up the stream of Wadi Feifa for a few minutes to reach a spring which creates a worthy shower. Further up, the vegetation is dense and the going is rough.

Backtracking to the confluence, walk downstream amidst partly burnt palm gardens. Along the stream are black basalt pebbles from volcanic outcrops around Tafila. Within an hour from the confluence a stream flows in from the south. Those who wish to continue to Wadi Khanzira should turn left here (see Route 28). Otherwise descend with the main stream.

It takes about two hours to reach a tiny gorge, cut in conglomerate — its walls are a mosaic of pebbles and boulders. A dam, diverting the stream to a water reservoir, is encountered 90 minutes from the gorge. If you have not arranged to be picked up at the dam, walk down the road passing traces of an ancient aqueduct as well as two ruined structures. The 'Araba Valley road is twenty minutes away.

Onn Crouvi

H.

Noya Shiloni

Avi Blum

I. H.

Top: Bedouin encampment below Rajef
Bottom: The Dead Sea viewed from Mukawir (Machaerus)

H.

Wadi Mujib's waterfall (R.11)

I. H.

I. H.

I. H.

I. H.

Avraham Izdarechet

Noya Shiloni

Yehoram Doron

Top Left: The Nabataean theatre of Wadi Sabra (R.51, 61)
Middle Left: Roman-Nabataean copper mine (the cave of the Ghula. R.62, 64)
Left: A bell-shaped Edomite cistern, Jabel el Quseir (R.50)
Top Right: A Nabataean cistern, Humeima (R.59-60)
Second Right: Leopard trap, Jabel Barza (R. 52-53)
Third Right: The rock relief of Sela' (R.29)
Bottom Right: Rock engraving of the ostrich-like Houbara, atop Umm el Biyara (R.47)

25. Wadi Umruq
Map 18

A waterfall and a pond reached within a 15-minute walk from the main road. A nice desert cooler.

Type of route: One-way and back.
Altitude difference, Distance and Walking time: 50 m ascent and descent, less than 1.5 km, 1 hour.
Rating: Easy.
Special equipment: None.
Guides: Not really needed. Try the local people at Mamura junction.
Water: A pond and a waterfall.
Season: Year-round. Be aware of flash flood risk, especially during winter!
Getting there and back: Leaving the Dead Sea road turn east towards Tafila at Mamura junction. The trail starts 1 km from the junction where the grade of the road gets steeper.

Leave the road, descending a short distance into the wadi to the south. Looking back towards the junction a strange pile of stones, probably an ancient guard post along the 'Araba road, rises above the terraces of the wadi.

Heading east, ascend through cultivated fields following plastic water pipes. At the head of the pipes, 15 minutes ahead, there is a small dam. Once past the dam you reach an 8 m waterfall dropping into an attractive pond.

Retrace your steps to the starting point.

26. Wadi Khanzira
Map 18

Wadi Khanzira drains a large area south of Tafila. The peaks of the area rise some 1,500 m above sea level, whereas the wadi's outlet on the bottom of the Rift Valley is at 300 m below sea level. Three major tributaries, with perennial streams, feed the lower reaches of the wadi. All three are narrow sandstone canyons surrounded by jagged topography.

This route enters the wadi very close to the point where the three tributaries join together. Abundant water vegetation, perennial ponds, dripping springs and narrow gorges are all there.

Type of route: One-way.
Altitude difference, Distance and Walking time: 600 m descent, 15 km, 8 hours.
Rating: Moderate. Expect wet shoes.
Special equipment: None.
Guides: Might help. Try the village of Sinfaha.
Water: A perennial stream which starts about 1 hour from the trailhead. Several dripping springs. Consider carrying 3 liters each.
Season: Spring and fall. Summer is also fine though not on especially hot days.
Getting there and back: Leave Tafila by the bus to Feifa or a taxi, descending towards the Dead Sea along a steep scenic road. After 16 km a sign reads "Mamura 10 km". One hundred m after the sign a toothed fence stretches along the left-hand side of the road. The trail starts at the small wadi behind the fence.
The trail ends at the outlet of Wadi Khanzira close to the 'Araba road. If you have not arranged to be picked up, hitch a ride to Mamura junction and from there to Tafila. To reach the end of the trail with a vehicle, head south from Mamura junction, cross a bridge after 3 km, and turn left into a side road. The road deteriorates into a dirt track after 1 km. After an additional kilometer it ends at the water reservoir of Wadi Khanzira.

Leave the road, descending into the small wadi behind the toothed fence. Within 15 minutes a large cairn is seen on an indistinct col to your right. The cairn marks the descent into a short gully which soon drops into a wide sandy wadi. A 25-minute walk down this wadi brings you to a string of easily negotiable dry falls. Below the falls you go through a narrow passage between boulders, after which oleander and reed appear for the first time.

Within about 70 minutes from the toothed fence you arrive at a flowing tributary of Wadi Khanzira. A little stream with abundant water vegetation creates here a dense jungle, and the going is difficult. Proceed downstream through the bush, until a small, dry tributary joins from the **north** (right) within about 30 minutes. Opposite this confluence you climb **south** (left) towards a flat terrace. Continue levelly along goat trails paralleling the main streambed, before climbing a short distance in order to cross a small side wadi with a lone palm tree. Soon after, veer left (south) to climb towards an obvious saddle. From the saddle, descend south reaching another flowing tributary of Wadi Khanzira about two hours from the trailhead.

A few minutes downstream are red narrows, whose walls are only 3 m apart. Running water fills the whole width of the narrows, creating elongate shallow pools — a good place for a cool desert bath.

The narrows open after 20 minutes before closing once again. This time they are carved into white sandstone. The confluence with the densely vegetated stream you came through is 45 minutes away from the head of the red narrows.

Proceed downstream in the shade of tamarisk and oleander. A gushing spring emerges from a crevice on the left-hand side of the canyon, about an hour from the confluence. As you proceed, more and more gardens cling to the canyon's vertical walls. An enormous red boulder lies in the middle of the streambed, 30 minutes away from the spring. Soon afterwards dripping greenery covers the rock face on the left.

The first sign of human activity is a water pump located on the left-hand side, 30 minutes from the boulder. Just beyond, a trail climbs south to reach an artificial reservoir. Ignore the trail and proceed within the canyon for 20 minutes to reach a little waterfall hidden amidst boulders.

A tamarisk-studded river terrace starts further downstream. Adhere to its left side to reach a jungle of reed, which can be crossed following goat tracks. It takes 20 minutes to get through this section and arrive at a concrete dam. The water collected here is used for irrigating fields in the northern part of the 'Araba Valley. Leave the dam, following a dirt track and an ancient aqueduct. The main road is 25 minutes away.

27. Wadi Khanzira, a short route
Map 18

An easy route through a stream with a little hidden waterfall, dripping springs and a colorful canyon.

Type of route: One-way and back.
Altitude difference, Distance and Walking time: 100 m ascent and descent, 4 km, 4 hours.
Rating: Easy. Expect wet shoes.
Special equipment: None.
Guides: Not really needed. Try the local people at Mamura junction.
Water: A perennial stream and dripping springs. Those who choose not to drink from them should carry 2 liters each.
Season: Spring and fall.
Getting there and back: Heading south from Mamura junction, cross a bridge after 3 km and turn left (south) towards a side road. The road ends after 2 km at the water reservoir of Wadi Khanzira. This is where the trail starts and finishes. The first half of the road is negotiable to all types of vehicle. You can reach Mamura junction using the local bus from Tafila to Feifa.

Follow the road and the ancient aqueduct on its left-hand side to reach a water reservoir and a dam. Bypass the dam and climb to a terrace on the right. Cross a dense bush of reeds following goat trails, which emerge out of this jungle 20 minutes away from the starting point.

Proceed upstream for another 20 minutes to reach a waterfall which is hidden amidst giant boulders. A dripping spring, maidenhair fern and plenty of shade can be found above it.

Garnished by hanging gardens, the canyon's red walls draw closer 30 minutes away from the waterfall. If you have the time you can proceed upstream according to Route 26. Otherwise retrace your steps to reach the starting point.

28. From Wadi 'Aima to Wadi Khanzira
Map 18

This two-day trek links two impressive canyons, offering an elevated camping site with wide vistas. See Routes 24 and 26 for more details.

Type of route: One-way.
Route:
> **Day 1:** Wadi 'Aima and Wadi Feifa. Camping site near the Feifa-Khanzira watershed.
> **Day 2:** Wadi Khanzira to the 'Araba Valley.

Rating: Moderate. **Abseiling is unavoidable.** Expect wet shoes.
Special equipment: Two 20 m ropes and ordinary abseiling gear.
Guides: Might help. Try the village of 'Aima.
Water: Perennial streams along most of the route. There is no water near the camping site. Consider carrying 4.5 liters each.
Season: Spring and fall. Summer is also fine if you ascend to the camp in late afternoon hours and start walking early on Day 2.
Getting there and back: To reach the trailhead see Route 24. The end point is described in Route 26.

Day 1
Altitude difference, Distance and Walking time: 600 descent, 450 m ascent, 11 km, 10 hours (1 hour to the first dry fall, 8 hours from the foot of the second dry fall to the end of the trail).
Falls: Four. Three dry falls and one waterfall. The first two falls require abseiling.
Water: Perennial stream. Abundant dripping springs. **There is no water near the camping site!** Fill up before leaving Wadi Feifa with at least 4.5 liters each.

Follow Route 24 to reach a fork where a side wadi flows in from the south, about 7 hours from the trailhead. From here onwards there is no more water until Wadi Khanzira. Fill up for five walking hours and an overnight camp.

Climb a short distance up the west bank of the side wadi to reach a faint trail contouring about 20 m above the streambed. Below is a dense bush of reeds, making progress in the streambed itself almost impossible. Within an hour the vegetation disappears and the trail descends into the wadi.

Proceed up the wadi bed for 15 minutes to reach a not-so-obvious trail on the west bank, discernible by a supporting wall. Above this wall the trail is very faint but the steep rocky slope is well-cairned. It takes 25 minutes to reach its apparent top on a flat shoulder.

Turn south, climbing up along a gully with a faint trail. Avoid going all the way up and instead veer west within 15 minutes from the edge of the last steep ascent. Reaching a flat shoulder continue west, taking care not to lose or gain altitude. Skirting the peaks to your south, and crossing a few shallow wadis, aim toward an elongate dome to the west. Before reaching the dome turn south, and proceed towards an obvious low saddle located 40 minutes away from the last steep ascent. The road from

Tafila to the Dead Sea is close by. Level sandy patches just below the saddle make an excellent camping site with attractive views.

Day 2:
Altitude difference, Distance and Walking time: 600 m descent, 15 km, 8 hours.
Falls: None.

Water: A perennial stream and several dripping springs in Wadi Khanzira. The stream is reached within about 90 minutes from the camping site.

Reaching the Tafila-Dead Sea road, pass the sign "Mamura 10 km" to reach a toothed fence to the left. From here onwards proceed according to Route 26.

29. Sela' – The Rock of Edom
Map 19

Surrounded by sheer cliffs and deep abysses, the isolated rock massif of Sela' is an extraordinary Edomite stronghold. Located halfway between Tafila and the Dana Nature Reserve, amidst rugged sandstone landscapes, the place combines intriguing archeology with amazing natural beauty. High above the cliffs, the rock mesa is carved with stairways, cisterns, watch-towers, ritual (?) basins and many thick sherds of Iron Age pottery.

What made people live in a place so inaccessible? During the last few years more and more high-perched Edomite sites are being discovered, and yet their motives are still a mystery.

Sela' was inhabited by Edomites between the 8th and the 6th centuries BCE. Nabataeans followed, and in Medieval times it saw human activity once again.

The Bible describes the war of Amaziah, king of Judah, against the Edo-mites: "He (Amaziah) slew of Edom in the Valley of Salt ten thousand, and took the Sela' ("the Rock") by war" (II Kings 14: 7); "And ten thousand the tribesmen of Judah captured alive, and brought them unto the top of the Sela' and cast them down from the top of the Sela', that they all were shattered" (2 Chron. 25: 11-12). Some scholars identify the biblical Sela', "the Rock", with Umm el Biyara, a high cliff located in Petra. Others claim that the geographical context in which Sela' is mentioned, fits the Dead Sea region far more than the region of Petra. If the Valley of Salt is the Dead Sea, then the Edomite site below the village that is today still called Sela' – is a good candidate for the biblical Sela', the more so since it is only a few kilometers south of the historical Edomite capital, Bozra.

In 1995 a remarkable rock relief was discovered in Sela' by Dr. Hamad Qatamine from Mauta University. Located on a vertical cliff high above the gateway to the stronghold, the relief shows a standing figure, three symbols of divinity and a cuneiform inscription, all in Mesopotamian style. The standing figure is holding a long staff and wears a peaked conical crown (tiara). Though the cuneiform inscription is badly damaged, the words "I am Nabonidus, king of Babylon" were deciphered with near certainty (reported by E. Raz).

The relief is the only archeological testimony that Edom had fallen under Babylonian rule at the time of Nabonidus, the last king of Babylon (555–539 BCE), and suggests that herewith came an end to the Edomite kingdom.

Type of route: One-way and back.
Altitude difference, Distance and Walking time: About 100 m ascent and descent, 2 km, 3 hours.
Rating: Easy.
Special equipment: None.
Guides: Might help. Fahed Abu Haiman, the appointed guardian of the site, will be happy to show you around.
Water: Consider carrying 1 liter each.
Season: Year-round.
Getting there and back: First, you have to reach the village of 'Ein el Beida. Starting by a local bus either from Tafila or Qadisiyya (above Dana Village), it takes about 30 minutes to get there.
From 'Ein el Beida a half-tarred road, branching westwards from the King's Highway, leads to the site within 2 km. The road passes through the village of Sela' and then descends steeply almost 400 m. Ask the local people for a ride (5–10 JD a round trip).

Built in the old style and commanding magnificent vistas, the village of Sela' is now falling apart. Many families have left the place in favor of the more prosperous village of 'Ein el Beida. Looking west from the lower part of the village, you see the deep canyon of Wadi Khanzira carving its way to the Dead Sea Valley amidst sheer cliffs (see Route 26). The ancient site of Sela' is seen below, a steep-walled mesa, well guarded by vertical cliffs. A once well-tarred road descends steeply towards the site. Reaching a junction, turn right and proceed to the end of the road a few hundred metres ahead.

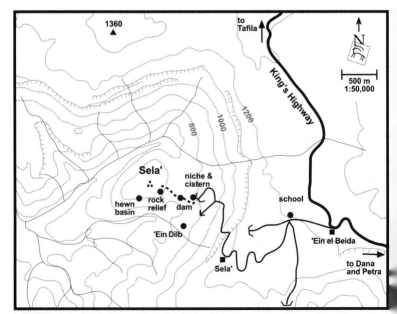

Map 19: Route 29. Sela' — The Rock of Edom

Where the road ends, a niche, probably used as guard post, is carved into the white sandstone. In front of the niche is a shallow cistern. Proceed south for a few metres and soon an aqueduct appears to your right. Head west, following the aqueduct through a labyrinth of white sandstone domes, which leads to a saddle. Just before the saddle, carved stairs appear for the first time. To the right of the stairway are a water reservoir and a dam.

Looking west, a sheer cliff rises above the saddle incised by a prominent cleft, which provides access to the hilltop. Cross the saddle to ascend a newly built stairway, which still uses ancient hewn steps. The top is reached in some 20 minutes.

Once up you emerge straight beneath a prominent rock which probably served as a watchtower overlooking the entrance, with a hewn cistern at its top and several ritual(?) basins around it.

Continue westwards past a hewn niche with grooves that might have held wooden beams. Traverse the highest point of the plateau and veer south towards a hewn basin, perched above a sheer drop.

Sites like Sela' back the Edomites' reputation for dwelling atop impossible rocks. Raging prophetically against the Edomites, Jeremiah writes (49: 16) "Though you build your nest as high as the vulture, thence I will bring you down".

The western edge of the hilltop provides excellent views towards the Dead Sea Valley.

Once you are back at the saddle, raise your head and look west towards the cleft you have just descended. The Babylonian relief can be spotted to the left of the cleft on a vertical rock face, at about two-thirds of the height between the saddle and the hilltop.

30–35. Dana Nature Reserve
Map 20

A spectacular blend of mountain and desert landscapes, as well as an extraordinary botanic diversity, make Dana Nature Reserve one of its kind. The reserve stretches over 300 sq. km from the edge of the Edom Plateau down to the 'Araba Valley. Its altitudes vary within short distances from 1,650 m above sea level to 150 m below, creating different climatic conditions and habitats. The reserve is dissected by deep canyons, winding below lofty sandstone massifs with overwhelming views. The white sandstone at the reserve is sculpted into domes and valleys blanketed by vegetation. To date, 700 species of plants have been recorded in the reserve as well as 200 birds and 36 mammals. The big mammals, though rare, include Nubian ibex (wild mountain goat), wolf, golden jackal, striped hyena and red fox.

The botanic diversity of Dana combines Mediterranean, desert ('Saharo-Arabian'), steppe ('Irano-Turanian') and subtropical ('Sudanian') plants. Trees include red juniper, oak, pistacia and even cypress, all from the Mediterranean zone. Subtropical trees such as acacia, *Moringa* and jujube grow on the lower reaches of the reserve.

The reserve offers accommodation in two campsites (Rummana and Feinan), a guesthouse and two simple hostels.

The Dana region involves both its nomadic and sedentary inhabitants in its conservation program. When the reserve was established in 1993, traditional pasture lands were taken from the Bedouin. As compensation a livestock fattening scheme and a project for processing skins were established. The village of Dana and its traditional stone houses are now integrated in the reserve. Its dwellers used to cultivate terraces of fruit trees using ancient irrigation methods. Over the years, as this agriculture was gradually abandoned, the villagers moved to Qadisiyya, which is closer to the King's Highway and offers a better livelihood. When the reserve was established, efforts were made to bring the village of Dana back to life. Nowadays there are about 25 families living in the village and the terraces are again cultivated. The fruit crops are bought by the reserve, processed in a fruit-drying center and sold in a designated shop. Other socioeconomic projects, which cater to the welfare of the local people, include crafting of silver jewelry and pottery. Rangers and guides are usually drafted from among the local community.

Facilities in the reserve

Rummana Campsite: A high-altitude campsite (1,200 m), on a mountain surrounding overlooking spectacular scenery. The campsite can host up to 60 people in 20 tents. Each tent is equipped with mattresses and blankets. Toilets and cold showers are available. Stock up with food supplies before you come. Alternatively, a fully equipped kitchen provides meals for groups of 6 people and more. Two Bedouin-style tents are available for meals. Camping fees include 5 JD for tent hire plus an additional 7 JD per person for mattresses and blankets. Entrance fee to the reserve is 5 JD. The campsite is closed from the first of November to the first of March.

Getting to Rummana Campsite: The easiest approach is by taxi from Qadisiyya or Tafila. Driving along the King's Highway turn west 5 km north of Qadisiyya. Drive west for another 6 km to reach the tower at the entrance to the campsite. Visitors are transported from the tower to the campsite by a shuttle truck. Vehicles are not allowed to enter the campsite.

Feinan Campsite: A low-altitude campsite (400 m), surrounded by jujube trees, at the outlet of Wadi Dana to the 'Araba Valley. The camp can host up to 24 visitors in 6 tents. Each tent is equipped with mattresses and blankets. Toilets and hot showers are available. Stock up with food supplies before you come. A fully equipped kitchen provides meals for groups of 6 people and more. Visitors can use the kitchen to cook their own meals. A Bedouin tent is available for meals. A research center is attached to the campsite. Camping fees are the same as in Rummana Campsite. The campsite is open throughout the year.

Getting to Feinan Campsite: Leave Tafila towards the 'Araba Valley. Turn left at Mamura junction and continue south for about 35 km until the village .of Qureiqira is signposted to the left. Reaching the campsite from the village involves a 14 km drive along a dirt track. The track is negotiable by high-clearance vehicle, which can be organized in Qureiqira (see map 17).

Dana guesthouse and visitor center: This compound includes the offices of the reserve, a research center, workshops and a guesthouse. Built within the village of Dana, its quality of design, as well as its superb positioning above the crags, is worthy of praise. The guesthouse can host up to 23 people in 9 rooms. Most of the rooms are doubles and triples and are equipped with a balcony overlooking the re-

serve. Toilets and hot showers are shared. A restaurant provides meals upon advance order. Information about the reserve is posted within the guesthouse. A nature shop sells nature-designed jewelry, jams, pottery, dry fruits and other products made by local inhabitants, who are part of the socioeconomic projects of the reserve. A conference room is also available. The prices for a room vary from 20 to 45 JD. Tel: 03-2270497/8. Fax: 03-2270499.

Dana Hotel: A simple hostel run by the community of Dana Village and located within the village. The hostel can host 18 people in 6 rooms. In summer it is possible to sleep in a Bedouin tent or in tents which are set up on the roof. Toilets and showers are shared. A fully equipped kitchen can provide meals for groups. Visitors can use the kitchen to cook their own meals. The price for a bed is 5 JD. Tel: 03-2270537.

Dana Tower Hotel: A privately owned hostel located within the village of Dana. The hostel can host 10 people in 6 rooms. A Bedouin tent is available in summer. Toilets and showers are shared. A fully equipped kitchen can provide meals for groups. Visitors can use the kitchen to cook their own meals. The price for a bed is 4 JD. Tel: 03-2270237.

Getting to Dana Village: To reach the village from Petra take the bus to Shawbak and continue with a second bus to Qadisiyya. Turn west at the northern end of Qadisiyya to reach Dana within a few minutes' drive (a local minibus connects the two villages). A taxi from Petra to Dana costs about 8 JD. To approach Dana Village from the north you can use the bus from Tafila to Qadisiyya

Entrance fees
5 JD for foreigners, 1 JD for Jordanians. Entrance fees are payable at the guesthouse and at the campsites (Feinan and Rummana).

Routes and guides
Three short routes (Routes 30–32) are offered in the vicinity of Rummana Campsite. These routes are closed between 1/11–1/03. One longer route, also closed during the same period, connects Dana Village with Rummana Campsite. Two full-day routes connect the highlands with the lowlands and are open year-round (Routes 34–35). Another route which is open year-round leads from Dana Village to the Edomite stronghold Shaq er-Rish. Inquire at the visitor center for more details.

Guides can be booked at the visitor center, and might be required for the longer treks.

The Syrian Serin

About 800 pairs of this bird species breed in the elevated areas of Dana Nature Reserve, which constitutes the southern boundary of its distribution. The nearest breeding population is at Jabel esh-Sheikh (Mount Hermon) about 400 km to the north.

This little bird nests on juniper trees and can be recognized by its yellow tint and its short black beak. It is a relative of the canary, which was probably domesticated from the European Serin. The Syrian Serin is another example of the Dana reserve's ecological uniqueness.

30. The Cave Trail
Dana Nature Reserve
Map 20

The trail leads to caves which were used as Bedouin dwellings and goat pens. It offers fine views towards Wadi Dana and the village. A brochure about the trail is available in the reserve.

Rating and duration: 4 km, 1.5 hours, easy.
Getting there and back: The trail starts and ends at Rummana Campsite.

31. The Campsite Trail
Dana Nature Reserve
Map 20

A short route amidst white sandstone domes and hollows lush with vegetation. A brochure about the trail is available in the reserve.

Rating and duration: 2 km, 1 hour, easy.
Getting there and back: The trail starts and ends at Rummana Campsite.

32. Jabel Rummana Trail
Dana Nature Reserve
Map 20

The trail stretches from the campsite to the summit of Jabel Rummana (1,330 m) and offers fine views towards the 'Araba Valley and the reserve. A brochure about the trail is available in the reserve.

Rating and duration: 100 m ascent and descent, 3 km, 2.5 hours, easy.
Getting there and back: The trail starts and ends at Rummana Campsite.

33. From Dana Village to Rummana Campsite

Dana Nature Reserve
Map 20

A short route, which can be walked in both directions. Starting from Dana Village you pass traditionally irrigated terraces of figs, pomegranates, olives, apples, grapes, palms and almonds. Along the route there are good views into the deep canyon of Wadi Dana. Strolling through a fairytale landscape of white domes, you get a full measure of the extraordinary plant world of the reserve.

Type of route: One-way.
Altitude difference, Distance and Walking time: the trail is mostly level with a few ups and downs, 4 hours, 5 km.
Rating: Easy.
Special equipment: None.
Guides: Might help. Inquire at the visitor center.
Water: None. Consider carrying 1.5 liters each.
Season: The trail is closed between 1/11–1/03. Do not follow this route on hot summer days.
Getting there and back: The trail starts at the village. Arrange to be picked up from Rummana Campsite or hitchhike back. There is no 'official' transportation from the camp to the village.

Follow the street beyond the mosque to its end, where you should veer west (left), and descend a short distance along a clear trail. The path soon levels, heading north amidst groves of fruit trees.

Follow the path past two clumps of tall poplar trees. Turn left (west) in front of a lone poplar and descend toward two aged olive trees. Do not descend the stairs immediately beyond. Instead turn right (north) and proceed along a well-cairned trail.

The trail undulates gently for about 3 hours before it reaches the road to Rummana Campsite. Turn left to arrive at the campsite within a few minutes.

34. From Dana Village to Feinan Campsite
Dana Nature Reserve
Map 20

This is one of two routes which traverse the reserve from top to bottom. As you descend through Wadi Dana (1,200 m to 400 m) the climate, vegetation and landscape change continually. The route runs along a dirt track.

Type of route: One-way.
Altitude difference, Distance and Walking time: 800 descent, 12 km, 5 hours.
Rating: Easy.
Special equipment: None.
Guides: Not really needed, but inquire at the visitor center.
Water: Year-round springs. Consider carrying 2 liters each.
Season: Year-round, though summer may be too hot.
Getting there and back: The route starts at Dana Village and ends at Feinan Campsite in the 'Araba Valley (see page 131), where you can easily get a pickup truck ride to the village of Qureiqira and the 'Araba road.

Follow the main street of Dana Village westwards to reach the head of a winding track. Descending into Wadi Dana the track overlooks sheer red cliffs and domes of white sandstone. The grades become less steep within 45 minutes.

After an additional 45 minutes, a side wadi with a little spring crosses the track. It provides shaded spots under giant junipers. About 1 hour further, ancient ruins are seen on the north bank of the wadi. A second spring which supplies water to Feinan Campsite is reached within an hour from the ruins.

Continue through Bedouin encampments, granite hills and jujube trees to reach Feinan Campsite within 30 minutes.

35. From Wadi Hamra to Hammam Dathneh
Dana Nature Reserve
Map 20

A spectacular route descending from the Edom Plateau to the 'Araba Valley through constantly changing landscapes. Dana Nature Reserve at its best! The route starts in a maze of white domes, but soon red cliffs take over. A major tectonic fault, which crosses the route, is to be blamed for its varied landforms and colors. You can see here bushes of wormwood, juniper trees, acacia, pistacia, and many other species of different origin. An elevated saddle provides imposing panoramas of the 'Araba Valley while Wadi Hammam Dathneh offers a lush oasis and a sacred spring.
The trail ends at the ancient copper mines of Feinan.

Type of route: One-way.
Altitude difference, Distance and Walking time: 900 m descent, 100 m ascent to cross a saddle, 15 km, 9 hours.
Rating: Moderate. Expect wet shoes along the lower reaches of the route.
Special equipment: None.
Guides: Recommended. Inquire at the visitor center.
Water: 'Ein en-Nawatif is a small dripping spring, some 30 minutes from the trailhead. A year-round stream flows through Wadi Hammam Dathneh and Wadi Ghuweir. Wadi Hamra is dry. Consider carrying 3 liters each.
Season: Year-round. Avoid hot summer days. Be aware of flash flood risk, especially during the winter!
Getting there and back: Drive through the village of Qadisiyya, located on the King's Highway above Dana Village. At the southern end of the village, near its last house, a side road branches to the west. 100 m from the junction there is a signpost of Dana Nature Reserve. The trail starts about 1 km beyond the signpost where the tarmac ends. You can reach this spot with a taxi from Qadisiyya.
The trail ends at the archeological site of Feinan (see Route 38).

Following the dirt track which starts where the tarmac ends, veer left at the first junction and left again within 100 m. The sandstone domes among which you walk are the watershed between Wadi Hamra to the south and a nameless wadi to the north.

The track ends after a few minutes above a saddle as wide as a football field. Ignore it and instead descend to the southwest with no obvious trail, aiming towards a low pinnacle of white sandstone.

A short descent brings you to a little hollow from where you should climb westwards to a col, which is marked by the pinnacle. Slipping over the col, descend along a steep rocky slope towards a wide ledge. Turn left (east) at the ledge to reach a stone-strewn area about 20 minutes from the trailhead. The ruins are the remains of an Edomite village.

A short walk up through the ruins leads to a little dripping spring, called 'Ein en-Nawatif. Leaving the spring, backtrack towards a prominent out-crop with a rock-hewn chamber. Climb west to a very low saddle before descending into Wadi Hamra.

Follow the wadi bed for a few minutes until goat trails commence on the south bank. These gain altitude in order to avoid a steep slope covered by wormwood bushes. After a short ascent, descend back towards the wadi bed, 40 minutes after entering Wadi Hamra.

Do not proceed along the wadi bed but take a clear trail climbing on the south bank. The trail levels after 10 minutes, permitting a good overview of the red sandstone cliffs on the north bank. Leaning on the red rocks, are dark flint strata in an almost vertical position. The notable difference between the south and north banks of the wadi is caused by a major fault.

Soon the trail descends again, crossing a side wadi which comes from the south. The trees in this wadi erupt from white rocks, flecked with black flint concretions. Proceed downhill towards a low but prominent saddle, just above the bed of Wadi Hamra.

From the saddle descend west to cross a side wadi. Do not continue along the trail on the left (east) bank of Wadi Hamra! Instead, descend into Wadi Hamra's bed and follow it for 50–100 m until a side wadi joins from the right (northwest). Turn right, ascending along the left-hand side of this side wadi while ignoring a contouring trail.

Follow the ascending trail carefully. Though it is well used, it has some misleading hairpins. Crossing a virtual saddle the views towards the 'Araba Valley soon open up. The real saddle lies 30 minutes from the wadi bed, 200 m south of the obvious seam line between red rocks at one side and gray ones at the other. It takes about 3–4 hours to reach the saddle from the trailhead.

Leave the saddle, descending west

through a gallery of vertical layers studded with juniper trees. The trail winds steeply towards a shoulder with gentler slopes, 10 minutes from the saddle. Cross a side wadi and progress almost levelly above the major wadi to the right (north). There is no obvious trail but numerous goat trails line the slope. Aim towards a yellow rocky shoulder opposite a black hill (which is not capped by red sandstone). The shoulder is reached within 50 minutes from the saddle. It is marked by a high cairn.

Wadi Hammam Dathneh is first seen from this shoulder. The wadi's south bank consists of red sandstone, its north bank of black igneous rock, and in the middle is a green jungle of lush vegetation. Descend toward a little red dome with a wide saddle and a great cairn. Round the dome from the left following a donkey trail, and continue along the crest towards a black dome. Ignore the little gully which descends towards the oasis. Instead, proceed westwards on the crest itself for 100 m and then descend diagonally along a spur. The trail meets the wadi within 40 minutes of the yellow rocky shoulder, opposite an elevated clear patch on the south bank.

Palms, oleander, sugarcane, willow, Euphrates poplar and *Ficus* trees crowd the wadi below while *Moringa* and acacia trees thrive on the slopes. The latter are representatives of the Rift's subtropical vegetation. Juniper trees are still around, representing the uplands and their Mediterranean climate.

Cross the stream and ascend shortly to the clear patch, which is marked by tall palm trees. Behind the trees hides a tiny, warm spring whose waters issue from a little crevice. The spring is sheltered by palm branches and ornamented by strips of cloth. Its water is considered sacred and believed to bequeath help and good health on all who drink it.

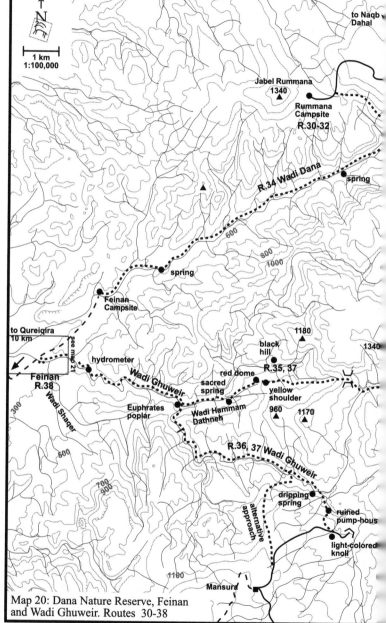

Map 20: Dana Nature Reserve, Feinan and Wadi Ghuweir. Routes 30-38

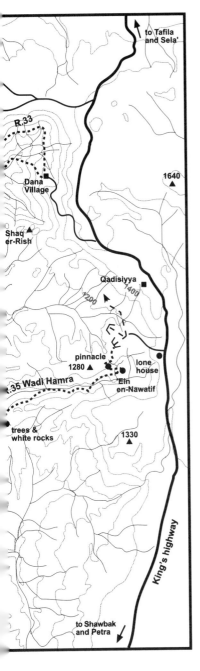

Backtrack to the north bank of the wadi and proceed through a short section of thick vegetation with no obvious trail. Within 15 minutes a side wadi joins from the north. Cross the wadi and progress on a well-used trail amidst pink granite boulders. The trail descends to the stream about 15 minutes further. Proceed in the water close to the north bank. Within a few minutes the trail climbs to the right and descends into Wadi Ghuweir opposite a clump of Euphrates poplar trees which marks the confluence of the two wadis.

The magnificent gorge of Wadi Ghuweir (see Route 37, Day 2) commences upstream from the confluence. If you have the time it is well worth a visit.

Advance downstream, crossing and recrossing the stream from one side to the other. The wadi is wide and progress is easy. A ruined hydrometer is reached after 60 minutes. Soon afterwards the wadi opens towards the 'Araba flats and within 30 minutes from the hydrometer a major track crosses it.

A prominent hill covered with piles of stones rises on the north bank of the wadi. The hill and its surroundings are part of ancient Feinan, which was once one of the largest copper centers in the Near East (see Route 38).

Walking northwards along the track you arrive within 45 minutes at Feinan Campsite (see page 131). To the southwest the track leads to the village of Qureiqira, 11 km away. Bedouin encampments, where pickup trucks may be arranged, are scattered along the track to the campsite.

36. Wadi Ghuweir
Map 20

Wadi Ghuweir descends from the Shawbak Plateau through a spectacular red sandstone *siq* whose lower reaches are garnished by hanging gardens. Its water flow changes with the season, but even in the summer it is a splendid route. At the outlet of the wadi are the ruins of Feinan, an ancient center of copper mining and smelting.

Type of route: One-way.

Altitude difference, Distance and Walking time: 500 m descent, 11 km, 8 hours.

Rating: Moderate. Expect wet shoes. In rain-rich years it may be necessary to cross two small ponds by swimming.

Special equipment: Bring plastic bags for your backpack, in case the ponds along the wadi are full. A waterproof bag should be handy for valuables.

Guides: Might help. Try the village of Mansura or the souvenir shop in front of Shawbak Castle.

Water: A little year-round stream along part of the way. Several springs. Consider carrying 3 liters each.

Season: Spring, summer and fall. Winter is also fine though the stream water will be cold. Be aware of flash flood risk!

Getting there and back: From Shawbak, take a taxi or a local bus to the village of Mansura, reached within a 30-minute drive. Ask the local people for guidance in order to find a half-tarred road which descends northeast into Wadi Ghuweir. Ordinary vehicles can negotiate this road easily (there is an alternative approach along a dirt track which is constantly in very bad condition. It reaches the wadi about 2 km northwest of the approach which is described below). Continue down the road, ignoring a side track which branches to the left (this is the head of the alternative approach), to reach the level of a light-colored knoll located to the right of the road, about 3.5 km away from its head. Soon afterwards a second track branches to the left. This is where the trail commences.

The trail ends at Feinan (see Route 38).

Take left at the fork, following the track through a sooty goat pen, to reach a ruined pumping house within 30 minutes. From here on the trail follows the wadi bed. A short walk leads to a dripping spring whose surroundings consists of dark flint layers and yellow limestone. White sandstone appears 50 minutes later, eventually giving way to a magnificent narrow gorge of purplish-red sandstone. The walls of the gorge converge to only a few metres apart, and are ornamented with red iron oxide paintings.

Cascades and easily negotiable falls follow, leading to a huge boulder which is stuck between the walls of the canyon, about 3 hours from the spring. Behind this boulder you may encounter two seasonal ponds where you may have to swim, though usually your gear can pass dry and safe.

As the gorge widens beyond the ponds, spectacular gardens of palm trees, maidenhair ferns and *Ficus* cling to its red sandstone walls. Enjoying the tropical atmosphere it takes about 90 minutes to reach a low waterfall. Bypass it on the left and proceed for 15 minutes before the wadi suddenly emerges into a terrain of rugged igneous hills. A clump of Euphrates poplar marks the confluence with Wadi Hammam Dathneh, which flows in from the east.

Continue according to Route 35.

37. From Wadi Hamra to Wadi Ghuweir
Map 20

A two-day trek combining the superb landscapes of Wadi Hamra and Wadi Hammam Dathneh with the spectacular gorge and the hanging gardens of Wadi Ghuweir. The trek offers a striking variety of landscapes.

The first day goes through Dana Nature Reserve. For registration and entrance fees contact Dana's visitor center.

Type of route: Almost circular.
Route:
  Day 1: Wadi Hamra and Wadi Hammam Dathneh. Camping site at the confluence with Wadi Ghuweir.
  Day 2: Wadi Ghuweir to the village of Mansura.
Rating: Moderate. Expect wet shoes in Wadi Hammam Dathneh and in Wadi Ghuweir. In rainy years two small ponds may have to be crossed by swimming.
Special equipment: Bring plastic bags for your backpack, in case the Wadi Ghuweir ponds are full. A waterproof bag may be handy for valuables.
Guides: Might help. Ask at Dana's visitor center.
Water: Wadi Hammam Dathneh and Wadi Ghuweir have perennial streams. The proposed camping site is located at their confluence. Wadi Hamra is dry. Consider carrying 3 liters each.
Season: Year-round, though the water in the streams may be cold in winter. Be aware of flash flood risk, especially during winter!
Getting there and back: To reach the trailhead, see Route 36. The trail ends in the village of Mansura, 30 minutes' drive from Shawbak. You may arrange for a ride to Shawbak with the local inhabitants.

Day 1
Altitude difference, Distance and Walking time: 800 m descent, 100 m ascent to a saddle, 11 km, 8 hours.
Water: 'Ein en-Nawatif is a small dripping spring located 30 minutes away from the trailhead. Wadi Hamra is dry. Year-round streams flow through Wadi Hammam Dathneh and Wadi Ghuweir.

Follow Route 35 to reach the confluence of Wadi Hammam Dathne and Wadi Ghuweir, where you find several level patches suitable for camping.

Day 2
Altitude difference, Distance and Walking time: 750 m ascent from the confluence to Mansura, 10 km, 8 hours (the last 2.5 km are a 350 m ascent along a half-tarred road).
Water: Year-round stream and springs along part of the way.

Advancing up an oleander-packed stream it takes 20 minutes to reach a low waterfall, which can be bypassed from the right. As you continue upstream the red walls of the sandstone gorge are ornamented with spectacular gardens clinging to the rock. The gardens comprise mostly maidenhair fern, palms, sugarcane, *Ficus* trees, and the orchid *Epipactis veratrifolia.*

About 90 minutes from the waterfall the vegetation disappears and the walls of the gorge draw closer. Here you may have to cross two ponds before reaching a giant boulder, stuck high above your head.

Cascades and low falls soon follow. Though they are all passable, you will need the help of your companions to get your backpack up. As the cascades disappear the walls of the canyon are closer than ever, winding upwards with spectacular 'paintings' of red iron oxides.

About 2 hours away from the giant boulder, white sandstone takes over, eventually giving way to gray limestone. Follow the wide canyon for an additional hour past a little dripping spring on the right (south) bank. Soon after, Wadi Hamra joins from the north. Ignore it, and continue a short way towards an abandoned pumping house.

Leave the wadi following a ruined track on its south bank. The track passes by a sooty overhang and meets with a half-tarred road, 45 minutes away from the wadi bed. Turn right and up, following this road which is still used by the villagers of Mansura. The village is about 1 hour away.

38. Feinan's copper works
Map 21

Feinan was one of the largest copper works in the ancient Near East. The site is located in the 'Araba Valley at the end point of the treks of Wadi Dana, Wadi Hamra (Wadi Hammam Dathneh) and Wadi Ghuweir.

What remain today are ruins of two Byzantine churches, an aqueduct and a water reservoir and smelting furnaces. The site has been exploited since the 7th millenium BCE but the major copper production took place during the Early Bronze Age (middle of the third millennium BCE), the Iron Age (9–5th centuries BCE), and the Roman Period (2–4th centuries CE).

Giant mounds of more than 200,000 tons of slag attest to copper production on an industrial scale. One can imagine endless caravans of pack animals, carrying juniper beams from the uplands to stoke the furnaces. The enormous amount of charcoal, produced over the years, must have played a significant role in the deforestation of the area.

Copper production in Feinan reached its peak under the Edomites (during the 9–5th centuries BCE) when mining and smelting techniques attained high professional level and probably influenced the economic and political power of the Edomites. It could well be that King David conquered Edom to gain control over the mines, and that King Solomon was involved in their development. Feinan is mentioned in the Bible by the name Punon as one of the stations of the Israelites when they wandered from Egypt to Cana'an (Numbers 33: 42).

Archeological sites in the vicinity of Feinan include Khirbet en-Nahas, Khirbet Jariyeh, and Khirbet Ghuweibeh.

Duration: Allow about 1 hour to explore the main ruins.
Guides: Bedouin encampments can be found 1 km north of Feinan.
Season: Year-round.
Getting there and back: Driving along the 'Araba road, turn east towards the village of Qureiqira about 35 km south of Mamura junction (connecting the 'Araba road with Tafila, see map 17). From Qureiqira you need a high-clearance vehicle to reach Feinan by an 11 km dirt track. Arranging a pickup truck at the village is quite easy (about 5 JD). If you have reached Feinan from the mountains and you want to get to Qureiqira, the Bedouin on the north bank of the wadi can usually help. There is an early-morning bus from Qureiqira to 'Aqaba.

Approaching Feinan from Qureiqira, leave the vehicle just before the track crosses Wadi Feinan (also called Wadi Ghuweir). Head east towards a ruined flourmill, which marks the end of an aqueduct. Follow the aque- duct to reach a large ruined water reservoir, which once collected water from the nearby stream of Wadi Ghuweir.

Proceed east towards heaps of darkish slag, the leftovers of the copper

Maim Anner

H.

Top: Wadi Ibn Hammad (R.13)
Bottom: Bedouin cemetery at the foot of Jabel Ras 'Athud (R.57, 61)

Yehoram Doron

I. H.

Lior Weiss

Avi Blum

Top Right: Myrtle bushes, Wadi Weida'a (R.15)
Right: Butter preparation

Top Left: Upper canyon of Wadi Hasa (R.19)
Left: Wadi Manshala (R.2)

ik Chudy

H.   Haim Anner

op: Wadi el Hidan's basalt canyon (R.12)
eft: The black summit of Jabel Feid (R.41)
ight: 'Paintings' of iron oxides on the walls of Wadi Ghuweir (R.36)

Two of Wadi Feid's 12 waterfalls (R.40)

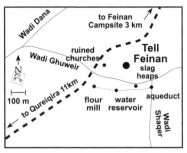

Map 21: Route 38. Feinan's copper works

smelting process. Further eastward the aqueduct crosses Wadi Shaqer over an arched bridge.

Looking north, a prominent hill (Tell Feinan) rises on the opposite bank of Wadi Feinan with ruins of two Byzantine churches on its western slopes. The church fathers Eusebius and Hieronymus describe Punon as a bishopric, and a place where slaves and prisoners worked hard to manufacture copper.

Cross the wadi toward the churches. Proceed eastwards through a small gully to reach some reconstructed smelting furnaces, on the slope to your left.

A local Bedouin school as well as a center for livestock fattening are located in Wadi Dana about 1 km to the northeast. Further ahead is the lower campsite of Dana Nature Reserve (Feinan Campsite).

Shawbak and Petra areas
From Wadi Ghuweir to Wadi Musa

Rugged black mountains and narrow black gorges which are carved in igneous rocks give the area between Wadi Ghuweir and Wadi Musa a special character, not found elsewhere in Jordan. South of Wadi Ghuweir a steep mountain front rises above the flat 'Araba Valley. Crowned with the majestic peaks of Jabel Feid and Jabel Abu Mahmud, the ridge extends 15 km southwards, towering to more than 1,100 m above sea level, almost 1,000 m above the valley below.

Above the black mountain front stretches a dissected plateau dominated by sandstone bluffs. Petra, the fabulous Nabataean capital, is located here, hidden among cliffs of red sandstone.

Wadi Feid, Wadi Qunai and Wadi Musa are the largest wadis in the region. Perennial streams flow through Wadi Feid and Wadi Musa while the seasonal Wadi Qunai houses huge potholes and springs. The lower runs of these wadis form spectacular canyons with juniper trees clinging to their crags. All the wadis in this region reach the 'Araba Valley but eventually drain into the Dead Sea.

The botanic diversity of the area is remarkable and, except for Dana Nature Reserve, is not equaled elsewhere in Jordan. Mediterranean plants grow here side by side with desert shrubs, creating a unique atmosphere of a forested desert. Near the small settlement of Bir ed-Dabaghat the Edom Plateau is covered with open oak forest (*Quercus calliprinos*) and not far from there is a rare concentration of *Pistacia atlantica* trees.

The largest township on the Edom Plateau in the region is the village of Shawbak, located near the impressive Crusader castle Montreal. Lower down is the town of Wadi Musa, which has lately undergone accelerated development as the gateway to Nabataean Petra. This is the biggest tourist center in Jordan, with fancy hotels as well as budget ones, restaurants and other visitor facilities. The Bedouin who used to dwell among the rock-carved monuments of the ancient city, were removed from the site in 1985 to a small settlement, built nearby by the Jordan government. Not far from Petra is Jabel Harun where, according to tradition, Aaron the brother of Moses is buried.

In the 'Araba Valley there are only two small settlements. Qureiqira is a farming community growing tomatoes and watermelons, near the ancient copper mines of Feinan. A few km to the south, near the outlet of Wadi Qunai, is the village of Bir Madhkur.

In ancient times the region was inhabited by the Edomites, and later by the Nabataeans. Edomite sites include the impressive strongholds of Umm el Biyara and Ba'ja, perched atop high sandstone cliffs. Nevertheless, it was the Nabataeans who bequeathed the renowned monuments of Petra.

Petra is today the crown jewel of tourism in Jordan, and despite the enormous numbers of visitors its charm has not faded. The capital of the Nabataean kingdom is a magic place with overwhelming rock-carved sepulchral monuments. From a secluded, cliff-surrounded nomad refuge, Petra became a major station for trade caravans on their way from South Arabia to the ports of the Mediterranean, besides being a cultic center and the residence of the Nabataean kings.

Many Nabataean sites are scattered around Petra. These include "Little Petra" with its rock-carved facades; caravanserais such as Bir Madhkur in the 'Araba Valley; elevated temples such as atop Jabel Qarun and Ras Naqb Sleisel, and agricultural terraces, wine presses and water reservoirs. Ancient caravan routes descend from Petra to the 'Araba Valley and continue westwards through the Negev Desert to the Mediterranean ports.

Only by leaving or approaching Petra from the desert, like the Nabataean caravans in the old days, can one grasp its importance.

The following routes are suggested in this region:

Route	Days	Rating	Season	Description
39. Umm el 'Ammad Cave	1 (5 hours)	moderate	spring fall winter	Roman copper mine, beautiful sandstone surroundings.
40. Wadi Feid	1 or 2 (11 hours)	strenuous incl. abseiling	spring summer fall	Majestic black canyon cutting through igneous rocks, 12 waterfalls, pools, junipers.
41. The Black Mountains	4	strenuous	spring fall winter	Awe-inspiring summits, spectacular views, black canyons in igneous rocks, potholes.
42. Canyons and ancient caravan routes	5	strenuous incl. abseiling	spring	Demanding trek, canyons in igneous rock, potholes, dry falls and waterfalls, rewarding views, Nabataean ruins.
43. Ba'ja Edomite stronghold	1 (3 hours)	strenuous	all-year	Shoulder-wide cleft leading to the summit, sheer sandstone bluff, Edomite cisterns.
44. Little Petra and its surroundings	1 (9 hours)	easy to moderate	all-year	Rewarding views of the 'Araba Valley, Nabataean monuments and ruins, beautiful valleys of sandstone.
45. From Little Petra to Petra	1 (3 hours)	easy to moderate	all-year	Red sandstone valley, alternative approach to Petra.
46. Wadi Musa	1 (11 hours)	moderate incl. abseiling	spring summer fall	Excellent canyoning, black gorge, 5 waterfalls, pools, vertical rock faces, junipers.
47. Jabel Umm el Biyara	1 (3 hours)	moderate	all-year	Excellent views of Petra and the 'Araba Valley, feeling of antiquity.
48. Wadi Mudhlim	1 (2 hours)	easy	all-year	Alternative route out of Petra, narrow *siq*.
49. Jabel Harun	1 (8 hours)	easy	all-year	Superb views of the 'Araba Valley and Petra, the tomb of Aaron, brother of Moses.

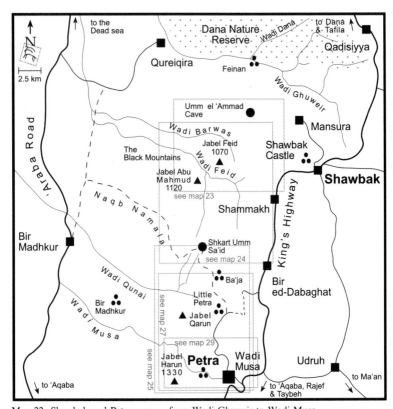

Map 22: Shawbak and Petra areas — from Wadi Ghuweir to Wadi Musa

39. Umm el 'Ammad Cave
Map 23

Umm el 'Ammad is a small copper mine from the Roman period, located a few km south of the copper production center of Feinan, and about 8 km northwest of Shawbak. The site is a man-made cave, an impressive technical monument exhibiting the excellent mining skills of the Roman period. The cave floor area is 120 by 55 m and its ceiling is supported by numerous sandstone pillars reaching 2.5 m in height. These gave the cave its name, "Mother of Pillars". The archeologist Nelson Glueck first described the cave in the early 30's of the twentieth century.

The route to the cave offers fine views towards the 'Araba Valley.

Type of route: One-way and back or one-way.
Altitude difference, Distance and Walking time: 350 m descent, 100 m ascent and back, 4 km, 5 hours. (It is possible to end the hike in Feinan — ask the local Bedouin for guidance).
Rating: Moderate.
Special equipment: None.
Guides: Might help. Try the village of Shawbak or the souvenir shop at the entrance to Shawbak Castle.
Water: None. Consider carrying 3 liters each.
Season: Spring, fall and winter.
Getting there and back: You will need a high-clearance vehicle to reach the trailhead, as well as for picking you up at the end of the route. Finding one in Shawbak should be quite easy (about 20 JD, including the waiting time at the trailhead). Driving south along the King's Highway pass Shawbak, and after 3 km turn west towards the villages of Rarqa and Jahir. From Rarqa continue north towards the village of Mansura. After an additional 3 km a dirt track branches to the left, descending steeply towards a flat shoulder which is perched along the escarpment. Once at the shoulder turn right (north) and proceed levelly for 300 m to reach another fork. Turn left and descend until the track suddenly ends. There are wonderful views along the track, as well as tall pistacia and juniper trees.

From the end of the track follow an obvious trail leading west along a white sandstone plateau. A large cairn with Arabic inscriptions marks the right way. Walk downhill to a saddle and into the wadi to the south-west. After about 50 minutes of descent, look for a dirt track on the north bank of the wadi. The track crosses a prominent saddle, ending shortly afterwards at the entrance to Umm el 'Ammad cave. Once you have spotted the track climb towards its edge, about 100 m above the wadi bed.

The mouth of the cave is quite small and its floor is covered with goat droppings. However, once inside, you can wander around comfortably. Beams of light which penetrate the darkness of the cave produce an extraordinary effect. Looking at the red sandstone walls it is easy to notice diagonal chisel marks, as well as green specks of copper ore. The copper ore was probably taken to Feinan for smelting (see Route 38) as there are no signs of copper works near the cave.

From the cave retrace your steps to-wards the beginning of the route. Alternatively you can descend along the track for about one hour to reach the north bank of Wadi Malaqa, where a vehicle can pick you up and take you to Feinan.

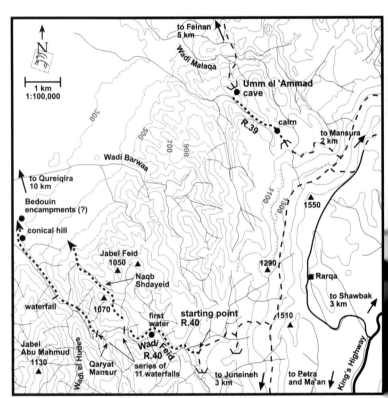

Map 23: Routes 39, 40. Umm el 'Ammad Cave and Wadi Feid

40. Wadi Feid
Map 23

The black gorge of Wadi Feid is one of its kind. Carved into massive igneous rocks, its twelve waterfalls drop one after the other between majestic cliffs, whose crags are dotted with junipers. Beneath the falls are numerous sparkling pools.

It is advised to spend the night at the trailhead and start walking in the early morning hours. Alternatively, if you do not want to rush it, consider splitting the route over two days by spending the night between the waterfalls.

Type of route: One-way.

Altitude difference, Distance and Walking time: 550 m descent, 7 km, 11 hours (1 hour to the first waterfall, 1.5 hours from the eleventh waterfall to the outlet).

Rating: Strenuous. **Abseiling is unavoidable.** The route includes ponds to be crossed by swimming.

Falls: Twelve waterfalls(!). Falls 1, 6 and 12 can be bypassed quite easily.

Special equipment: Two 30 m ropes and ordinary abseiling gear. A waterproof bag can be useful.

Guides: May help with the approach to the first waterfall. Try the 'Azazma Bedouin who live near the trailhead.

Water: A perennial stream starts about 30 minutes from the trailhead. Consider carrying 1.5 liters each.

Season: Summer is ideal. Spring and fall are fine but the water can be cold.

Getting there and back: You will need a high-clearance vehicle to reach the trailhead, as well as to pick you up at the end of the route. Arranging a pickup truck in Shawbak should be quite easy (30 JD for the whole day).

The trailhead is located above Wadi Feid at the beginning of a camel path called Naqb Shdayeid. Make sure you find a Bedouin driver who knows the place – the tracks are not that obvious. Driving south along the King's Highway, turn right to the village of Hewaleh (see map 24) at the signposted junction, 8 km from the junction to Shawbak Castle. Continue straight through the village to reach a hairpin bend and a junction after 3 km. Go right, and soon the views open up to the west. After about 2.5 km the half tarred road ends at the wadi of 'Ein Juneineh near a small spring surrounded by orchards and several abandoned stone houses. Follow the dirt track northwards ignoring a branch to the left after about 500 m. About 1.5 km beyond the branch you cross Wadi Shammakh near a concrete-built pool. To the right (east), about 200 m from the track, is a tiny waterfall feeding an aqueduct. Ignore several side tracks and proceed levelly for another 3 km before turning left (west) down a series of steep switchbacks. At the end of the switchbacks turn left and after a short level drive veer right. Descending along another series of switchbacks you reach a side wadi. Ascend a short way before descending westwards once again. Leave the vehicle on the wide shoulder, where the track levels.

The route ends at the outlet of Wadi Feid (whose lower reach is called Wadi Abu Sakakin), 10 km from the nearest road. Usually you may find Bedouin who can provide a lift towards the village of Qureiqira or the 'Araba road. There is an early morning bus from Qureiqira to 'Aqaba. If you prefer to avoid the risk of not finding a lift, arrange to be picked up by those who drop you at the trailhead. Any Bedouin in Qureiqira will know the way towards the outlet of Wadi Feid (Wadi Abu Sakakin). The driver should wait near a conical hill, on the north bank of the wadi, about 500 m from the end of his track. The vehicle itself cannot reach the hill. Camping near the outlet of the wadi and walking to the road on the following day is another possibility.

Leave the track, descending into Wadi Feid along a fine trail. On the western horizon Wadi Feid cuts through two distinct black massifs: Jabel Feid on the north and Jabel Abu Mahmud on the south. Walking about 30 minutes among sandstone outcrops, you reach a little stream surrounded by oleander, willow, tamarisk and reed. You can proceed along the streambed or climb to the right and progress along an ancient rock-hewn aqueduct. After about 20 minutes a side wadi joins from the north, near a ruined compound, which was probably the destination of the aqueduct. This is the place to camp if you want to start abseiling in the early morning of the next day. Not far are the ruins of the Edomite stronghold Qaryat Mansur (see Day 2 of Route 41). Ignore a steep trail that ascends to Jabel Feid (Naqb Shdayeid) and continue downstream. A little pool perched above the first waterfall is ten minutes away.

Waterfall 1: 25 m. It is possible to by-pass the waterfall from the left.
Waterfall 2: Three steps: 10 m, 5 m and 5 m. There are small ponds beneath the two upper steps.
Waterfall 3: 25 m. A small pool is located below the waterfall.
Waterfall 4: 20 m. Two steps: 17 m and 3 m. A pistacia tree grows at its head.
Waterfall 5: 35 m. A willow tree grows at its head.

Waterfall 6: 5 m. It is possible to by-pass the waterfall from the right.
Waterfall 7: 30 m. A willow tree grows at its head.
Waterfall 8: 20 m. Contour a short distance on the right bank to reach a convenient abseiling point. Immediately below the waterfall is a 7 m step.
Waterfall 9: 30 m. A horseshoe waterfall.
Waterfall 10: 45 m. A beautiful pool and a *Ficus* tree are perched at its foot, just above the next waterfall.
Waterfall 11: 10 m. Beneath the waterfall there is a small pool.

From here onwards, ropes are no longer needed. The wadi takes a 90-degree turn and proceeds through a pool with oleanders, before turning sharply once again, where a dry wadi joins in from the left. Proceed downstream to reach the twelfth waterfall and a small pool within about 1 hour. Passing the waterfall from the right, it takes about 15 minutes before the water disappears, and a similar amount of time before the wadi opens towards the 'Araba Valley.

Ascend northwards along an obvious donkey trail to reach a terrace with a prominent conical hill. If you arranged to be picked up, the driver should be waiting here. Otherwise, proceed northwards along the trail and you might find some Bedouin willing to help with a lift. If you plan to walk to Qureiqira, follow Day 4 of Route 41.

41. The Black Mountains
Map 24

Looking eastward from the 'Araba Valley a steep, black mountain front rises 1,000 m above the plains just south of Wadi Ghuweir. Two lofty peaks, Jabel Feid (1,150 m) and Jabel Abu Mahmud (1,120 m), dominate the skyline of the ridge, and offer superb views of the 'Araba Valley and the Negev Desert. Deep canyons, including Wadi Feid, Wadi el Hudes and Wadi Barwas, slice the ridge. Carved into hard igneous rocks Wadi Feid breaches Jabel Abu Mahmud ridge and descends in a spectacular series of waterfalls towards the 'Araba Valley (this route skirts the waterfalls, to abseil the waterfalls see Route 40). At its upper reaches are the ruins of the Edomite stronghold Qaryat Mansur. Wadi el Hudes lies beneath Jabel Abu Mahmud and is the most obvious approach to the mountain. Last is Wadi Barwas, named for the fruit of the red juniper tree. As its name suggests, impressive junipers crowd the slopes of the wadi. Its upper reaches are in red sandstone country, but further down igneous rocks take over and springs feed a small stream. In summertime the stream dries out after a few hundred metres, not reaching the wadi's outlet to the 'Araba Valley. The lower part of the wadi is a tiny, beautiful gorge.

Type of route: One-way.
Route:
>   **Day 1:** Shkart Umm Sa'id, Wadi el Hudes, Jabel Abu Mahmud. Camping site at Wadi el Hudes.
>   **Day 2:** Lower reaches of Wadi el Hudes, lower reaches of Wadi Feid, Jabel Feid, Qaryat Mansur. Camping site at the upper reaches of Wadi Feid.
>   **Day 3:** Pools at the upper reaches of Wadi Feid, Wadi Barwas. Camping site at Wadi Barwas outlet. Alternatively you can abseil down the waterfalls of Wadi Feid according to Route 41.
>   **Day 4:** From the outlet of Wadi Barwas to the village of Quarei-qira (walk or ride).

Rating: Strenuous. Steep ascents with no obvious trail.
Special equipment: None.
Guides: Might help. Try Abu Gasem, who usually encamps in winter and spring about 200 m north of Shkart Umm Sa'id.
Water: Consider carrying at least 3 liters.
Season: Spring and fall. Winter usually brings days with excellent vistas. However it can get very cold, not to mention the risk of flash floods.
Getting there and back: From Petra take a taxi towards Little Petra (about 5 JD). The trailhead is at Shkart Umm Sa'id, 8 km north of Little Petra, beside the half-tarred track of Naqb Namala. Only high-clearance vehicles can get there, so look for a Bedouin pickup truck in Little Petra or the nearby settlement el Beida (about 5 JD). The trail ends at the 'Araba Valley near the outlet of Wadi Barwas,

10 km from the small village of Qureiqira. You can either walk to the village, or be lucky enough to find Bedouin goatherds, who may offer you a lift. The dirt track that leads to Qureiqira is more like a trail and is permanently in bad condition. The ride takes about an hour. From Qureiqira there is a daily bus to 'Aqaba, departing in the early morning (around 6 a.m.).

Day 1
Altitude difference, Distance and Walking time: 300 m descent to the foot of Jabel Abu Mahmud, 450 m to the summit and back, additional 200 m descent to camp, 11 km, 10 hours.
Water: 'Ein el Hudes spring is about 2 hours from the beginning of the route. Another small spring is located near the camp.

The trail commences at Shkart Umm Sa'id, a level patch at 1,000 m altitude, located beside a hairpin bend in the dirt track of Naqb Namala. This area was used as a campsite in ancient times, and pottery sherds as well as flint tools are found all over the place.

"Amidst snow and biting cold wind we returned to our elevated camp and a heavy fall continuing throughout the night, the mountain paths soon became impassable, and we found ourselves unable to leave the spot. With six inches of snow on the ground... and no material whatever for making a fire, our position was not an enviable one." (E. H. Palmer who camped at the head of Naqb Namala, 1868)

In winter and spring families from the 'Amarin tribe pitch their tents here, herding their goats in the area. A few tens of metres north of the track rises a prominent bluff of red sandstone (1,150 m) with a small ravine on its west face. Water may be found behind a dam at the outlet of the ravine.

Head north on an obvious path towards a rounded hill rising from a saddle. The path stretches along the east bank of Wadi Qunai's tributary and the progress is quite level. It takes about 20 minutes to reach the saddle which offers fine views of Jabel Abu Mahmud and Jabel Feid.

Descend north into Wadi el Hudes along a white sandstone slope. After about an hour and a half, you reach ancient terraces and ruined structures, built above a side wadi coming down from the east. The spring 'Ein el Hudes issues here, surrounded by oleander, Euphrates poplar and reeds. Proceed along the wadi bed for ten minutes to reach dry falls with several potholes. Pass the falls on their left and progress along the left bank aiming towards the west flank of a remarkably stratified hill. Once past the hill, about 30 minutes beyond the falls, the path descends gently towards a side wadi which joins from the west. This is where the approach to Jabel Abu Mahmud begins.

Bear up, avoiding forks to the left and aiming towards a prominent saddle just south of the first pinnacles. The last section involves slogging up on stable scree with no obvious path, but with plenty of goat droppings to show you the way. The saddle is reached in about 80 minutes. Here there is a small level patch and a strange pile of stones, possibly a leopard trap. Head north and up along goat trails that cross the crest of the ridge and continue along the contour on the eastern face, a few metres below the crest. Reaching a saddle, bypass the next peak on the left to reach another saddle. Here you have to descend east and then climb straight to the summit, which is surrounded by a rocky playground and

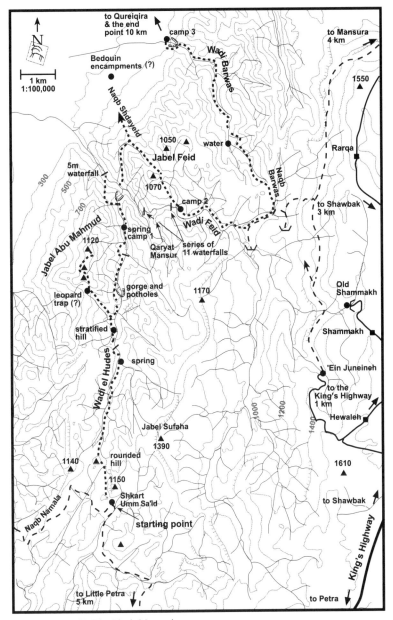

Map 24: Route 41. The Black Mountains

impressive juniper trees. The whole exercise along the crest of the ridge takes about one hour.

Almost 1,000 m of steep drop separate the peak from the plains below, and the views are breathtaking. The central Negev Desert of Israel rises on the western side of the 'Araba Valley, while to the north and south are vast expanses of desert wilderness. To the south is a prominent peak with a white structure. This is Jabel Harun where according to tradition Aaron, brother of Moses, was buried. East of this mountain is Petra, obscured by red sandstone bluffs. Closing the horizon to the east are the peaks of the Edom Plateau, rising to 1,700 m and more. The descent back toward Wadi el Hudes takes about two hours.

Proceed down the wadi for about 20 minutes to reach an impressive red gorge, after passing two low dry falls. The gorge ends with a 15 m dry fall, worth seeing. Retrace your steps for 15 minutes and climb west towards a low pass. The trail descends into the wadi bed 30 minutes after the beginning of this bypass. Short of going down the wadi, bear up towards the fall to enjoy a string of potholes before you continue. Backtracking from the potholes, walk along the wadi bed for a few minutes, before bypassing another fall on the left bank. After about 30 minutes a little spring appears with oleander and reed around it. Nearby are level patches suitable for a camping site.

Day 2

Altitude difference, Distance and Walking time: 100 m ascent to a col followed by 150 m descent to Wadi Feid, 800 m ascent to Jabel Feid, 450 m descent to Wadi Feid's, upper reaches, 6 km, 8 hours.

Water: Wadi Feid is a perennial stream. There is no water along the ascent to Jabel Feid. Water is available again near the camping site.

From the spring continue down the wadi to reach a low dry fall within a few minutes. This is the beginning of a short but impassable gorge, which must be skirted in order to reach Wadi Feid. Climb up on loose scree to your left (west) to reach a not-so-obvious col after 20 minutes.

From the col the sheer south face of Jabel Feid is seen rising majestically above Wadi Feid. A steep ravine descends from the mountain into the wadi below, ending abruptly with dry falls. The ascent to the mountain involves bypassing these dry falls from the east and progressing along the ravine towards the summit. Leave the col, descending on faint goat trails along a 30-minute steep slope. The route is not marked by cairns so take care not to lose the trail.

Wadi Feid is a true oasis and it is worthwhile to spend some time here before climbing Jabel Feid. Should you wish to end the trek, the outlet to the 'Araba Valley is about 30 minutes downstream (see Route 40). Just below the intersection between the goat trail you came on and the wadi is a 5 m waterfall feeding a small pool. If you have the time, you can also walk upstream in the shallow water for less than an hour to reach a tight left bend where a 50 m waterfall and magnificent pools await you.

After refreshing, head towards the confluence of Wadi el Hudes and Wadi Feid (10 minutes from the lower waterfall, 50 minutes from the upper one), marked by a big round boulder on the south side of the streambed. From the confluence go downstream about 50 m and then climb upon rocky slabs to your right (north). Soon afterward you will notice goat trails bearing up along a gully towards a wide spur on your left (west). 15 minutes suffice to reach the spur, from where you should descend into the obvious ravine to the west. Continue north along the ravine bed leaving it only once to pass a steep section along the left bank. The ravine makes a sharp curve to the east after about an hour and meets a fine camel path called Naqb Shdayeid. The path progresses in the ravine before it climbs with well-built serpentine bends towards a narrow cleft to the right. Shortly beyond the cleft the path crosses to the left bank and ascends to a saddle at 950 m. The saddle is reached after 1 hour along the camel path.

Two peaks can be reached from here, one to the north and one to the south. Climb south for 20 minutes to reach Jabel Feid's southernmost peak, rising to 1,070 m and located just above a sheer drop to Wadi Feid. Wherever you look, the views are magnificent. You can easily pick out Jabel Abu Mahmud and Wadi el Hudes. On the western horizon rises the Negev Desert in Israel and below it stretches the 'Araba Valley with a narrow long ridge rising slightly above the plains. The village Qurei-qira, where this trek ends, lies beneath this ridge. Around the peak several pinnacles point fingerlike towards the sky.

Retrace your steps to the saddle and bear up and north on a stable talus slope to reach the northern peak after about 40 minutes. This peak is 1,150 m high, offering spectacular views to the north. Looking at the 'Araba Valley it seems that the valley floor extends to the northeast to form a plain protruding the mountain front. The outlets of Wadi Ghuweir and Wadi Dana can be seen reaching the plain near the ancient copper works of Feinan (see Route 38). Copper was manufactured in Feinan mainly in the Roman-Nabataean period and the Iron Age (around the 1st millennium BCE), when it might have been one of King Solomon's mines.

It takes about 20 minutes to return to the saddle. From the saddle it is

another 45 minutes down Naqb Shdayeid's eastern part and into Wadi Feid. Flat terraces close to Wadi Feid's streambed make an ideal camping site.

Qaryat Mansur
Not far from the suggested camping site is the recently discovered Edomite stronghold of Qaryat Mansur (probably 8–6th centuries BCE). Follow the obvious contouring trail on the south bank of Wadi Feid for 10 minutes to reach the crest of an east-to-west spur separating Wadi Feid from its southern tributary. A prominent saddle lies 100 m to your west. Above the saddle are remnant of black walls which once encircled the stronghold. Perched above deep abysses on the western edge of the spur, the site offers dramatic views. It is not known why the Edomites saw need to dwell in such inaccessible crags.

Day 3
Altitude difference, Distance and Walking time: 250 m ascent to the watershed with Wadi Barwas, 600 m descent from Wadi Barwas to the 'Araba Valley, 9 km, 7 hours.
Water: Wadi Feid dries out about 20 minutes upstream from the camp, but a year-round spring is located in Wadi Barwas, 3 hours away. Near the suggested camping site there may be no water! Fill up in advance with enough water for camping and a 10 km early morning walk next day.
Alternative route: Abseiling down the waterfalls of Wadi Feid —see Route 40.

Before heading up along Wadi Feid, walk down for a few minutes to reach a waterfall. At the top of the waterfall are small pools, perfect for a morning bath. This is the head of a magnificent black gorge with a series of 12 waterfalls described in Route 41. Bearing back up, adhere to the north bank to avoid the oleander and Eu-phrates poplar thicket along the stream. The trail, which follows an ancient aqueduct, reaches a small side wadi coming from the north about 20 minutes later. This is where the water disappears, so fill up your containers. Proceed east along the dry wadi for another 20 minutes to reach a triple fork of wadis.

Climb east along a clear trail wind-ing up the slope towards a dirt track. Turn left and proceed along the track until it descends into the wadi to your left. Here you may find a num-ber of Bedouin encampments of the 'Azazma and Howeitat tribes. Leaving the track follow the wadi bed northwards for about 10 minutes until a low saddle emerges on your left. The saddle, which is 10 minutes further ahead, is marked by red sand-stone which lies side by side with grayish-yellow limestone.

From the saddle, descend west along a well-cairned donkey trail called Naqb Barwas. The trail goes down to the wadi and then climbs to the south bank where it continues 50 m above the wadi bed. Pistacia trees are abun-dant here, as well as huge junipers. After 500 m of level progress, the trail crosses to the north bank. Soon reed and oleander appear for the first time and water issues in the wadi. Instead of going down to the stream, stick to the north bank and climb a short distance to cross a side wadi.

Soon after, the trail crosses to the south bank through dense brush of Euphrates poplar, oleander, reed and *Ficus* trees. This is a marvellous spot to rest and enjoy the shallow stream, about 75 minutes downstream from the saddle.

After the rest, continue on the left bank until the water vegetation disap-pears, allowing you to descend back into the wadi bed. The stream may be dry further ahead, so keep an eye on it and fill up with water in advance.

This might be the last water source until the end of the trek.

After about one hour from the dense vegetation, the wadi veers west and shortly afterwards it passes through low cascades. A 4 m fall marks the head of a short impassable gorge. To bypass it, climb left aiming towards a low pass.

The outlet of Wadi Barwas is reached within minutes from the pass. At the entrance to the gorge, which you just bypassed, is a jujube tree and above it are narrows leading to a low dry fall. You may find water under the fall.

The entrance to the gorge is a good place to camp but it might be worth-while to continue 2 km southwest over stony gravel fans towards possi-ble Bedouin encampments. Should you find Bedouin, you might arrange an early morning ride to the village of Qureiqira.

Day 4
Altitude difference, Distance and Walking time: Level progress. 10 km. 3 hours.
Water: None.

Start this walk as early as possible to avoid the heat of day and save a lot of effort. Wherever you are camped, simply raise your head to the north-west and you will see a narrow ridge rising slightly above the plains. The village of Qureiqira (see map 22) is lo-cated beneath the eastern flank of this ridge about 5 km from its southern tip. Head towards the ridge, crossing small wadis and walking on stony flats until eventually the houses of the village come into view. Don't neglect to look back at the sheer mountain wall behind you to see Jabel Feid and Jabel Abu Mahmud rearing up from the plains.

Once you reach Qureiqira you'll find a small shop but no restaurant and no official place to stay. The only bus leaves for 'Aqaba at 6 in the morning so you will probably want to hitch a ride towards the main 'Araba road 15 km away, where you will have to wait for another ride.

The simple story about the creation of the world
Subach Aziz (translated by the author)

When the creation was over, God leaned back, enjoying the end of a day and looking at his work — beautiful and glistening (and still a bit wet). "The trouble is," he thought, "I haven't got the time to look after all the things I've created". And so God raised his voice (in a sound of silence) and called his ministers, so he could divide the world among them.

First came Ocean. "You that came first will get most of the world's area", said God. "You will have lots of water, storms, plenty of creatures, from the world's smallest to the whale. Yours are abysses and the riches of the world. All the restless nomads will come to you."

Second came Forest. "It's good you came on time", said God. "I was waiting for you to take all the trees, the woodlands, the streams and the rivers. You will have all the rain forests, the bush, springs and hidden paths, giant snakes, alligators and colorful butterflies. All the adventurers, all the seekers of trouble and treasure will come to you".

The Mountain minister got high peaks, narrow paths and everlasting snow. All the lovers of solitude, all the poets and thinkers, would come to him.

The Steppe minister got vast expanses and fast horses (as well as many other things). All the lovers of freedom would come to him.

That is that, thought Good Old God (who was quite tired and wanted to go home). But then, late and last, came a poor old guy: The Desert. God was silent and the Desert was silent. God raised his eyes and said "You are so very late, I've given all that is worthy to the others". The Desert smiled for a while and said "What you give is yours forever, and what you keep is lost, and all that you got to give is worthy". God smiled silently and said "I haven't got plenty of water to give you, son (and he said it as if the word was pulled out of his heart), only a few springs and dry wadis, a few bushes, bare rocks". He opened the wind sack and a hot, easterly desert wind leaped out. "Only thirst and hunger are left for you, son", and God shook the sack and all the sands of the desert were scattered. Thus all the creatures of the night were wakened, small and weather-beaten. And the Desert took what was given, and Good Old God smiled silently, and the Desert smiled back.

And God said "A hard land I've given you, but I shall make it to be a journey land. All the restless nomads will come to you, all the freedom lovers, all the lovers of solitude, all the seekers of trouble and treasure, all the adventurers, all the prophets and poets. And since you are so poor, so hard and so bitter, you shall be the test of all the truly big things".

So evening came and morning came, a new day.

42. Canyons and ancient caravan routes around Petra
Map 25

Steep canyons, carved in black igneous rocks, descend from the region of Petra towards the 'Araba Valley. Wadi Musa carries beautiful pools and waterfalls, while Wadi Qunai and Wadi Umm Hashba possess magnificent dry falls and potholes which may carry water after floods. Trekking through those canyons requires abseiling skills.

Wadi Umm Hashba is Wadi Qunai's biggest tributary, draining one of the highest regions in Jordan. The wadi develops downward into a narrow gorge, with gleaming rock faces, ponds and dry falls. Great juniper and pistacia trees with a variety of birdlife can be seen in Wadi Qunai. Wadi Musa is doubly blessed: Not only does it harbor the magic city of Petra, but it is also Jordan's southernmost perennial wadi. On its lower reaches lies the mysterious Pond Temple; a Nabataean site that poses questions not yet answered by excavation.

Ancient caravan routes (such as Naqb Namala, el 'Aqeb and Sleisel) link the region of Petra with the 'Araba Valley. These routes negotiate steep topography by built switchbacks, used by the Nabataean caravans on their voyage to the Mediterranean shores. The main port for caravans passing through Petra was probably Little Petra, where rock-carved monuments are hidden in a valley of white sandstone.

The walking days of this route are long and include steep ascents. Considering your full backpack and ropes this is a very strenuous trek.

> **Type of route:** Almost circular.
> **Route:**
> > **Day 1:** Jabel el 'Aqeb, Wadi Qunai, Wadi Muslim. Camping site at Shkart Umm Sa'id.
> > **Day 2:** Wadi Umm Hashba. Camping site at the confluence of Wadi Muslim and Wadi Umm Hashba.
> > **Day 3:** Naqb Qarun, Jabel Qarun, Little Petra, Wadi Marwan. Camping site in Wadi Musa.
> > **Day 4:** Wadi Musa lower reaches (often called Wadi Siyyagh). Camping site beneath Naqb Sleisel.
> > **Day 5:** Naqb Sleisel to the region of Little Petra.
> **Rating:** Strenuous. **Abseiling is unavoidable.** The route includes ponds, to be crossed by swimming.
> **Special equipment:** Two 40 m ropes and ordinary abseiling gear. A waterproof bag can be useful.
> **Guides:** Might help. Try 'Ali Jmeidi or other Bedouin from the village of the Badul, near Petra. Though they have probably never abseiled before, they know the area very well.
> **Water:** Consider carrying at least 3 liters each.
> **Season:** Spring is the best. Fall is alright, though water in the potholes will be scarce.

Getting there and back: The starting point is at Jabel el 'Aqeb. To reach this hill with a vehicle you need a pickup truck, which can be arranged (about 5 JD) in Wadi Musa or in Beida, a small settlement near Little Petra. From Little Petra head north on the half-tarred road of Naqb Namala. Passing the sewage project after 4 km, turn left, climbing a short way towards a pass. Proceed south for 2 km towards the prominent dark hill of Jabel el 'Aqeb. To reach the hill on foot follow Route 44. You can camp nearby but there is no water around.
The trail ends on the tarmac road connecting Little Petra with Petra.

Day 1

Altitude difference, Distance and Walking time: 650 m descent, 450 m ascent, 9 km, 11 hours (1 hour to the first fall, 3 hours from the last fall to camp). An early start is a must.

Falls: There are ten dry falls in Wadi Qunai. Falls 2,5,6,8,10 require abseiling.

Water: Abundant potholes. A tiny spring underneath the fourth fall. Another spring issues near the confluence of Wadi Muslim and Wadi Umm Hashba. Water might be hard to find at the suggested camping site of Shkart Umm Sa'id. If there are no Bedouin around to offer you water, continue towards the potholes of Wadi Umm Hashba.

Located at the edge of Petra's dissected plateau, Jabel el 'Aqeb offers superb panoramas towards the 'Araba Valley. East of its hilltop, a steep wadi plunges northwards. Scramble down this wadi among giant boulders and with no obvious trail, to reach Wadi Qunai within 40 minutes. Scarlet igneous rocks, junipers and pistacias create here a special atmosphere punctuated by the twittering of birds.

Continue down, passing within 20 minutes a side wadi which joins from the south. Upon reaching a fall, pass it on the left along a clear trail descending towards a series of potholes. Soon after a second fall comes into sight.

Fall 2: 15 m.

Fall 3: 15 m. The fall can be bypassed along goat trails on the right. The trails descend on loose scree to the bottom of the fourth fall.

Fall 4: 15 m, plunging to a pothole.

Continue along the smooth rocky surface of the right bank to reach a surprising pool, encircled by oleander and reed and fed by a tiny spring.

Fall 5: A series of four steps. The fourth step is 15 m high. It is possible to descend the upper steps by holding on to a hiker's rope.

Fall 6: 10 m, plunging to a pothole.

Fall 7: 8 m. The fall can be bypassed from the right. Below the fall there is a row of potholes.

Fall 8: A 25 m chimney. A pothole and a giant juniper tree are located below the fall.

Fall 9: Two steps of 5 m, which are easily bypassed.

Fall 10: 40 m, plunging to a pothole.

A wide wadi joins Wadi Qunai from the north, a short distance from fall 10. Turn right into this wadi to arrive at another fork after 15 minutes. To the right is wadi Umm Hashba and to the left is Wadi Muslim. Water issuing here from the gravel soon disappears again. Take left into Wadi Muslim, passing a graded fall after 20 minutes and arriving at another fall within another 20 minutes. Climb through the fall to reach a third low fall 15 minutes afterwards.

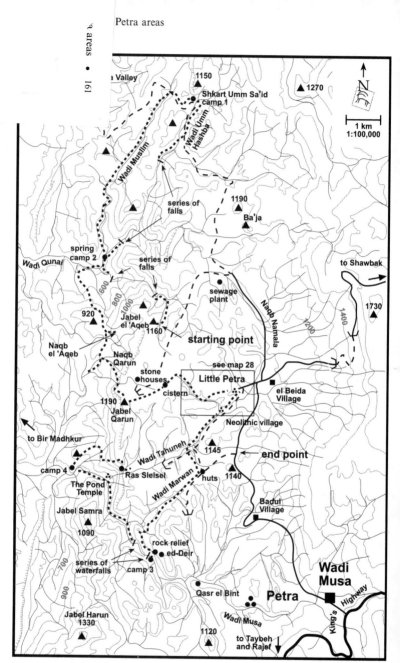

Map 25: Route 42. Canyons and ancient caravan routes

Proceeding among juniper and pistacia trees you reach the dirt track of Naqb Namala within 80 minutes from the third fall. The track marks a Nabataean route that connected Petra with the 'Araba Valley. Veer right, ascending towards the flat shoulder of Shkart Umm Sa'id where a prehistoric site was recently excavated. It is a fine place for camping, with good westward views, though it may well prove to be cold and windy. Usually there are Bedouin in the vicinity, who can provide drinking water. Otherwise, check the small dam hidden in a ravine which descends westwards from the red bluff (1,150 m) to the north. If you have not found water, continue downhill along the track and camp near the potholes of Wadi Umm Hashba (see Day 2).

Day 2

Altitude difference, Distance and Walking time: 500 m descent, 5 km, 11 hours (1.5 hours to the second fall (the first can be bypassed). The camping site is a few minutes away from the last fall). An early start is recommended.

Falls: There are thirteen dry falls in Wadi Umm Hashba. Falls 2, 8–12 require abseiling.

Water: Plenty of potholes which may contain water. The only year-round spring is located near the camping site, just beneath the confluence with Wadi Muslim

Follow the dirt track of Naqb Namala southwards until it climbs to the left about 20 minutes away from the camping site of Shkart Umm Sa'id. Proceed down the wadi bed, crossing a few low dry falls and potholes (an alternative water source in case there is no water in Shkart Umm Sa'id). The first noteworthy fall can be bypassed by ascending to the right. After a short ascent the trail forks:

one branch continues uphill and the other descends back into the wadi. As you descend into the wadi, its grades become less steep. A second fall is encountered about 1 hour from the dirt track of Naqb Namala.

Fall 2: 25 m. A wide seasonal pond, 15 m in diameter, is located below the fall.

Fall 3: 8 m. The fall can be bypassed from the right.

Fall 4: 5 m. The fall can be bypassed from the left.

Fall 5: 3 m. The fall can be bypassed from the left.

Fall 6: A huge boulder blocks the wadi, creating a 2 m chimney on the left-hand side. Below the boulder is a pothole, which may have to be crossed by swimming.

For a short distance the wadi becomes less steep. After easily passing several potholes you reach two potholes which are perched above a 5 m fall (fall 7). Do not take the tempting trail, which climbs to a low col on the right. Instead, descend into the wadi which soon becomes a gorge with silk-smooth rock surfaces. Slide down using a hiker's rope to reach the eighth fall.

Fall 8: 40 m. A willow tree, which has survived many floods, grows at the foot of the fall. Further below a savage ravine joins in from the left. Sparkling pools and gleaming rock faces have created here a spot of rare beauty.

Fall 9: 10 m. The nearest anchor is 15 m away from the fall.

Fall 10: 15 m. A 10 m pothole is located below it. Swimming may be unavoidable.

Fall 11: 10 m. Abseil through a narrow passage to the left. Three potholes below the fall may have to be swum.

Fall 12: 25 m. There are no natural

anchors close by. Chocks and cams may be handy.

Further down the wadi the grades diminish, but potholes are still common.

Fall 13: 10 m. It is possible to descend this fall without a rope.

The confluence of Wadi Muslim and Wadi Umm Hashba is reached within a few minutes. Nearby there is a little spring and several possible camping sites.

Day 3

Altitude difference, Distance and Walking time: 700 m ascent to Jabel Qarun, short ups and downs, 200 m descent to Wadi Musa, 15 km, 8 hours plus 2 hours for visiting Little Petra.

Falls: None.

Water: Drinking the water of Wadi Musa is not recommended. Fill up before leaving Little Petra.

Descend towards Wadi Qunai and turn right (west) down the wadi. The trail leaves the wadi and climbs southwards upon a dark conglomerate, 50 m before sandstone rock appears on the south bank. Crossing some low shoulders you arrive at a sandy hollow with ancient man-made terraces. Leave the hollow, and ascend southeast towards a prominent saddle. The saddle, which is crossed by a fault, is reached 90 minutes after leaving Wadi Qunai.

Shortly after the saddle the trail branches. Disregard Naqb el 'Aqeb, which climbs steeply to the left. Instead descend a short distance before ascending gently to a second saddle. Once at the saddle, descend towards two shallow wadis whose upper reaches are crowded with junipers.

Immediately after crossing the second wadi, Naqb Qarun winds its way upward. After 15 minutes of steep ascent you come into sandstone surroundings and continue levelly to the south. Crossing a small wadi, keep as-

cending to pass through a rock corridor that leads to a Nabataean terrace. Continue uphill to the hilltop of Jabel Qarun, about 50 minutes from the beginning of Naqb Qarun.

A completely ruined Nabataean temple overlooking dramatic scenery stands on the top of Jabel Qarun. From here you proceed to Little Petra according to Route 44.

After filling your containers leave Little Petra, heading southwest along the dirt track of Wadi Tahuneh. Passing the ruins of a Neolithic village proceed for about 20 minutes before reaching a confluence of tracks and wadis. Turn left following the dirt-track which climbs on the south bank. Continue southwards heading towards two huts standing at the foot of a dominant rock massif. Reaching the huts and an olive grove, cross a shallow wadi and then leave the track, ascending a short distance to the watershed of Wadi Marwan. It takes about 30 minutes to reach the watershed from Wadi Tahuneh.

Proceed according to Route 46. The proposed camping site is located on a man-made terrace in the streambed of Wadi Musa beside olive trees and a year-round stream (Its water is not recommended for drinking). It is about 2 hours from the watershed of Wadi Marwan.

Day 4

Altitude difference, Distance and Walking time: 350 m descent, 4 km, 8 hours (2 hours from the last fall to the camping site).

Falls: There are five waterfalls in Wadi Musa. All of them require abseiling.

Water: A perennial stream. The water in the upper reaches of Wadi Musa is not recommended for drinking. Potable water is available beneath the confluence of Wadi Musa and Wadi Tahuneh.

Follow Route 46 to the confluence of

Wadi Musa and Wadi Marwan. If you want to skip the last day of the trek, turn right and proceed according to Route 46. Otherwise go straight ahead. Beyond the confluence with Wadi Marwan an ancient aqueduct is seen on the right bank. Follow the aqueduct and within 40 minutes Wadi Tahuneh joins from the right.

On the north bank of the wadi, overlooking several round ponds, are the Nabataean ruins of the Pond Temple. Broken column, triglyphs, capitals and stone arches protrude partly from the ground. Lying in the streambed is a giant boulder with three hewn niches, possibly made to hold idols. Palm trees overlook the site from now disused terraces. The pond temple at this enigmatic location, is still unexcavated.

Leaving the temple continue down the wadi, struggling with boulders and dense vegetation for about 50 minutes. Plastic pipes and terraced plots are the first signs of Bedouin. Pass a side wadi joining from the north and climb towards an elevated hut on the north bank. This is the residence of Muhammad 'Ali el Jmeidi of the Badul tribe. Ask permission to camp on one of the terraces nearby. Water is available from the plastic pipes.

Day 5
Altitude difference, Distance and Walking time: 500 m ascent, 6 km, 4 hours.

Falls: None.
Water: None.

Start early and you will avoid the heat of the day. From the terrace, head northeast towards a shoulder just above Wadi Musa. The not-so-obvious trail of Naqb Sleisel proceeds east towards the escarpment, crosses a shallow wadi and ascends steeply with a southeast trend. The uppermost part of this trail is stone-supported, but it still takes about 2 hours to reach the top of the escarpment. Naqb Sleisel is considered by some as the main Nabataean caravan route, connecting Petra with the 'Araba Valley. Its steep grades, as well as the existence of easier routes such as Naqb Namala and Naqb Qarun, cast doubts on this claim.

Follow the edge of the escarpment southwards for a few minutes to reach the ruined Nabataean temple of Ras Sleisel, situated on a prominent rocky outcrop. It is the third temple along this route and your last vista towards the desolate region to the west.

Leaving the ruins, descend a short way into Wadi Tahuneh and proceed up along its bed. Reaching a major fork of wadis and tracks within about 30 minutes, take right (south) following the familiar track of Day 3. Walk southwards for 500 m before veering east following one of the branches of this track. The road connecting Little Petra and Petra is only 20 minutes away.

43. Ba'ja Edomite stronghold
Maps 26, 27

Ba'ja is the site of an Edomite stronghold, located atop a sandstone bluff (1,230 m), 5 km north of Little Petra. Surrounded by sheer cliffs, the access to the site demands a head for heights as well as climbing skills. It makes one wonder what cause led the Edomites to dwell here.

The site has to date not been excavated. Among the ruins are bell-shaped cisterns, sacrificial basins, ruins of walls and great amounts of pottery sherds. Its dense vegetation includes juniper, oak and pistacias as well as other Mediterranean species, which have escaped the Bedouin hunger for firewood. Its inaccessibility protects it from grazing and woodcutting.

Two other archeological sites, Ba'ja I and Ba'ja II are located at the foot of the bluff. Those were dated to the Nabataean and the Neolithic periods, respectively.

Type of route: One-way and back.
Altitude difference, Distance and Walking time: 150 m ascent and descent, 1–3 km, 3 hours.
Rating: Strenuous. A short section demands climbing skills.
Special equipment: A 20 m hiker's rope.
Guides: Recommended. Try Hamdan Salem from the 'Amarin tribe. His tent is usually located a few hundred metres south of the hill. Bedouin from the vicinity of Little Petra also know the ascent.
Water: None. Consider carrying 2 liters each.
Season: Year-round.
Getting there and back: Take a taxi from Petra to the new sewage plant, 4 km north of Little Petra (about 6 JD). The remaining 2 km from the sewage plant to the site are for high-clearance vehicles only. It is an easy walk.
Passing the sewage plant, cross a shallow wadi about 5.5 km from the main road. Soon afterwards, a track branches to the east, leading to a prominent red bluff with a stone building at its foot. Make arrangements to be picked up here or near the sewage plant.

The route to the summit follows a narrow cleft a few metres north of the structure. The cleft, not wider than one's shoulders, is blocked by a number of vertical walls. Though there are carved grooves on its walls, a rope can be of help.

Reaching a densely vegetated hollow at the head of the cleft, proceed up towards an overhang with boulders on its right. Scramble up through a narrow passage between the boulders, emerging at the bottom of a scree slope.

Slog up towards a vertical rock face. Bear left, proceeding levelly for about 100 m towards a col of white sandstone. Leave the col by a short, steep descent into a densely vegetated valley with three hidden cisterns. After having located the cisterns, head up towards a saddle with a built wall. This spot is reached within an hour from the bottom of the hill.

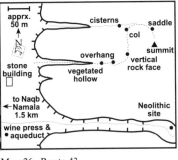

Map 26: Route 43.
  Ba'ja Edomite stronghold

The access to the peaks is straightfor-
ward. Rocky knolls with carved sacrificial basins and imposing views
ornament the summit. To the west
stretches the 'Araba Valley with the
Negev Desert at the horizon. To the
south are red sandstone bluffs in the
vicinity of Petra and a section of the
King's Highway, between the settlements of Wadi Musa and Taybeh. To
the north lies the tilted plateau of Jabel Sufaha. The east is a fantastic
maze of sandstone domes.

The only route back is a retrace of
your steps to the bottom of the hill.

44. Little Petra and its surroundings
Maps 27, 28

Little Petra, or as it is called in Arabic, Siq el Barid, is far more than Petra's little sister. Amidst white domes of sandstone, on either side of a hidden valley, lies an archeological wonderland. Impressive facades of tombs and temples are hewn into the rock and traces of aqueducts and cisterns are seen everywhere. The place possesses an extraordinary peacefulness.

Little Petra was probably the major caravanserai of the Nabataean capital. It is easy to imagine the sounds and smells of old days, when traders, caravan masters, drovers and local dwellers roamed about, chatted, negotiated, argued and prayed.

Mediterranean trees such as oak, juniper, carob and pistacia thrive here in small sandy valleys among typical desert plants such as the desert broom, and though the place does not look like a desert, the annual rainfall says it is. Not far west from Little Petra, the plateau ends with a steep escarpment falling towards the 'Araba Valley and offering rewarding views. At the edge of the plateau is Jabel el 'Aqeb, and nearby is a ruined Nabataean temple at the top of Jabel Qarun.

Type of route: Circular.
Route: Little Petra, Jabel el 'Aqeb, Jabel Qarun, Little Petra.
Altitude difference, Distance and Walking time: 100 m ascent, undulating terrain to Jabel el 'Aqeb and Jabel Qarun, 100 m descent back to Little Petra, 11 km, 9 hours.
Rating: Easy — Moderate.
Special equipment: None.
Guides: Might help. Ask at the entrance to Little Petra.
Water: None. Consider carrying 3 liters each.
Season: Year-round.
Getting there and back: The trail starts and ends at the entrance to Little Petra, 6 km away from the city of Wadi Musa (about 4 JD for a taxi).

Save the visit to Little Petra for the end of the route. Backtrack about 100 m from the site's entrance and bear north into a wide valley with white cliffs and ancient terraces where barley is still cultivated today. Ignore a side wadi which joins from the west, and continue north. At the edge of the valley, about 20 minutes from the starting point, a fine trail ascends to the saddle on the right. Once at the saddle veer left towards a promi- nent knoll. The view from the knoll takes in a vast plateau with the distinct dark hill of Jabel el 'Aqeb at its western edge.

Leave the knoll, descending west towards Jabel el 'Aqeb. As you cross the plateau, you may encounter Bedouin encampments of the 'Amarin tribe. Once at the hill of Jabel e 'Aqeb, cross a saddle, and climb northwards to a better situated top Located at the edge of the plateau

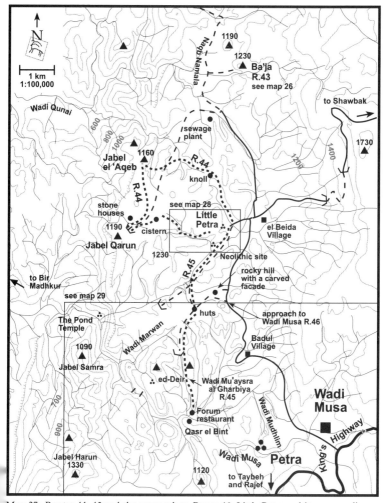

Map 27: Routes 44, 45 and the approach to Route 46. Little Petra and its surroundings

about 50 minutes away from the knoll, it provides wide open vistas of the 'Araba Valley.

Below the escarpment, light colored rocks lean on the dark slopes of Jabel el 'Aqeb. This contact is due to a north-south fault, parallel to the Dead Sea Rift. Ancient trails take advantage of the relatively graded topo-graphy created by these faults, in order to negotiate the difference in altitude between Petra and the 'Araba Valley. Naqb el 'Aqeb, descending on the slope below, is an example of such a trail.

The dark ridge of Jabel Abu Mah-mud rears up on the north with Jabel Feid looming behind it. Closer are

Wadi Qunai's upper reaches, negotiable only with the aid of ropes. Jabel Harun's white mosque is the most prominent feature to the south.

Return to the plateau and contour south along a low shoulder and then along a dirt track to reach a faint junction. Turn right, and within minutes a number of well-built but deserted houses will come into view, about 40 minutes from Jabel el 'Aqeb. Beside the houses is a Nabataean cistern.

The prominent hill of Jabel Qarun overlooks the houses from the south. It is a short walk to the summit where ruins of a Nabataean compound overlook superb scenery. The view from the peak takes in the lower reaches of Wadi Musa as well as the settlements of Taybeh and Wadi Musa. A small built basin implies that the place may have been used as a temple.

Leaving Jabel Qarun, cross the plateau heading east, towards the northern side of a prominent rock massif about 20 minutes away. This is the

head of a small wadi, which drains towards Little Petra. Nearby there is a Nabataean cistern which still collects runoff water.

The wadi offers a variety of rock shapes and carries lush vegetation. Mediterranean trees such as oak, pistacia and juniper as well as many desert shrubs, and the endemic bush *Daphne linearifolia*, distinguished by its narrow leaves and its strong aroma, grow along its bed. The large number of species that grow together in this arid biotope is indeed remarkable.

Descending a rocky slope, follow cairns to negotiate some steep rock ledges. A series of Nabataean terraces is crossed within less than an hour from the head of the wadi. On the left-hand side of the last terrace is a great oak tree, which marks the entrance to the hidden valley of Little Petra.

Before entering Little Petra it is worthwhile to visit some of the Nabataean water installations. Follow the sandy wadi until it suddenly narrows

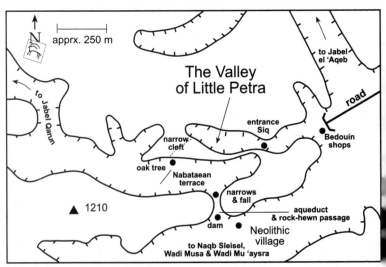

Map 28: Routes 42, 44, 45. Little Petra

to a steep little gorge. In order to reach a sandy hollow below the narrows, climb a few metres to the right, contour for a short stretch and descend into the hollow using some hewn grooves and a juniper tree.

The hollow is blocked by a dam. Facing the dam, go left to a narrow rock-hewn passage that marks the beginning of an aqueduct. The ruins of an 8,000 years old Neolithic village can be seen through the passage but a vertical drop prevents easy approach.

Retrace your steps to the oak tree that marks the entrance to Little Petra. Climb a short way to reach a natural cleft, which leads into the site. On both sides of the valley are rock-hewn facades of sepulchral monuments, water reservoirs and stairways. The wadi bed was paved and a central aqueduct stretched along it. One of the monuments has preserved frescoes in which plant designs and the figures of Pan and Eros are discernible.

Little Petra could have supplied all the needs of a travel-weary caravan, including plenty of water, abundant shade, temples and gathering places. Caravans were probably not allowed into the city of Petra itself, just as trucks are not allowed into city centers today.

The outlet of Little Petra valley is a narrow *siq*, which was, and still is, the main entrance to the site. Near the *siq* are souvenir stalls and Bedouin selling booths. To reach the Neolithic village (el Beida), turn right, descending a short way along Wadi Tahuneh.

Oak (*Querqus calliprinos*)

45. From Little Petra to Petra
through Wadi Mu'aysra al Gharbiyya
Maps 27, 29

An unusual entrance to Petra through a scenic ravine with rock-carved monuments. Purchase entry tickets at the main gate before taking this route.

> **Type of route:** One-way.
> **Altitude difference, Distance and Walking time:** Undulating, 100 m descent, 3 km, 3 hours.
> **Rating:** Easy — Moderate.
> **Special equipment:** None.
> **Guides:** Not really needed. Ask at the entrance to Little Petra.
> **Water:** None. Consider carrying 1.5 liters each.
> **Season:** Year-round. Be aware of flash flood risk, especially during the winter!
> **Getting there and back:** The route starts at Little Petra, 6 km away from the settlement of Wadi Musa (about 4 JD for a taxi). The route ends at Petra near the Forum restaurant.

Leaving Little Petra walk southwest, descending along Wadi Tahuneh, past the ruins of the Neolithic village, to reach a confluence of tracks and wadis within about 30 minutes. Go left following the major track, which climbs southwards. Proceed southwards, along the plateau, heading towards two huts below a prominent rock massif with a sheer north face. Once you reach the huts, continue along the track, rounding the rock massif from the right. The head of

Wadi Mu'aysra is a few minutes from the huts and about 30 minutes from Wadi Tahuneh.

The trail manoeuvers amidst rocks marked by occasional red paint spots. Rock-carved Nabataean monuments are reached within 40 minutes from the watershed. Stick to the left bank following a clear trail, which leads to a flat shoulder with comprehensive views of Petra. The ancient city is minutes away. You will enter it just behind the Forum restaurant.

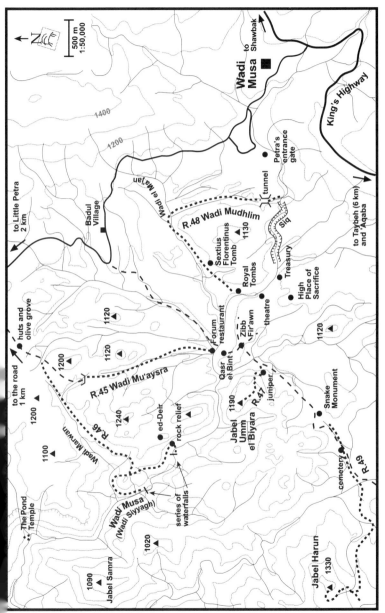

Map 29: Routes 45–49. Petra's basin

46. Wadi Musa
Maps 27, 29

"Further towards the west the ravine has never been explored and no one could tell in what direction the waters, when swollen, find their way through the cliffs." (Edward Robinson, 1838)

Wadi Musa which flows from Petra towards the 'Araba Valley, is the southernmost perennial wadi in the Kingdom of Jordan. Within the wide valley of Petra, it is hard to imagine the savage appearance of its lower reaches where it leaves the sandstone and starts cutting deep into hard igneous rock. Five waterfalls are spaced along its gorge, shadowed by pinnacles and juniper trees, which are mirrored in its streambed pools.

The route approaches and leaves Wadi Musa through Wadi Marwan, and with an early start it can be completed in a day. However if you don't want to rush, divide the route over two days, spending the night beneath the second waterfall. Should you choose this option, consider descending towards the Pond Temple, a mysterious Nabataean site that is still unexcavated (see Day 4 of Route 42). At the upper reaches of Wadi Musa is an intriguing Nabataean rock relief.

Type of route: Circular.
Altitude difference, Distance and Walking time: 300 m descent and ascent, 10 km, 11 hours (2.5 hours to the first fall. 3 hours from the last fall to the end of the route).
Rating: Moderate. **Abseiling is unavoidable.** Ponds along the wadi have to be crossed by swimming.
Falls: Five waterfalls. Abseiling all the falls is recommended. Bypassing the falls may prove to be dangerous.
Special equipment: Two 30 m ropes and ordinary abseiling gear. A waterproof bag can be useful.
Guides: Might help with the approach to the first waterfall. Try 'Ali Jmeidi or other Bedouin from the village of the Badul.
Water: Perennial stream and pools. The water is not recommended for drinking. Consider carrying 3 liters each.
Season: Summer is ideal. Spring and fall are also fine.
Getting there and back: Take a taxi from Petra toward Little Petra (about 4 JD). The trail starts 5 km north of the settlement of Wadi Musa (2 km south of Little Petra), where a track branches to the southwest. To identify the fork, look for a whitish-pink rocky hill with a carved facade (see map 27), located to the left-hand side of the road to Little Petra. The trail ends at the same place. Hitching a ride back to Petra is quite easy. Be aware that the lower reaches of Wadi Musa are often called Wadi Siyyagh.

Follow the dirt track heading southwest towards two huts, which can be seen from the main road beneath a prominent rock massif with a shee eastern face. The huts and a youn olive grove are reached after a 3(

minute walk. Cross a shallow wadi and then leave the track, climbing a short way to the watershed of Wadi Marwan.

To reach Wadi Musa the trail contours above Wadi Marwan, skirting the rock massif of Jabel ed-Deir, famous for the impressive facade of 'the Monastery' located beneath its summits.

Passing a lone juniper to your left, descend into the wadi, arriving within minutes at a flat area with several man-made terraces. Leave the wadi by climbing left on an obvious trail, which soon proceeds levelly. The scenery gets wilder as you progress.

When it is no longer possible to contour, avoid the ascending trail and lose some altitude towards a lower and fainter trail. The new trail proceeds very close to the contact between the red sandstone and the dark igneous rock. Continue levelly towards a prominent saddle beneath a toothed crest.

Cross the saddle, turn left and progress along the contour towards a shallow col with a small igneous outcrop to its right. From the col, it is possible to see stands of olive, palm trees and willows in Wadi Musa. It takes about 90 minutes to reach this point from the head of Wadi Marwan.

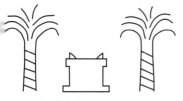
Rock-relief of a Nabataean altar

Before descending into the wadi, look north towards a vertical rock face, located a few tens of metres opposite and above the olive terrace of the wadi bed. With some effort, you should be able to spot a rock-carved

relief, about 1 m by 1 m, depicting a Nabataean altar flanked by two palm trees. The altar might be related to the Pond Temple, located at the lower reaches of Wadi Musa.

Descending into Wadi Musa along steep scree, you reach the wadi bed just below the olive terrace. The first waterfall is a few minutes ahead.

Waterfall 1: 30 m. A drainpipe of light-colored travertine laden on purple rocks. Beneath the waterfall is a 5 m pool.

Waterfall 2: 15 m. A deep elongate pool lies beneath the waterfall inside a narrow cleft, to be crossed by swimming. Should you decide to spend the night in Wadi Musa, the poolside is an ideal site for camping.

Waterfall 3: 15 m. Beneath the fall is a 5 m pool, which cannot be crossed without swimming.

Waterfall 4: 25 m. A spectacular travertine gutter over a giant boulder. The fall drops into a shallow pool located at the head of a gorge. Shortly beyond the fall a boulder blocks the gorge. Crawl beneath it or try and climb over it.

Waterfall 5: A series of three waterfalls. The first is 10 m high with a pool, which can not be crossed without swimming. The second is 5 m high with another deep pool. The third is 2 m high.

A small wadi joins from the left just after the fifth fall. Soon afterwards a trail commences on the right bank, climbing toward a low col about 5 minutes later, before descending into Wadi Marwan.

Proceed along the wadi for a few minutes until a steep side wadi joins from the left. This is where a stone-supported trail climbs to the right. Shortly afterwards it crosses the wadi, climbs on the left bank and descends back to the wadi bed, in front of a giant boulder serving as a shelter for goats. It takes about 30 minutes to reach this spot from Wadi Musa.

Leaving Wadi Marwan, ascend upon the right bank of a steep wadi, which joins from the right. The lower section of the trail is not obvious. Aim towards prominent supporting walls further up. These attest that the trail was probably a well-tended Nabataean route towards the Pond Temple.

It takes about 30 minutes to clear the ascent and reach the already-known saddle and toothed crest. From here onwards the route follows the same trail you came along. Climb a short way to reach an overhang and continue levelly towards the head of Wadi Marwan about 45 minutes away. It takes another 30 minutes to reach the road from the watershed of Wadi Marwan.

47. Jabel Umm el Biyara
Map 29

"In looking at the wonders of this ancient city, one is at a loss, whether most to admire the wildness of the position and natural scenery, or the taste and skill with which it was fashioned." (Edward Robinson, 1838)

Jabel Umm el Biyara which looms above Petra's colonnaded street, is reached by an impressive winding rock-carved staircase. An Edomite stronghold, including cisterns and storage houses, was unearthed on its summit. It is here that a seal impression "Qosgabar, king of Edom", was found (dated to the 7th century BCE).

Its unique panoramas and air of solitude, together with an atmosphere of antiquity, make Umm el Biyara one of the more attractive high places in the vicinity of Petra.

Type of route: One-way and back.
Altitude difference, Distance and Walking time: 300 m ascent and descent, 5 km (to and from Qasr el Bint), 3 hours.
Rating: Moderate.
Special equipment: None.
Guides: Might help. Ask near the temple of Qasr el Bint.
Water: None. Consider carrying 2 liters each.
Season: Year-round.
Getting there and back: The trail starts and ends at Petra.

From the temple of Qasr el Bint, climb southeast towards a lone pillar called Zibb Fir'awn. Leave the pillar, heading southwest towards Jabel Harun along the middle of three tracks. The trail to Umm el Biyara branches from the track 50 m after it crosses a wadi. Skirt a sandstone outcrop, aiming towards a prominent juniper, which is located south of the carved facades.

The trail ascends to an elevated rock terrace, passes some carved niches, and enters a cleft with hewn stairs. It takes about one hour to reach the peak along a winding route with dramatic panoramas. Follow the cairns carefully! The trail takes some surprising hairpin bends.

At the northwestern edge of the summit plateau is a graceful rock engraving of a *Houbara* (a small ostrich-like bird). Cross a little ravine and climb to the highest point of the plateau for rewarding views westwards.

Proceed southwards along the eastern cliffs, which offer comprehensive panoramas of the Petra basin. Along your way there are bell-shaped cisterns, which gave the mountain its name — 'the mother of cisterns'. Not far to the west are the excavated ruins of an Edomite complex with rooms and storage houses.

Retrace your steps to Qasr el Bint.

48. Wadi Mudhlim
Map 29

An alternative exit from Petra through an impressive gorge, which is narrower than the *Siq*.

Type of route: One-way.
Altitude difference, Distance and Walking time: 70 m ascent, 3 km (From the Royal Tombs to the head of the *Siq*), 2 hours.
Rating: Easy. Expect wet shoes during winter and spring.
Special equipment: None.
Guides: Not really needed. Ask near the Royal Tombs.
Water: None. Consider carrying 1.5 liters each.
Season: Year-round. Be aware of flash flood risk, especially during winter! The upper drainage of Wadi Musa is diverted into Wadi Mudhlim.
Getting there and back: The trail starts and ends at Petra.

Leaving the Royal Tombs, walk northeast along the foot of the cliffs. Pass the Sextius Florentinus tomb and proceed for about 750 m, until a narrow side wadi cuts the cliffs near a ruined stone wall.

As you go right into Wadi el Ma'jan, notice the carved niches, which once housed Nabataean idols. After some 100 m, a boulder blocks the main gorge. Veer right, into the narrows of Wadi Mudhlim. At the headwater of this wadi, about an hour ahead, is a 90 m tunnel. Go through it, to emerge at the head of Petra's *Siq*. The tunnel, as well as a dam at the entrance to the *Siq*, were constructed by the Nabataeans to divert the flood waters of Wadi Musa. The same diverting system is still used today.

49. Jabel Harun
Map 29

"The road from Shawbak to 'Aqaba... lies to the east of Wadi Musa; and to have quitted it, out of mere curiosity to see the wadi, would have looked very suspicious in the eyes of the Arabs. I therefore pretended to have made a vow to slaughter a goat in honor of Aaron, whose tomb, I knew, was situated at the extremity of the valley and by this stratagem I thought that I should have the means of seeing the valley on my way to the tomb. To this my guide had nothing to oppose; the dread of drawing upon himself, by resistance, the wrath of Aaron, completely silenced him." (J. L. Burckhardt, 1812)

Jabel Harun is, according to tradition, Mount Hor where Aaron, brother of Moses, died and was buried. The mountain rises to 1,330 m, offering magnificent views towards Petra and the 'Araba Valley.

The Bible describes the dramatic death and succession of Aaron: "At Mount Hor near the frontier of Edom, the Lord said to Moses and Aaron, Aaron shall be gathered to his father's kin... Take Aaron and his son Eleazar, and go up to Mount Hor. Strip Aaron of his robes and invest Eleazar his son with them, for Aaron shall be taken from you: he shall die there... There Aaron died on the mountain top." (Numbers 20: 23–28).

The tradition that relates Mount Hor with the region of Petra is mentioned by the historian Josephus Flavius as early as the 1st century CE. The grave of Aaron is held as one of the most sacred places among the local Bedouin tribes and has attracted many pilgrims over the ages. The Swiss traveller Burckhardt came to Jabel Harun in 1812, disguised as a Muslim, and pretending to have taken a vow to sacrifice a goat at Aaron's tomb. His visit led to the rediscovery of Petra by the western world.

A white-plastered mosque is built upon the summit, sheltering the sepulcher of Aaron. According to an inscription above the entrance, the mosque was built in the 13th century by the Mamluke Sultan Ibn Qala'un. The remains of an old church can be seen inside the mosque, and ruins of a Byzantine monastery are located just below the summit.

The guardian of Aaron's tomb is usually around to open the mosque for visitors.

Type of route: One-way and back.
Altitude difference, Distance and Walking time: 150 m descent and ascent from the entrance of Petra to Qasr el Bint, 450 m ascent and descent to Jabel Harun, 16 km, 8 hours.
Rating: Easy.
Special equipment: None.
Guides: Not really needed. Ask near the temple of Qasr el Bint.
Water: None. Consider carrying 3 liters each.
Season: Year-round.
Getting there and back: The trail starts and ends at the entrance to Petra. From the temple of Qasr el Bint you follow a dirt track to the foot of the mountain. It may be possible to hitch a pickup truck ride and thus save 2 km in each direction.

Follow Petra's colonnaded street to reach the temple of Qasr el Bint. Climb southeast along an obvious trail leading soon to a lone pillar called Zibb Fir'awn. Near the pillar is a triple junction. Taking the middle and most prominent track, cross a wadi and continue along its west bank. The red cliffs of Jabel Umm el Biyara loom to your right (west). Soon the track crosses to the east bank, reaching the snake monument within a few minutes. The carved snake forms the cap of a square monument (it is not that obvious at first glance). Proceed 50 m beyond the monument and climb left (south), reaching a flat valley within about 1.5 hours from the entrance to Petra.

Straight ahead there is fenced agricultural land with olives and eucalyptus trees. Continue along the track, with the fence on your left. Within 5 minutes Jabel Harun comes into sight, with the prominent white mosque at its peak.

A lone juniper tree marks a Bedouin cemetery on the right. It takes another 10 minutes before the track descends steeply into a wadi and climbs to the opposite bank. Immediately afterwards leave the track towards a little built structure to your right. From the structure follow the well-cairned trail uphill. Ascending along

a shoulder, it takes about 25 minutes to reach a fork of trails. Take right, descending a short way before winding up towards a flat saddle, 20 minutes ahead.

Bear right (east) towards the foot of a sandstone bluff, where the final ascent to the summit begins. Passing above an arched cistern, climb some rock-hewn steps to reach the summit within 15 minutes.

Once up, the views are breathtaking. To the east is the town of Wadi Musa connected by the King's Highway to the villages of Taybeh and Rajef further to the south. The red mountains of Petra can be seen to the northeast and it is even possible to spot the Nabataean rock monument upon Jabel ed-Deir ('the Monastery'). To the west is a steep drop of more than 1,000 m towards the 'Araba Valley, beyond which the land rises again towards the ranges of the Negev Desert in Israel.

Inside the mosque, covered with fabrics, is the sepulchral monument of the prophet Aaron. A stairway leads to a space below the floor where a few burial niches were found. The walls of the mosque include fragments of columns and slabs of marble, once part of the Byzantine church that used to stand here.

The mountains of Rajef and Humeima
From Wadi Musa to Wadi Rahma

There are many trekking possibilities in this region, ranging from day trips to long demanding expeditions. Though the wadis still flow from the high plateau towards the 'Araba Valley, the topography is more intricate, with high mountains rising sporadically along the way. Numerous wadis bear north to south, at right angles to the major drainage pattern. This seemingly chaotic pattern is caused by faults that run parallel to the 'Araba Valley. There are numerous springs and potholes in the region but no year-round streams. Water is precious.

On the southeastern edge of this region is the Humeima Plateau (known as el Hisma), a wide rolling terrain of sand and loess. This landscape is bordered on the north by the escarpment of Ras en-Naqb, rising 200–350 m above the sand flats.

Insular sandstone massifs, intersected by narrow canyons, stretch below the King's Highway between Wadi Musa and Rajef. The massifs provide marvellous wandering opportunities and their canyons, though dry, are deep and scenic. Rising southwest of the sandstone inselberg terrain is an elongate limestone range called Jabel Naqb el 'Aunat. A labyrinth of spectacular narrows, draining into Wadi Quseib, lies on the western side of the range. Further south, at the outlet of Wadi Sik and Wadi Rakiya, is a field of magnificent red sand dunes. Great potholes are found in Wadi Khubat, and at the southern boundary of the region is Wadi Rahma with its high dry falls. Most of the wadis that wind toward the 'Araba Valley terminate in mud flats and do not reach the Dead Sea.

Hotel accommodation is available only in Wadi Musa and Taybeh but it is usually possible to find a place for the night in several other villages along the King's Highway. The only accommodation in Taybeh is the luxurious Taybet Zaman Hotel. Constructed of the renovated old stone houses of Taybeh, it is built as a traditional village. In the 'Araba Valley there are only the village of Risha, and Rahma Village further to the south.

Below the escarpment of Ras en-Naqb, a few km west of the modern village of Humeima lies ancient Humeima, a Nabataean city famous for its water system. Several other Nabataean sites are found in the region. South of Petra, at Wadi Sabra, there is an impressive rock-hewn theatre, and at the outlet of Wadi Tajra are the ruins of the small Nabataean village of es-Sadeh. Caravan routes connected Humeima with Petra through those sites.

High-perched Edomite strongholds are found beneath Taybeh and Rajef, in Jabel el Quseir and Umm Ala.

The following routes are suggested in this region:

Route	Days	Rating	Season	Description
50. Jabel el Quseir Edomite stronghold	1 (5 hours)	moderate	all-year	Spectacular sandstone domes, Edomite cisterns, tiny narrows.
51. From Petra to Taybeh	2	moderate	spring fall winter	Remote archeological sites, superb views, narrow *siq*, mazes of white sandstone domes.
52. The Rajef Inselbergs	3	moderate	all-year	Mazes of domes, rewarding views, narrow sandstone canyons, springs.
53. Around Rajef — Jabel Barza, Wadi Hurma, Wadi Abu el 'Uruq	1 (11 hours)	strenuous	all-year	Jabel Barza's rock labyrinths, narrow *siq* in Wadi Abu el 'Uruq.
54. Around Rajef — Jabel Juleif, Wadi Tajra, Wadi Abu el 'Uruq	1 (9 hours)	strenuous	all-year	Rewarding views from Jabel el Juleif, narrow *siq* in Wadi el 'Uruq.
55. The White Narrows and the Dark Gorge	1 (5 hours)	moderate	all-year	Water-filled potholes, shoulder-wide dark gorge.
56. Ein es-Sadeh	1 (5 hours)	moderate	all-year	Hidden waterfall, Nabataean ruins, impressive views from the Edomite stronghold Umm Ala.
57. Across southern Edom from Dilagha to Humeima	4	strenuous water is scarce	spring fall winter	Spectacular views, majestic dune field, narrow sandstone and igneous canyons.
58. The sand dunes of Wadi Rakiya	1 (4 hours)	easy	all-year	Majestic dune field.
59. Jabel Humeima	1 (7 hours)	moderate	all-year	Impressive views, Nabataean cisterns.
60. Humeima from the Horn of the Gazelle	1 (4 hours)	moderate	all-year	Fine views, Nabataean cisterns.
61. From Petra to Humeima	6	strenuous water is scarce	spring fall winter	Extremely rich variety of landscapes, summits, canyons and sand dunes.
62. Wadi Khubat	1 (10 hours)	moderate	spring fall	String of water-filled potholes.
63. Wadi Rahma	1 (10 hours)	moderate incl. abseiling	spring	Huge potholes, impressive dry falls.
64. From Wadi Khubat to Wadi Rahma	3	strenuous incl. abseiling	spring	Fine views, dry falls, water-filled potholes, rich variety of landscapes.
65. Jabel Sor	1 (3 hours)	easy	all-year	Easy climb, fine views.

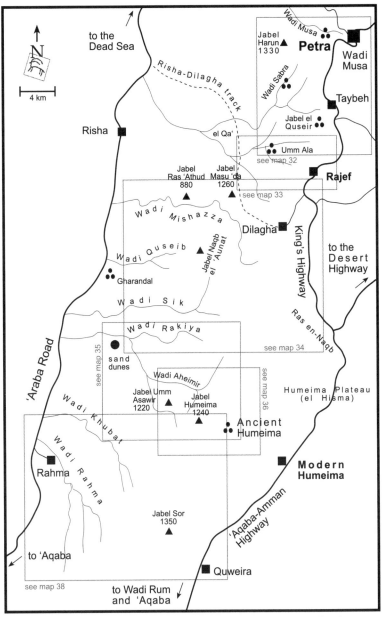

Map 30: The mountains of Rajef and Humeima — from Wadi Musa to Wadi Rahma.

50. Jabel el Quseir Edomite stronghold
Map 31

A short route easily accessible from the King's Highway, offering superb views, a narrow gorge and an intriguing Edomite stronghold. Built on Jabel el Quseir (1,150 m), amidst a spectacular landscape of white sandstone domes, the Edomite site includes bell-shaped cisterns, ruins of walls and sacrificial basins. Ascent to the site involves walking on steep rock surfaces.

Type of route: One-way and back.
Altitude difference, Distance and Walking time: About 350 m descent and ascent along a dirt track. Additional ups and downs from the track to Jabel el Quseir. 7 km. 5 hours. A pickup truck ride can save time and effort. The route will then be 3 km long and will take about 4 hours.
Rating: Moderate.
Special equipment: None.
Guides: Might help. Try the village of Taybeh.
Water: None reliable. Potholes might hold seasonal flood water. Consider carrying 3 liters each.
Season: Year-round. Be aware of flash flood risk, especially during the winter!
Getting there and back: Leaving the town of Wadi Musa, drive 8 km south along the King's Highway to reach the village of Taybeh. You can use the local buses between Wadi Musa and Taybeh or take a taxi (about 4 JD).
Just behind the well-known hotel of Taybet Zaman a dirt track commences. The track descends steeply for 2 km toward a valley dotted with domes, called el Batha. The trail starts and ends just before the steep grades of the track diminish.
To avoid the steep descent and the ascent on the way back, it is possible to arrange a pickup truck in Taybeh.

Descend 30 minutes along the dirt track towards a plateau studded with domes. To spot Jabel el Quseir, look south towards a white domed block, which is separated from the main ridge to the east by a deep saddle. To reach the summit you have to descend into a wadi, climb to a minor saddle and only then ascend towards the saddle you can see from here. The whole exercise takes about 80 minutes.

To the west a side wadi descends southwards into Wadi Tibn. For the shortest approach to Jabel el Quseir, walk above this wadi until a good trail descends into its bed.

Should you descend into this wadi immediately you will soon reach a narrow gorge where a landslide blocked the erstwhile course of the wadi. If you do not mind getting your gear wet, it is possible to descend through the short gorge by negotiating potholes and low dry falls. Alternatively, cross the first landslide reaching a hollow whose southern side is blocked by another landslide.

A second gorge carves it way on the right-hand side of the landslide. Though it is not possible to descend through the gorge without abseiling, it is worthwhile to enter it. Descend a

5-m chimney between boulders, and continue down a number of low falls. Soon the walls of the gorge draw closer, creating a virtual ceiling above your head. Backtrack and cross the landslide. Reaching the foot of the landslide, it is recommended to enter the lower end of the gorge where a natural red amphitheater has only a narrow cleft toward the blue sky. If you left the track by the shorter route it will take you 15 minutes to reach this spot.

Proceed a short distance down the wadi bed until a wadi joins from the east. Turn east, and after a short walk turn right into a side wadi marked by ancient man-made terraces. Ascend a short way towards a saddle from where Jabel el Quseir is clearly seen. Looking hard you can

spot a stone wall below the summit. Beyond the wall is a rock-hewn cave.

From the saddle go downhill, turn right (west) at the wadi and within minutes turn left (south) ascending along a side wadi toward the main saddle of Jabel el Quseir. Below the saddle, above a big juniper tree, a pile of white stones on the sandstone slope to your right marks the ancient trail to the summit.

Leaving the wadi bed, veer right following the stones uphill. Contour for 100 m before climbing steeply through a little rocky gully. The entrance to the stronghold, which is guarded by a wall, is reached within minutes. Above the wall is a rock-hewn room, which looks like a guard post.

On the top of Jabel el Quseir are

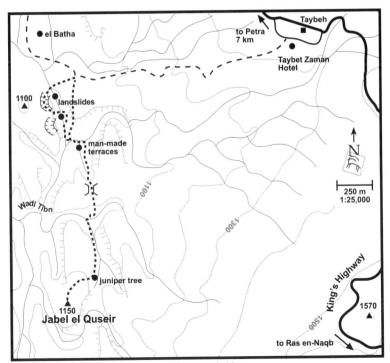

Map 31: Route 50. Jabel el Quseir Edomite stronghold

bell-shaped cisterns, sacrificial basins and masses of pottery sherds. Most of the sherds are several cm thick.

The summit consists of domes and small depressions with no drainage. Some of the depressions are so perfect that they could have been water reservoirs. Who were the people that chose to live here and why? All we know is that the site was used by the Edomites probably during the 8–6th centuries BCE.

The views from the top are magnificent. To the west, Wadi Tibn carves its way towards Wadi Sabra. The village of Taybeh can be seen on the east. Further to the south, perched above the escarpment, is Prince Hassan's summer palace. Below it are the sandstone massifs of Jabel Juleif and Jabel Barza (Routes 52–54). A labyrinth of white domes stretches to the north with the conical peak of Jabel Harun looming on the far horizon.

Heading back to Taybeh, avoid the wadi with the landslides. At the confluence of the landslide wadi and the wadi you are coming from, climb north on a talus slope with a well-defined trail. It takes about 60 minutes from the summit of Jabel el Quseir back to the dirt track.

51. From Petra to Taybeh
Petra, Jabel Harun, Wadi Sabra, Wadi Tibn
Map 32

This two-day route visits remote archeological sites in the southern suburbs of Petra. Jabel Harun (see Route 49) offers rewarding views over the 'Araba Valley and the mountains of Petra, and preserves under its mosque the traditional tomb of Aaron, brother of Moses. Wadi Sabra is a wide canyon in red sandstone. Located in the middle of nowhere, its ancient Roman-Nabataean theatre is an architectural jewel. Wadi Tibn offers a narrow *siq* and impressive juniper and pistacia trees. If you have the time you can also climb to Jabel el Quseir. At its peak is an Edomite stronghold surrounded by a maze of white domes (see Route 50).
The approach to Jabel Harun is through Petra. Entrance fee to Petra is 20 JD for one day or 25 JD for two days.

Type of route: One-way.
Route:
    Day 1: Petra, Jabel Harun, Wadi Sabra. Camping site in Wadi Sabra.
    Day 2: Wadi Sabra, Wadi Tibn, Jabel el Quseir, Taybeh.
Rating: Moderate.
Special equipment: None.
Guides: Might help. Try asking at the village of the Badul or inside Petra, near the temple of Qasr el Bint.
Water: There are small springs along the route and near the camping site. Consider carrying 3 liters each.
Season: Spring, fall and winter. Be aware of flash flood risk, especially during winter!
Getting there and back: The starting point is at the official entrance to Petra. The trail ends at the village of Taybeh, on the King's Highway (see Route 50).

Day 1
Altitude difference, Distance and Walking time: 300 m ascent to Jabel Harun, 500 m descent to the theatre of Wadi Sabra, 12 km, 7 hours.
Water: Water is available only near the camping site in Wadi Sabra.

Follow Route 49 to Jabel Harun. From the summit retrace your steps towards the major wadi below. Turn right (south) and continue up for a few minutes, passing two little side wadis that join from the left. Where

the third side wadi joins, leave the main wadi and turn left (south). Continue southward and then southeast to reach a saddle within 10 minutes.
Descend southwards along an obvious camel path into a tributary of Wadi Sabra. It takes about an hour to reach the confluence with a second tributary which joins from the left. The theatre of Wadi Sabra is 20 minutes ahead.
Carved in red sandstone, the theatre still has some 150 stone seats. Above it is a sophisticated water system,

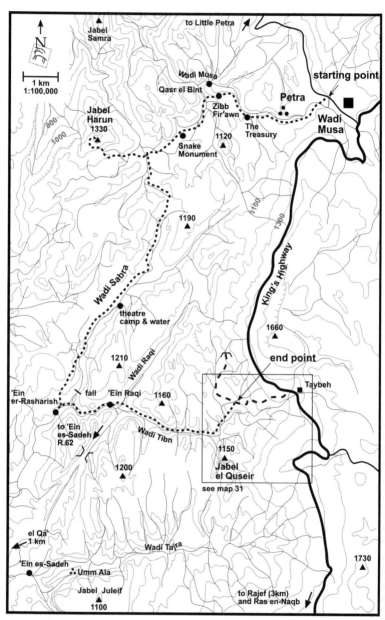

Map 32: Route 51. From Petra to Taybeh

regulating the seasonal flow of two ravines, which descend from Jabel el Jatum. Half-buried pillars and capitals protrude from the wadi bed not far below the theatre.

Some consider the Wadi Sabra site a suburb of Petra, where water games were held. The proximity of the water system to the theatre is the main reason for this suggestion. Others claim that it was a Roman garrison or a Nabataean copper mining center.

Suitable camping spots can be found near a little spring, a few minutes below the theatre.

Day 2

Altitude difference, Distance and Walking time: 100 m descent to Wadi Tibn. 500 m ascent to Taybeh. 12 km, 6 hours. Climbing Jabel el Quseir will add 2 hours.

Water: 'Ein er-Rasharish spring is about 1 hour away from the camp. 'Ein Raqi spring is one more hour away.

From the theatre proceed down the wadi for 20 minutes until a side wadi joins in from the west. Take right, climbing up and leaving Wadi Sabra along a well-trodden camel path. Reaching a col descend back to the wadi bed after 30 minutes. The whole exercise is needed in order to avoid a 30 m dry fall.

A few minutes down the wadi lies a spring, known as 'Ein er-Rasharish (spring of poplars), being crowded with Euphrates poplar. Backtrack from the spring and continue up the wadi to reach the confluence of Wadi Sabra and Wadi Tibn. Leaving the confluence, turn right (east) slogging up among boulders, pistacia trees and potholes to reach a little spring called 'Ein Raqi within 40 minutes. The junction between Wadi Raqi and Wadi Tibn is a few minutes away.

Proceed east through the narrow gorge of Wadi Tibn. After about 40 minutes the gorge widens and oleander bushes appear. Continue up through potholes and low dry falls for about 75 minutes to reach a confluence of wadis forming a T-junction.

Turn left (north) to reach another junction after a few minutes. If you want to climb to the Edomite stronghold atop Jabel el Quseir, go right and soon afterwards turn right (south) again into a wadi with ancient man-made terraces (see map 31). From here onwards follow Route 50.

To reach Taybeh, follow an obvious trail which starts at the junction and climbs north on a yellowish talus slope. Within a few minutes you will reach a dirt track coming down from the village of Taybeh. Unless you have arranged to be picked up, it takes about 45 minutes to arrive at the village.

52. The Rajef Inselbergs
Map 33

The King's Highway between the villages of Taybeh and Rajef affords a rare
vista of steep sandstone inselbergs with sheer side cliffs, crowned with mazes
of domes and little valleys. The inselbergs are dissected by narrow canyons
which hide springs and groves of fruit trees.

The route goes through several canyons and ascends the inselbergs of Jabel
Juleif and Jabel Barza, both offering rewarding views. Ruins of a Nabataean
village and an Edomite stronghold are found in the lower reaches of Wadi
Tajra.

Type of route: One-way.
Route:
> **Day 1:** Rajef, Jabel Juleif, Naqb el Maiet, Wadi Tajra, Umm
> Ala. Camping site at 'Ein es-Sadeh spring.
> **Day 2:** Wadi Abu el 'Uruq, Jabel Barza, Wadi Hurma. Camping
> site at 'Ein Meshet.
> **Day 3:** The White Narrows, the Dark Gorge, Jabel Mas'uda.

Rating: Moderate.
Special equipment: None, though a 10 m hiker's rope can be of use.
Guides: Might help. Try asking in the village of Rajef.
Water: Consider carrying 3 liters each.
Season: Year-round. Be aware of flash flood risk, especially during
winter! Avoid walking on hot summer days.
Getting there and back: The trail starts at the village of Rajef,
located on the King's Highway, and served by a local bus from
Wadi Musa. The trail ends at the village of Dilagha, 7 km southwest
of Rajef. To reach Dilagha you will have to arrange a pickup ride
on the last day of the trek. There are infrequent buses from Dilagha
to Wadi Musa.

Day 1
**Altitude difference, Distance and
Walking time:** 900 m descent, two
short ascents of 100 m, 13 km, 7
hours. Ascending to the Edomite
stronghold Umm Ala will add 2 hours.
Water: Water is available in the lower
part of Wadi Tajra, 5 hours from the
trailhead, as well as near the camping
site.

A steep track with imposing views
descends westwards from the northern edge of the village of Rajef. To
the north is Wadi Tajra. Just above it
and to the south lies the massif of Jabel el Juleif, which looks like a red
carpet with white islands rising above
it. Further to the south is the narrow
gorge of Wadi Abu el 'Uruq and the
massif of Jabel Barza with its prominent white peak, rising above a labyrinth of hills to 1,130 m. Beneath Jabel
Barza and unseen are Wadi Hurma
and the Dark Gorge. Further away is
the gray ridge of Jabel Mas'uda
which marks the end of the trek.

Follow the dirt track till it ends at a
saddle, about an hour away from the
trailhead. From the saddle you can
follow a rewarding two-hour trail to
the western edge of Jabel el Juleif. Al

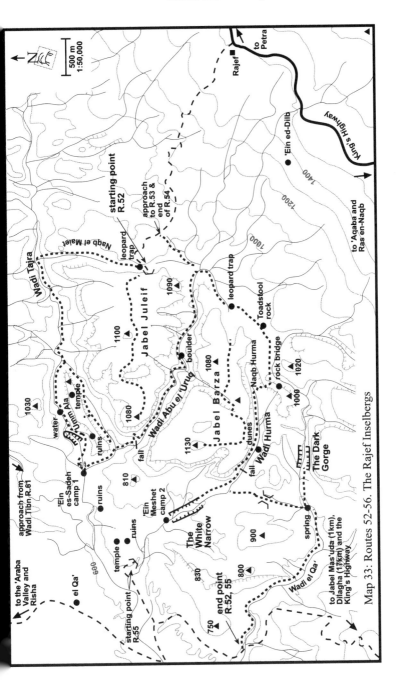

Map 33: Routes 52-56. The Rajef Inselbergs

ternatively you can descend straight into Wadi Tajra.

To reach the western edge of Jabel Juleif, go north about 100 m towards a rock-built Bedouin hoardplace, where you climb westwards. Adhere to the watershed of the massif, avoiding wadis which descend north or south. A white overhanging bluff, used as a goat pen, is reached within 30 minutes. Another 30 minutes take you to the western rim of the massif, where red cliffs drop towards yellowish hogbacks and the colorful plain of el Qa', home of the Sa'idiyin tribe.

On the western horizon stretches the 'Araba Valley with the elongate hill of Jabel Risha rising from its plains. A Sa'idiyin village which bears the same name is situated at its foot.

The narrow cliff of Umm Ala is separated from Jabel el Juleif by the deep wadi just below the observation point. Atop the cliff are ruined walls of an Edomite stronghold from the 8–6th centuries BCE.

Once back at the saddle, descend north past a leopard trap and into a small wadi which drains into Wadi Tajra. On the eastern (right) bank of this wadi runs a clear trail which is known as Naqb el Maiet. Notice the sandstone banks of the wadi which appear painted with purplish-red iron oxides. The vegetation includes large bushes of the endemic *Daphne linearifolia* (recognized by its elongate narrow leaves and its characteristic fragrance), oleander, juniper and *Ficus*.

The main wadi bed of Wadi Tajra is reached within less than an hour. Turn left and progress leisurely among cliffs of red sandstone. On the left bank are rock shelters, used by Bedouin shepherds. To the west rises a prominent cliff comprising the north face of Umm Ala stronghold. Not much survived from the Edomite structures that once stood there. The view from Umm Ala is impressive but it is similar to that of Jabel Juleif (If you want to visit the site follow Route 56). Oleander bushes appear in the wadi bed after about 40 minutes, and soon afterwards seeps of water issue on the wadi floor. Keep an eye out for a rock-built Bedouin hoardplace on the left bank, marking the beginning of a trail which leaves the wadi to skirt a series of falls.

Follow this trail uphill to reach a col with fine views. By now the red sandstone has given way to walls of black igneous rock. A Nabataean aqueduct can be traced, contouring the north bank of the wadi towards a ruined compound built of ashlar.

Once back in the wadi bed, head up towards the falls past a built arch which supports the aqueduct. Bypass the first dry fall from the right and climb through the second. After a short walk the sound of water can be heard as it drips down a perfect drainpipe of travertine.

Backtrack to the base of the first fall and bypass some narrows soon afterwards. The walls of the narrows have natural niches, which the Bedouin close with stone walls to make hoarding places. An olive grove garnishes the north bank of the wadi, where the small spring of 'Ein es-Sadeh issues. There are plenty of suitable sites for camping.

Around 'Ein es-Sadeh

Continue down the wadi for 15 minutes before climbing easily towards a low saddle to the south. From the saddle, ascend a short way westwards to the top of a low hill. Ruins of an east-to-west oriented compound suggest a Nabataean temple. From the hilltop one can see other ruins to the southeast. These, as well as the temple and the aqueduct, point to the presence of a significant Nabataean settlement. Considering the excellent location of the place with relation to

H.

ʻbya Shiloni

I. H.

Top: A maze of white sandstone domes viewed from the Edomite stronghold Baʻja (R.43)
Left: Wadi Musa (R.14)
Right: Hot shower, Wadi ʻAttun (R.8)

I. H.

Noya Shiloni

I. H.

Top Left: The thermal stream of Wadi Zarqa Ma'in winding towards the Dead Sea (R.5, 6)
Top Right: Abseiling in Wadi Karak (R.14)
Bottom: Jabel Barza (R.52, 53)

Onn Crouvi

H.

Onn Crouvi

Top: el Khazneh, Petra's 'Treasury'
Right: 'The Monastery', Jabel ed-Deir
Left: Petra's valley as seen from Jabel Umm el Biyara (R.47)

Noya Shiloni

Ittai Glaich

Yehoram Doron

Top: Wild palms sprouting from the walls of Wadi Hasa (R.20, 21)
Middle: View towards Jabel Umm Asawir from the sand dunes of Wadi Rakiya (R.57, 58, 61)
Bottom: Wadi Hasa, lower canyon

Petra and Wadi Sabra to the north and Humeima to the south, this is not unexpected.

On your way back towards the olive grove, you may explore an Early Bronze site located on the southern slope of the wadi, almost midway between the temple hill and the olive grove.

Day 2

Altitude difference, Distance and Walking time: 550 m ascent and descent, 12 km, 10 hours. The route can be shortened by 3 hours if it does not include the climb to Jabel Barza. **Water:** Water is available only at 'Ein Meshet, at the end of the day.

Wadi Abu el 'Uruq branches southwards from Wadi Tajra, very close to the proposed camping site. Ascending through Wadi Abu el 'Uruq you soon climb over a low dry fall to arrive at a triple fork after 30 minutes. Continue straight past a 5 m fall towards a graded 40 m fall. To bypass the fall, climb steeply over rock slabs to the left towards a hunting shelter overlooking the fall and its potholes.

Soon afterward the wadi gets narrower and its steep sandstone walls zoom higher. About 40 minutes from the fall you pass a big boulder and after an additional 30 minutes you reach a junction where a side wadi joins from the right. Take left, passing another boulder and proceeding in the main wadi bed to enter amazing narrows, which widen only about 10 minutes later.

Leaving the red narrows you reach a junction of wadis in white sandstone terrain. Turn right into a side wadi, which descends from the south. Adhering to its right (west) bank you soon reach a well-preserved leopard trap, located near a wide saddle.

From here, the side trip to the summit of Jabel Barza and back takes about 3 hours. Alternatively

you can continue straight towards Wadi Hurma.

To reach Jabel Barza from the leopard trap go west through a sandy valley, heading towards a low pass. A rock-built Bedouin hoardplace with a built staircase is located just before the pass. Beyond the pass a goat trail commences, passing next to a sooty overhang.

Bear west on the plateau to reach a wadi which drains to the north. The west bank of this wadi is an impassable vertical cliff. Veer left (south) heading up the wadi bed until its walls get gradually lower. With the aid of Bedouin-laid stones and a few juniper beams climb out of the wadi in a southwest direction.

Cross another wadi and continue west along the south rim of the Jabel Barza's plateau. The landscape is a sort of white labyrinth, taken out of a fairy tale. Look for goat droppings and occasional Bedouin-laid stones for direction — it is quite easy to get lost here.

On the south there is a sheer drop towards Wadi Hurma, offering fantastic views. To the southeast, just below the horizon, there is a natural rock bridge, shaped by erosion. The wadi is called Hurma, "gateway", for this feature.

Continue westwards to reach a built passage, supported by stones and wooden beams, perched above a deep abyss dropping into Wadi Hurma. Soon afterwards descend over steep rock ledges, aided by wooden poles stuck into the sandstone. Pass another supported section and then leave the trail and ascend to the right (northwest). Reaching the summit of Jabel Barza involves inching up on steep sandstone slopes, scaling many false peaks. It takes about 70 minutes to cover the distance from the leopard trap to the summit.

Standing at the summit is like flying over a maze. Below you there are numerous white domes, surrounded by sandy valleys which are crowded with vegetation.

Once back at the leopard trap, progress south through sandy flats, studded with rocky outcrops. Pass on the right of a toadstool rock with a rock-cut Bedouin hoardplace, and proceed carefully, following occasional cairns.

The well-cairned trail into Wadi Hurma (Naqb Hurma) descends on its south bank upon a steep rocky slope. Pass through a surprising cleft, which is only half a metre wide, to reach the wadi bed within 30 minutes from the sandy flats.

After the dramatic descent, the sandy bed of Wadi Hurma is peaceful. Within 10 minutes a side wadi joins from the southeast. At its upper reaches is the sandstone bridge seen from Jabel Barza.

Pass next to some sand dunes to reach a fall within 20 minutes. Bypass the fall along the north bank through a natural, multicolored rock gallery. It takes about 30 minutes before the trail drops back into the wadi. Do not take the actual wadi bed, which consists of white narrows. Instead proceed along the north bank to reach the spring of 'Ein Meshet within 20 minutes. Plastic pipes carry water from the spring to a concrete pool and from there to a fruit grove with olives, lemons, guavas and pomegranates. This is an excellent place for camping. Ask permission to stay if there is somebody around.

Day 3
Altitude difference, Distance and Walking time: Ups and downs. 500 m ascent towards Jabel Mas'uda. 6 km to reach a dirt track and an additional 6 km along the track towards Bedouin tents. 7 hours (4 hours without the walk along the track).
Water: Water is available at 'Ein Meshet and at a small spring near

the Dark Gorge, about 90 minutes from the trailhead.

Leaving the camping site, walk south retracing your steps of the previous day, only this time inside the white narrows instead of above them. These are studded with low dry falls and potholes where you may get wet feet. To enter the narrows, bypass a white fall on the left. The narrows widen after 20 minutes.

Head south (right) towards a saddle marked by a red sandstone cliff to the east, and a gentler slope of yellowish rocks to the west. The saddle is located on a major fault running north-to-south and dictating the location of most of the springs in this area. Descend south into the wadi of the Dark Gorge to reach a little spring hemmed in by water vegetation and shallow pools, about 30 minutes from the narrows.

Climb to the south bank of the wadi, turn east (left) and progress on a rocky ledge, just above the red canyon below. After a few minutes the trail crosses a side wadi which joins from the south, and soon afterward it reaches a fork of wadis. Instead of going down into the wadi, climb a few metres to the right to another rocky ledge located above the Dark Gorge. Follow this ledge, passing resting patches of ibex (wild mountain goat). After 10 minutes the narrow gorge below you is blocked by rockslide, making it possible to cross to its north side over a bridge of boulders. Continue along a very short exposed section on the north bank towards the head of the gorge.

Descend into the gorge through low dry fall, with a pothole that may contain water. Soon afterwards there is a 5 m chimney, which can be negotiated with mutual help. The gorge less then 1 m wide and its walls tower 30 m. Darkness take over within minutes as the rocky bridge that you ju crossed blocks the sunlight for the next stretch of 50 m. Re-emergence into sunlight is a dazzling experience.

Descend a low fall straight into a pothole and then another fall of a similar height. The whole gorge walk should take about 30 minutes.

Once out of the gorge, do not continue in the wadi bed (which is impassable) but climb left (south) and head back towards the spring. Do not descend to the spring. Instead progress on the south bank for a few minutes until a little ravine descends into the main wadi. Descend with it, follow a rock-hewn aqueduct and continue through deserted agricultural terraces towards a tall acacia tree. A major confluence of wadis is reached within 15 minutes from the spring.

Turn right at the confluence, descending for about 30 minutes until a dirt track crosses the wadi. This track connects the 'Araba Valley with the highlands. Infrequent pickup trucks pass through here on their way from the village of Risha in the 'Araba Valley to the village of Dilagha, not far from the King's Highway.

Reaching Dilagha involves a 900 m ascent and a 17 km walk! Instead, you can follow the track for 3 km, ascending 500 m to reach a spur of Jabel Mas'uda with excellent views. Proceed south for another 3 km and you will probably find Bedouin who can offer you a lift. The whole walk, from the intersection between the wadi and the track to the nearest Bedouin encampment, can be covered within 3 hours.

From Dilagha it is quite easy to hitch a ride towards the King's Highway.

53. Around Rajef

Jabel Barza, Wadi Hurma, Wadi Abu el 'Uruq
Map 33

Jabel Barza is a spectacular sandstone inselberg where one may spend hours roaming among white domes and sandy valleys. The descent into Wadi Hurma is steep and dramatic, but the wadi itself is peaceful and the going is easy. The ascent back to the vicinity of Rajef is through the impressive red gorge of Wadi Abu el 'Uruq. The route passes through the Nabataean ruins of 'Ein es-Sadeh.

Type of route: Circular.
Altitude difference, Distance and Walking time: 500 m descent and ascent. Additional ups and downs, 14 km, 11 hours. Without the ascent to Jabel Barza, the route is only 8 km long and takes about 7 hours to complete.
Rating: Strenuous.
Special equipment: None.
Guides: Might help. Try asking in the village of Rajef.
Water: Water is available at 'Ein Meshet and 'Ein es-Sadeh. Consider carrying 3 liters each.
Season: Year-round. Be aware of flash flood risk, especially during the winter! Avoid walking on hot summer days.
Getting there and back: The trail starts and ends below Rajef. The village, which is located on the King's Highway, is served by a local bus from Wadi Musa. Here you need to arrange a pickup truck ride along a 3 km dirt track, which descends steeply westwards before it ends at Ras Naqb el Maiet. The vehicle should pick you up from the same spot.

Descend southwards along a little gully about 400 m east of the end of the track. It takes about 20 minutes to reach a confluence of wadis, dominated by the lofty gates of Wadi Abu el 'Uruq's gorge. Cross Wadi Abu el 'Uruq and climb southwards on the right (west) bank of a sandy wadi. Just before you reach a saddle, there is a perfectly preserved leopard trap.

From here to 'Ein Meshet, continue according to the description of Route 52 (Day 2).

Once you reach 'Ein Meshet, con-

tinue down the wadi past a hut on the left bank. After about 20 minutes veer north (right) towards a wide saddle with Nabataean ruins at its flank. On the low hill to the west is a Nabataean compound, which was probably a temple.

Descend shortly towards Wadi Tajra, turn right and proceed for 10 minutes until Wadi Abu el 'Uruq joins from the right. Continue according to the description of Route 52 (Day 2).

From the head of Wadi Abu el 'Uruq gorge retrace your steps to the track.

54. Around Rajef
Jabel Juleif, Wadi Tajra, Wadi Abu el 'Uruq
Map 33

Jabel Juleif inselberg carries bluffs of white sandstone, offering rewarding panoramas. Descending through the red canyon of Wadi Tajra you reach the foot of a sheer cliff, where the Edomite stronghold of Umm Ala is located. Further downstream lies a hidden waterfall. Ruins of a Nabataean village and an aqueduct are located at the lower reaches of the wadi near a garden of fruit trees. The ascent back to the vicinity of Rajef is through the deep red gorge of Wadi Abu el 'Uruq.

> **Type of route:** Circular.
> **Altitude difference, Distance and Walking time:** 400 m descent and ascent, 9 hours, 13 km. Not including Jabel Juleif will reduce the distance to 9 km and the walking time to 7 hours.
> **Rating:** Strenuous.
> **Special equipment:** None.
> **Guides:** Might help. Try asking in the village of Rajef.
> **Water:** Water is available at 'Ein es-Sadeh. Consider carrying 3 liters each.
> **Season:** Year-round. Be aware of flash flood risk, especially during the winter! Avoid walking on hot summer days.
> **Getting there and back:** See Route 53.

From the edge of the track go north into Wadi Tajra, following Day 1 of Route 52. Once you reach Wadi Abu el 'Uruq follow the description of Day 2 of Route 52. When the gorge of Wadi Abu el 'Uruq finally widens you arrive at a junction of wadis. Take left and immediately afterwards left again. Continue through a wide wadi for a few minutes ignoring the first gully which ascends to the north. Take left at the second smaller gully and ascend with no obvious trail. Twenty minutes will bring you to the saddle and the dirt track where you started the trail.

55. The White Narrows and the Dark Gorge
Map 33

This short route is accessible with a high-clearance vehicle. The lower reaches of Wadi Hurma consist of sandstone narrows that might hold water after flash floods. The Dark Gorge, about 200 m long, is hardly more than shoulder-wide!

Altitude difference, Distance and Walking time: ups and downs, 6 km, 4 hours.

Rating: Moderate. Expect wet shoes.

Special equipment: A 10 m hiker's rope might be handy, though you may manage without it.

Guides: Might help. Try asking the local Bedouin who dwell along the Dilagha-Risha road, or in Dilagha itself. The names 'The Dark Gorge' and 'The White Narrows' are not used by the Bedouin. Be prepared for difficulties in explaining yourself.

Water: Water is available at 'Ein Meshet. An additional spring is located near the Dark Gorge. Consider carrying 1.5 liters each.

Season: Spring is the best period, with abundant water-filled potholes, though you can really follow this route year-round. Be aware of flash flood risk, especially during the winter!

Getting there and back: To reach the trailhead you have to get to Dilagha (see map 34). The village, 7 km southwest of Rajef, is served by infrequent local buses from Wadi Musa. A taxi from Wadi Musa will cost around 8 JD. Once in Dilagha you will need to arrange a pickup truck ride for a 30-minute drive (20 km) along a half-tarred road.

Leaving Dilagha with a pickup truck, turn right just before the white building of the police station, and then left immediately afterwards. Follow the road for 13 km to a col in Jabel Mas'uda with magnificent views. From the col, descend steeply to reach Wadi el Qa' after 4 km. This is where this route ends — arrange with the driver to wait here after he drops you.

To reach the starting point continue north, cross a shoulder and after 1.5 km from Wadi el Qa', turn right to a side track. Follow the track to its end to reach the lower reaches of Wadi Hurma, a few minutes away from 'Ein Meshet. The vehicle should return and wait in Wadi el Qa'.

The gardens of 'Ein Meshet are reached by a short walk from the end of the track. From here onwards follow Day 3 of Route 52.

56. 'Ein es-Sadeh
Map 33

The presence of water in 'Ein es-Sadeh has attracted many settlers over the ages. Near the spring are ruins of a small Nabataean village with houses, temple (?) and an aqueduct. The site is located halfway between Petra and Humeima along an important caravan route. The Edomites have also left their mark in the vicinity of the spring, occupying the lofty sandstone cliff of Umm Ala. Fruit trees are cultivated today at 'Ein es-Sadeh by a family from the Sa'idiyin tribe. Near the garden there is a little canyon with a tiny, hidden waterfall.

Type of route: Circular.
Altitude difference, Distance and Walking time: 200 m ascent and descent to Umm Ala and back, 5 km, 5 hours.
Rating: Moderate.
Special equipment: None.
Guides: Not really needed. Try asking in Dilagha or along the Dilagha-Risha road.
Water: A small spring at 'Ein es-Sadeh and a small waterfall further upstream. Consider carrying 3 liters each.
Season: Year-round.
Getting there and back: The trail starts and ends 20 minutes from 'Ein es-Sadeh. Follow the track from Dilagha to Jabel Mas'uda (see 'Getting there and back' Route 55, map 34). Descending from Jabel Mas'uda the track crosses wadi el Qa', climbs over a shoulder, and after 1.5 km it branches. Take right following the side track for 1 km until it bends to the right and climbs away from the wadi.

Leaving the track follow the wadi bed for about 30 minutes to reach the confluence of Wadi Tajra and Wadi Abu el 'Uruq. On the north bank is an olive grove and the small spring 'Ein es-Sadeh. Continue straight towards narrows with rock-built Bedouin hoardplaces. The narrows can be easily bypassed on the left (north).

Above the narrows there are Nabataean terraces and a ruined aqueduct. Follow the aqueduct to reach a low fall (probably dry) which can be bypassed from the right. Climb through a second half-dry fall to reach a hidden drainpipe waterfall within minutes. This is a good spot for a refreshing shower.

Retrace your steps to the head of the narrows and climb southwards on a well-defined trail leading to Wadi Tajra's upper reaches and to Umm Ala (alternatively you can b·cktrack to the vehicle). It takes about 20 minutes to reach a col with fine views into the canyon of Wadi Tajra. The upper reaches of the canyon are packed with giant oleanders hiding a tiny stream. Proceeding upstream among red cliffs the vegetation soon disappears.

Within 20 minutes from the col a side wadi joins from the right. Follow it to reach a low saddle beneath the northern face of Umm Ala. Slipping over the saddle, descend a short way with no obvious trail. Soon the wadi gets steeper and a trail commences on its right (north) bank. Follow this trail to its apparent end 10 minutes ahead (the trail actually continues a few metres down the slope). Instead of descending to the continuation of the trail climb straight up, scrambling for 15 minutes to reach the elongate flat top of Umm Ala's cliff.

The ruins of the Edomite stronghold include walls, buildings and a bell-shaped cistern, all located at the southwestern tip of the cliff.

The view from Umm Ala takes in the deep canyon of Wadi Tajra to the north while on the west is a colorful flat terrain called el Qa'. The grayish peak of Jabel Mas'uda rises to the south.

A conical hill looms at the north-eastern side of the Umm Ala's cliff with a ruined structure at its top.

Most of it has totally collapsed, but parts of its base, including hewn and built steps, are still intact. The dramatic location of this structure suggests that it was a place of worship.

Leaving Umm Ala, backtrack towards the trail you came on. Turn right (west) and progress levelly above the wadi. It takes about 20 minutes to reach the confluence of Wadi Tajra and Wadi Abu el 'Uruq.

Just before you reach the vehicle you may explore Nabataean ruins, located on a wide saddle on the south bank of the wadi. On the hill just west of the saddle is a west-to-east oriented structure, possibly a temple. This Nabataean site was probably an important station on the route between Petra and Humeima through Wadi Sabra.

57. Across southern Edom
from Dilagha to Humeima
Maps 34, 35

The route starts on the Edom Plateau, descends to the 'Araba Valley and then ascends back to the plateau. Along the way are narrow canyons of sandstone and igneous rocks, as well as towering peaks and vast expanses of colorful desert landscape. Ras 'Athud (880 m) and Jabel Umm Asawir (1,220 m) offer spectacular views of southern Edom. At the outlet of Wadi Rakiya is a sea of red sand dunes attempting to overwhelm stubborn rocky outcrops. The route ends at the ruins of the ancient Nabataean city of Humeima (see Routes 59–60). Bear in mind that it is one of the most arid regions along the Rift Valley. Water sources are scarce and walking distances are long. It is a demanding trek. Those who endeavor will be rewarded by an unrivaled variety of landscapes.

Type of route: One-way.
Route:
    Day 1: Naqb Dilagha, Wadi Mishazza, Ras 'Athud. Camping at 'Ein Mishazza spring.
    Day 2: Wadi Quseib's canyons. Camping at 'Ein Rakiya.
    Day 3: Wadi Rakiya, Wadi Aheimir's sand dunes, Wadi Aheimir. Camping at 'Ein Aheimir.
    Day 4: Jabel Umm Asawir, Humeima.
Rating: Strenuous.
Special equipment: None.
Guides: Recommended. Try asking in the village of Dilagha.
Water: Consider carrying 4.5 liters each. Water sources are very scarce!
Season: Spring, fall and winter. Be aware of flash flood risk, especially during the winter!
Getting there and back: The trail starts at the upper reaches of the village of Dilagha (see Route 55).
Upon reaching the first houses of the village, 3 km from the King's Highway, turn right from the main road into a good dirt track. Follow the track for less then 2 km to reach a junction, which is located on a saddle. This is the trailhead.
The trail ends at the ruins of the ancient city of Humeima, 9 km away from the Amman-'Aqaba highway. To be picked up see Routes 59–60. Alternatively you can find Bedouin encampments near ancient Humeima. Negotiating a pickup truck ride to the main road should be quite easy.

Day 1
Altitude difference, Distance and Walking time: 900 m descent, 300 m ascent and descent to the summit of Ras 'Athud, additional 100 m descent to the camping site, 19 km, 9 hours.
Water: The water of 'Ein Nukheileh is salty but potable. Better water is available only at 'Ein Mishazza.

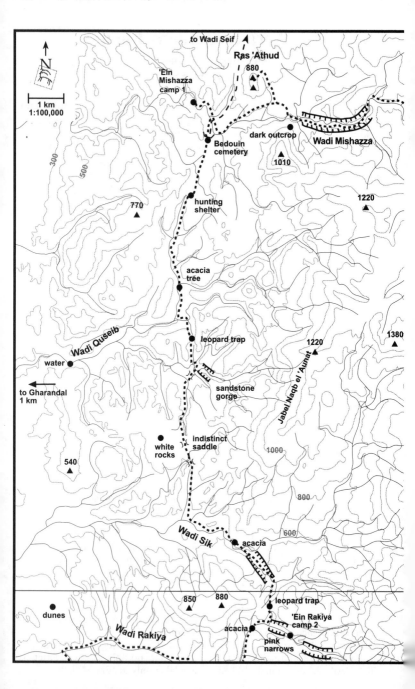

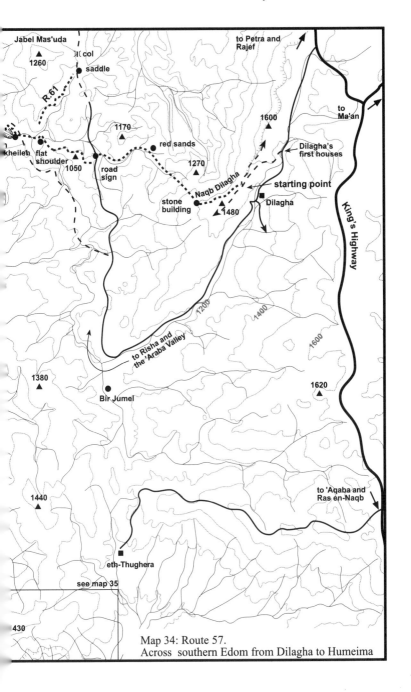

Map 34: Route 57.
Across southern Edom from Dilagha to Humeima

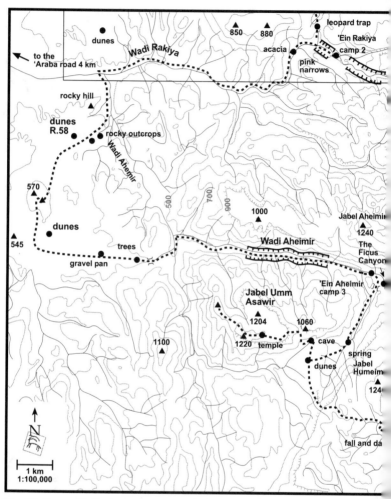

Map 35: Routes 57, 58. Across southern Edom from Dilagha to Humeima
and the sand dunes of Wadi Rakiya

Leaving the junction, head southwest along a wide camel path (Naqb Dilagha) contouring towards a low rounded knoll with a somewhat hidden pile of stones at its top. Below the path, the topography plunges with steep gradients. Jabel Mas'uda looms on the northwest, striped by yellow and black strata of limestone and flint. Further to the west and just south of the mountain are the lower reaches of Wadi Mishazza, where the proposed camping site is located nearby black peaks. To the north, the Rajef inselbergs create a maze of rounded domes.

Descend gradually through cultivated lands, past a stone building or

on the east. Continue parallel to the main wadi to reach a steep section where the wadi leaves the sandstone in which it was incised and enters a limestone environment. To bypass this section follow the stone-supported trail through vertical strata before descending back to the wadi bed. Shortly afterwards a half-tarred road crosses the wadi.

Leave the wadi and climb towards a road sign situated next to an earth ramp. The road is reached within 2 hours from the trailhead. Proceed on a sidetrack branching westwards from the road sign towards a low saddle. Leave the track at the saddle and contour northwestwards. The deep wadi below you is the upper part of Wadi Mishazza. Reaching another saddle descend north towards a flat-topped shoulder which is dotted with curious stone piles. At its north end is a little gully where a winding donkey trail descends straight to the confluence of two tributaries of Wadi Mishazza. It takes about 30 minutes to reach this confluence from the road.

Aim towards a disused dirt track, which crosses the wadi. Shortly after crossing the track the little spring of 'Ein Nukheileh appears, dripping into a limestone gorge below it. Bypass the gorge from the right. After 200 m the cliffs disappear, making it possible to descend into the lower end of the gorge upon angular scree. For the easiest descent bear eastwards as you reach the head of the scree.

Once in the wadi, walk down for about 15 minutes before a sandstone gorge develops. Its reddish-white walls draw closer together as you proceed. Pass two low dry falls and continue at ease, to reach the gorge outlet about 90 minutes away from its head.

As soon as you see a dark (igneous) outcrop on the left (south) bank, look for a faint trail, which climbs upon the opposite (north) bank. Reaching

your left. Soon, signs of agriculture disappear and the trail gets steeper, going through a series of switchbacks until the grades straighten out again, less than an hour from its head.

Cross a shallow wadi and proceed northwest along its right bank. Soon the trail crosses a side wadi, which joins from the direction of red sands some flats, proceed northwest towards a prominent mountain with two conical peaks, called by the Bedouin Ras 'Athud. To reach its summit follow goat trails along its eastern spur for about 30 minutes.

Looming some 300 m above its surroundings, the mountain offers magnificent scenery. To the northeast is the Shawbak Plateau. Beneath it is the tilted plateau of Jabel Sufaha and the impressive black mountains, Jabel Feid and Jabel Abu Mahmud. Closer, is Jabel Harun, recognizable by the white mosque at its summit. Dominating the skyline on the south is the table mountain of Jabel Umm Asawir. The village of Rajef and its inselberg landscape are seen on the east.

Descend to the base of the mountain and proceed southwards into Wadi Mishazza. Once in the wadi, walk down for about 40 minutes to reach the year-round water source of 'Ein Mishazza. Further down is a 3 m dry fall and some narrows with more water. There are plenty of fine camping sites around.

Day 2

Altitude difference, Distance and Walking time: Ups and downs, 17 km, 8 hours.
Water: 'Ein Rakiya is a perennial spring. Another spring is located off the route close to the outlet of Wadi Quseib to the 'Araba Valley. Potholes with water might be found at the upper reaches of Wadi Quseib.

Retrace your steps up the wadi for about 20 minutes, past a pebble-built fence on the south bank. Just beyond the fence, a ruined dirt track descends into the wadi near a lone acacia tree. Follow the track southwards to reach a Bedouin cemetery, seen from afar by its wooden poles that are wrapped with white rags. The graves are marked by simple headstones. The track used to connect the cemetery with nearby encampments of the Sa'idiyin tribe (Wadi Seif).

Follow a well-defined camel path stretching southwards from the cemetery to reach the watershed between tributaries of Wadi Mishazza and Wadi Quseib within 20 minutes. 200 m south of the watershed, a winding trail descends on the eastern rocky slope of a tributary of Wadi Quseib. At the head of the trail is a stone-built hunting shelter. Once in the wadi, it takes about 30 minutes of easy walking to reach the confluence with another tributary of Wadi Quseib, marked by a tall acacia tree.

Proceed south, and soon afterwards, when the wadi takes a tight bend to the west, turn left (east) into a side ravine with a small pothole. Reaching a T-junction 5 minutes later, veer south (right) along a fine camel path, climbing gently towards a saddle with a leopard trap.

Leaving the saddle descend a short way southwards, following a trail on the west bank of the wadi. Reaching a colorful sandy valley, turn left to reach the entrance of a red sandstone gorge, about 200 m ahead. Exploring the gorge is worthwhile. Backtracking to the entrance of the gorge, climb south on a donkey trail to reach a flat patch with abundant signs of campfires. Cross a shallow wadi and ascend along a clear trail towards a low saddle.

Slipping over the saddle, descend straight into the wadi to the south whose bed is a carpet of white sand and green vegetation. Within 30 minutes a side wadi joins from the left. Pass the confluence and climb left on a rocky slope with no trail. Reaching a white shoulder, head south towards another low and indistinct saddle.

Descend into the wadi to the south through a tiny gully. When the wadi veers westwards continue in the actual bed for 50 m and then climb left (south) to another white shoulder.

Leave the shoulder immediately, descending easily, but with no apparent trail, into the next wadi to the south. After 30 minutes of progress through white sand you glide into Wadi Sik.

An important dirt track once passed through Wadi Sik, connecting the oasis of Gharandal (in the 'Araba Valley) with the Edom Plateau. Nowadays the track is no longer negotiable.

Turn left (east) and continue upstream for about 40 minutes. Passing an acacia tree on the left, look for an overhang with modern Arabic inscriptions on the right. This marks the entrance into some white narrows. Turn right into the narrows towards another acacia tree. The narrows host two low dry falls which can be easily tackled with mutual help.

40 minutes later the wadi widens, and a side wadi carpeted with white sand joins from the right. Turn right, advancing along a clear trail on the right-hand side of the wadi. Shortly afterwards the trail descends into the wadi and climbs left to a hardly noticeable saddle. The pile of stones on the saddle is probably a ruined leopard trap.

Descend southwards, following a trail on the right-hand side of the wadi to reach Wadi Rakiya within 15 minutes. Turn left into pink narrows, and within ten minutes the spring of Ein Rakiya appears with its year-round puddles, surrounded by tamarisk and elecampane (*Inula*) bushes. The vicinity of the spring offers fine camping sites.

It is worthwhile to explore the sandstone gorge, which starts a few minutes above the spring. Giant boulders block the gorge about 1 hour away from the camping site.

Day 3

Altitude difference, Distance and Walking time: 23 km, 250 m descent, 900 m ascent, 9 hours.

Water: 'Ein Aheimir is the only reliable water source.

Walk down through the pink narrows passing a lone acacia tree and a Bedouin grave after 30 minutes. The wadi which joins from the left near the acacia, has a number of potholes. Wadi Rakiya widens after about 80 minutes from the camp, where a major tributary joins from the south. Bedouin encampments may be seen around.

It takes about one hour to reach the confluence of Wadi Rakiya and Wadi Aheimir, where sand dunes pile against rocky bluffs on the north bank of Wadi Rakiya.

Heading south into Wadi Aheimir, pass below a rocky hill on the right bank and continue towards some other rocky outcrops just ahead, about 30 minutes from the confluence. Aiming southwest, leave the wadi on the seam line between the dune field and the rocks. As you progress red sand dunes of exceptional beauty begin to dominate the landscape. Looking east the blend of colors is breathtaking. Silver-trunked *Haloxylon persicum* bushes dot the red sands, while black and yellow rocks dominate the horizon.

Follow the dunes for about 1 hour towards the highest rocky island to the southwest, rearing up from the red dunes. The views from its summit are spectacular. The conical double summit of Ras 'Athud is seen to the north while to the east rises the table mountain of Jabel Umm Asawir which consists of red sandstone strata, reclining horizontally upon black igneous rocks.

Just below the peak is a beautiful saddle whose southern slope consists of red sands. Leave the saddle descending southeast. Hiking through the sands, with some ups and downs, avoid the major wadi to the south. Instead ascend a short way eastwards to reach a large gravel pan. Traversing the pan bear east towards a clump of trees about 40 minutes away. Slip over a saddle and descend a short distance into a wide wadi, which joins Wadi Aheimir within 15 minutes.

Take right (east) at the confluence and proceed up along Wadi Aheimir. The run of the wadi is perfectly straight due to a west-to-east fault line. An impressive gorge is reached after 70 minutes, as the walls of the wadi draw a few metres apart. 30 minutes later water emerges and tamarisk and reed crowd the wadi. Proceed along the stream of 'Ein Aheimir, towards a *Ficus* tree which marks the entrance to a little canyon with potholes. There are plenty of level patches for camping in the vicinity of the canyon.

Day 4

Altitude difference, Distance and Walking time: 600 m ascent to Jabel Umm Asawir, 300 m descent and then another 300 m ascent, 15 km, 9 hours.
Water: Year-round water is available only in 'Ein Aheimir. Potholes with water may be found beneath the Nabataean dam of Wadi Qalkha.

Leaving the *Ficus* canyon, backtrack 100 m down Wadi Aheimir to embark on a donkey trail, which climbs to the south. Follow the trail along a white sandstone slope to reach a low saddle, crossed by a major north-to-south fault. Descend southwards into the sandy wadi to reach a fork about 40 minutes from the camping site.

Go straight (right) to arrive at a little spring. Pass a side wadi which joins from the right and ascend westwards (right) immediately afterwards. There is no trail, so simply slog up the steep slope to reach a watershed with red sand dunes. Once at the watershed bear northwest towards a prominent overhang. Bedouin from

the Jahalin tribe dwell here during most of the year. It takes about 90 minutes to reach the overhang from the *Ficus* canyon.

Skirt the cliffs westwards, cross a little wadi which descends from the north, and ascend along a fine camel path on its west bank. Reaching a saddle, climb left (west) upon a winding trail, which leads to the plateau of Jabel Umm Asawir within 40 minutes from the overhang.

Once on the plateau, proceed westwards adhering to the southern escarpment. Signs of intensive grazing are seen everywhere. Just beneath the highest area lies an ancient compound whose walls are about 1 m in height. Its east-to-west orientation suggests a temple. The views from above the 'temple' include the mountains of Humeima as well as huge flats, studded with rocky inselbergs, further to the east.

Proceed northwest to the edge of the plateau. Cross a deep saddle and ascend to a prominent top with a sheer 600 m drop on its western face. Below are the sand dunes of Wadi Rakiya in lively red hues. For the best views northwards return to the main plateau and proceed towards its northern tip. The summit of Ras 'Athud can easily be spotted.

Once back at the Bedouin overhang proceed towards the escarpment to the south following the rim of the sand dunes. It takes about half an hour to reach a junction of trails at the foot of the cliffs. Do not take the trails, which descend to the north or contour southwards. Instead, climb steeply on a not-so-obvious rocky trail. Reaching the head of the escarpment within 30 minutes you are rewarded with fine views over Jabel Umm Asawir and the wadi below.

Leaving the escarpment ascend southeast through a little wadi. Slip over a saddle and descend a short way into Wadi Qalkha. Follow the wadi to a dry fall, 40 minutes ahead. Skirt the fall on the left to reach an impressive Nabataean dam built of sandstone ashlar.

Proceeding between red walls for about 40 minutes, you emerge on the plains of Humeima. Once on the plains, bear north along a dirt track to reach the ruins of Humeima (see Routes 59–60) within 30 minutes from the outlet of the wadi.

58. The sand dunes of Wadi Rakiya
Map 35

At the outlet of Wadi Rakiya towards the 'Araba Valley lies a spectacular field of red sand dunes. Amidst the dunes rises an occasional rocky outcrop, not yet engulfed by the sands. Large silver-trunked bushes of *Haloxylon persicum* are about the only shrubs growing here.

Type of route: One-way and back.
Route: Strolling along the sand dunes of Wadi Rakiya.
Altitude difference, Distance and Walking time: About 200 m ascent and descent. 6 km or less, 4 hours.
Rating: Easy.
Special equipment: None.
Guides: Might help. Try asking in the village of Risha or Rahma.
Water: None. Consider carrying 1.5 liters each.
Season: Year-round.
Getting there and back: Leave 'Aqaba, heading north along the 'Araba road. 15 km beyond the junction to the village of Rahma, take a track going east into Wadi Rakiya. Driving along this track requires a high-clearance vehicle. Reaching a confluence of wadis after 7 km turn right to Wadi Aheimir, and drive southwards for an additional 1 km. This is the starting and the end point.

Leave the wadi and start walking to the southwest on the seam line between the dune field and the rocks. It takes about one hour along the dunes to reach the highest rocky 'island' on the southwest. See Day 3 of Route 57 for further details.

Leaving the 'island', backtrack to the vehicle.

59–60. Around Humeima
Maps 36, 37

Humeima was a remarkable Nabataean city with a sophisticated water supply system, located about halfway between Petra and 'Aqaba. This is the place to observe the famous Nabataean techniques for providing and conserving water in the desert. Among the ruins are at least 20 cisterns, and an aqueduct that was fed by two springs. Some of the water installations in Humeima are still used today by local Bedouin of the Howeitat tribe. In his account about the region, the historian Diodorus who lived during the 1st century BCE tells us:

"For in the waterless region, as it is called, they have dug wells at convenient intervals and have kept the knowledge of them hidden from the peoples of all other nations... thus they have for their use drinking water in abundance"

The city was probably founded by the Nabataean king Aretas III as early as the first century BCE. After the Roman annexation of Arabia, Humeima became a major station on the Via Nova Traiana, the great north-south highway connecting the Gulf of 'Aqaba with the city Bosra (in Syria). It remained an important garrison town into the Byzantine period. Two small churches were built here, and in the 6th century a bishop was appointed for the city. During the Early Islamic period Humeima was the residence of the 'Abbasid clan. The town took an active part in the revolt that led to the overthrow of the Umayyad caliphate.

Located beneath the escarpment of Ras en-Naqb, which rises to the north, Humeima offers a superb combination of desert landscapes. To the east and south is an extensive rolling area, stretching as far as the eye can see. Occasional inselbergs rise above the flats. To the west there are rocky uplands, ending westwards with an almost sheer drop. This is the watershed between steep wadis draining towards the 'Araba Valley and gently grading wadis leading to a sand pan south of Humeima.

The water supply system

Making their living in an arid region with a mean annual rainfall of 100 mm, the builders of Humeima had to develop a self-sufficient water system. Cisterns were hewn in the rock adjacent to catchment areas, usually at the outlet of clefts and small wadis, west of the city. Larger reservoirs were built with local stones. Most of the cisterns were roofed by slabs resting on transverse arches — a common method in Nabataean architecture.

Besides the cisterns, the city was supplied with water by an aqueduct from two faraway springs northeast of the city: the Qana Spring 14 km away, and the Jammam Spring, about 15 km away. The overall length of the aqueduct is 23 km, the longest Nabataean aqueduct discovered so far.

Getting there and back: From 'Aqaba drive north about 70 km, to reach the modern village of Humeima. Frequent local buses from 'Aqaba to Humeima are available. Taxi fare is around 10 JD. Leave the main road 1 km north of the village, near a cluster of houses and a small restaurant with a Coca Cola sign. Drive west on the side road until it ends after 11 km. From the end of the road walk westwards for about 700 m to reach the ruins of ancient Humeima. Though the road is not in good condition, a taxi driver with good will can negotiate it easily. Alternatively, you can organize a pickup truck ride in modern Humeima.

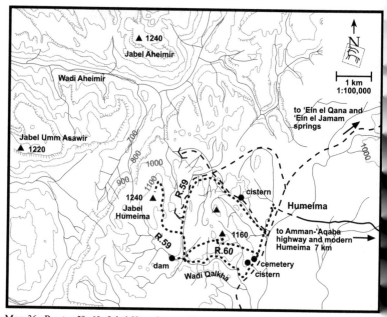

Map 36: Routes 59, 60. Jabel Humeima and Humeima from the Horn of the Gazelle

59. Jabel Humeima
through Wadi Qalkha and Wadi el Birkeh
Maps 36, 37

Jabel Humeima (1,240 m) looms almost 300 m above its surroundings, over-looking an impressive variety of landscapes. The summit is reached by a not-too-difficult scramble. Cisterns and dams near the mountain provide fine examples of Nabataean water management.

Type of route: Circular.
Altitude difference, Distance and Walking time: 300 m ascent and descent, 12 km, 7 hours.
Rating: Moderate.
Special equipment: None.
Guides: Might help. Try 'Awad Abu Muhammad or any other Bedouin, who encamp near ancient Humeima.
Season: Year-round. Avoid hot summer days.
Water: Not reliable. Consider carrying 3 liters each.
Getting there and back: The route starts and ends at ancient Humeima.

Starting the route at ancient Humeima, head south, passing a Bedouin cemetery after about 20 minutes. Just beyond the cemetery, a little rocky gully descends from the right (west) with a *Ficus* tree at its outlet. The gully houses a hewn cistern, once roofed by still-visible arches.

Proceed south, turning right into Wadi Qalkha. After about 40 minutes between red sandstone walls you reach a Nabataean dam, built of sandstone ashlar. Below the dam lies a pothole, which may contain water after seasonal floods. Climb the hewn stairs to the head of the dam, where Nabataean inscriptions are seen on the walls of the wadi. The water reservoir behind the dam is now filled with gravel. Further to the west is a series of potholes, which end with a 10 m dry fall.

Backtrack to the foot of the dam and turn north along a tributary of Wadi Qalkha. After about 500 m it is possible to climb the left bank of the wadi, using some rock slabs. Con-tinue west, crossing a low rocky shoulder which extends southwards from Jabel Humeima. Follow the sandy wadi below the west flank of the shoulder. Just before the sheer cliffs at the north end of the wadi block your way, climb back to the rocky shoulder you just crossed. Slogging up the shoulder, it takes about one hour to reach the summit of Jabel Humeima.

A huge cairn and a choice of views await you at the top. To the west the uplands of Humeima end with an abrupt escarpment. Wadi Aheimir begins its journey to the 'Araba Valley beneath this escarpment, run-ning along a major fault line parallel-ing the Rift Valley. Jabel Umm Asawir, a prominent table mountain, looms above Wadi Aheimir. Further to the west is the 'Araba Valley as well as parts of the Negev Desert in Israel. To the northeast, above the plains of Humeima, rises the Ras en-Naqb escarpment. The 'Aqaba-Am-man highway is clearly seen winding

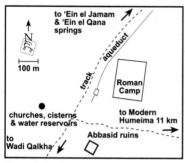

to 'Ein el Jamam
& 'Ein el Qana
springs

N

100 m

aqueduct

track

Roman
Camp

churches, cisterns
& water reservoirs

to Modern
Humeima 11 km

Abbasid ruins

to
Wadi Qalkha

Map 37: Ancient Humeima

along its steep slopes. To the east and southeast are impressive sandstone inselbergs, including Jabel Rum (1,754 m) and Jabel Umm 'Ishrin (1,753 m), the second-highest peaks in Jordan. The enormous flat area, of which Humeima is part, is drained by almost non-grading wadis that end at a sand pan near the village of Quweira.

Retrace your steps to the side wadi, which joins Wadi Qalkha in the vicinity of the dam. Turn north (left) up the wadi, to reach a saddle with a dirt track. Following the track northwards you reach a junction of tracks about 20 minutes away. Turn southeast (right) crossing a low shoulder to reach the impressive cistern of Wadi el Birkeh. The cistern, which may still contain water, is 6 by 10 m with a rock-cut stairway providing access to the water. The structure was roofed by 15 arches. From the cistern it takes about 30 minutes to reach the ruins of Humeima.

60. Humeima from the Horn of the Gazelle
Maps 36, 37

Wadi Qalkha with its splendid red walls holds an impressive Nabataean dam. A rocky knoll, called by the Bedouin of the Howeitat tribe Qarun el Ghazal (the Horn of the Gazelle), rises above the surrounding flats (1,160 m above sea level), affording a unique perspective over the ancient city and its surroundings.

Type of route: Circular.
Altitude difference, Distance and Walking time: 200 ascent and descent, 8 km, 4 hours.
Rating: Moderate.
Special equipment: None.
Guides: Not really needed. See Route 59.
Season: Year-round. Avoid walking on hot summer days.
Water: None. Consider carrying 3 liters each.
Getting there and back: The trail starts and ends in ancient Humeima.

Follow Route 59 to reach the Nabataean dam in Wadi Qalkha. From the dam, retrace your steps and turn left into the second wadi joining from the north. Within minutes veer east out of the wadi to reach a relatively flat shoulder. Proceed eastwards, crossing a few gullies while approaching the base of a prominent sandstone knoll which is called by the local Bedouin the Horn of the Gazelle (Qarun el Ghazal).

The knoll is best climbed from its southwestern flank. Scrambling up takes about 20 minutes.

The view from the hilltop includes the ruins of Humeima, surrounded by ancient agricultural terraces. From here it is possible to realize the extent of cultivation in the past. To the northeast the escarpment of Ras en-Naqb rises above the flats. Humeima's aqueduct started from the escarpment, carrying the water of two springs into the city. To the west rises Jabel Humeima with a great cairn at its peak. Numerous ridges adorn the southwest.

Retracing your steps to the bottom of the rocky knoll, walk east along the uplands to reach the flats of Humeima 15 minutes later. The ancient city itself is reached after an additional 20-minute walk.

61. From Petra to Humeima
Maps 29, 32, 33, 34, 35

This trek links Petra with the Nabataean settlement of Humeima. The views from Jabel Harun, Umm Ala, Jabel Mas'uda, Jabel Ras 'Athud and Jabel Umm Asawir are spectacular, and afford a true insight into southern Edom. The route combines ever-changing landscapes of sandstone bluffs, igneous peaks, deep canyons and rolling red dune fields as well as remote Nabataean and Edomite sites.

It is a challenging trek with long walking days and scarce water sources, but the effort is well rewarded.

Type of route: One-way.
Route:
- **Day 1:** Petra, Jabel Harun, Wadi Sabra. Camping site in Wadi Sabra.
- **Day 2:** Wadi Tibn, 'Ein es-Sadeh. Camping site in 'Ein es-Sadeh.
- **Day 3:** Jabel Mas'uda, Wadi Mishazza , Ras 'Athud. Camping site at 'Ein Mishazza.
- **Day 4:** Wadi Quseib's canyons. Camping site at 'Ein Rakiya.
- **Day 5:** Wadi Rakiya, Aheimir's sand dunes, Wadi Aheimir. Camping site at 'Ein Aheimir.
- **Day 6:** Jabel Umm Asawir, Humeima.

Rating: Strenuous. Long walking days and scarce water sources.
Special equipment: None.
Guides: Recommended. Try Muhammad en-Nimr or Muhammad Jmeidi at the village of the Badul near Petra.
Water: Consider carrying 4.5 liters each.
Season: Spring, fall and winter. Be aware of flash flood risk, especially during the winter!
Getting there and back: The route starts in Petra and ends at the ruins of Humeima. See page 211 for getting to and from Humeima.

Day 1
Maps: 29, 32.
Altitude difference, Distance and Walking time: 300 m ascent to Jabel Harun, 500 m descent to the theatre of Wadi Sabra, 12 km, 7 hours.
Water: Water is available only at the camping site in Wadi Sabra.

Follow Route 51.

Day 2
Maps: 32, 33.
Altitude difference, Distance and Walking time: 100 m descent to Wadi Tibn, 100 m ascent to a pass and 200 descent to 'Ein es-Sadeh, 10 km, 5 hours. An additional 4 hours are needed to explore the surroundings of 'Ein es-Sadeh (See Route 56).
Water: 'Ein er-Rasharish spring is about one hour away from the camping site of Wadi Sabra. 'Ein Raqi is about two hours away.

Follow Day 2 of Route 51 to 'Ein Raqi spring. Just beyond the spring, turn south into a small tributary of Wadi Tibn. Walk up the ravine to reach a pass within 40 minutes. Slipping over

H.

H.

tai Glaich

Top: Sand Dunes in Wadi Rakiya (R.57, 58, 61)
Middle: Moonscape between Wadi Quseib and Wadi Siq (R.57, 61)
Bottom: Deep canyons descending from the highlands of Humeima to the 'Araba Valley

Noya Shiloni

Avi Blum

Noya Shiloni

Top: Bedouin in Wadi Hasa
Left: Wadi Mukheiris (R.1)
Right: Hanging gardens in Wadi Karak (R.14)

Shai Reuveni

Top Left: Swimming in the gorge of Wadi el Hidan (R.10)
Top Right: Wadi el Hidan's majestic waterfall (R.12)
Bottom: The approach to Wadi Musa via Wadi Marwan (R.46)

I. H.

I. H.

Noya Shiloni

Top: View to the southeast from the summit of Jabel Rum (R.68)
Middle: Descending from Jabel Rum
Bottom: Heading back home

the pass, descend into a narrow ravine, which widens within an hour. Reaching Wadi Tajra after 1.5 hours from the pass, turn east (left) towards the nearby olive grove of 'Ein es-Sadeh.

The vicinity of the spring offers Nabataean and Edomite ruins as well as narrow canyons, looming cliffs and a tiny waterfall. It is a good place to camp. See Route 56 for details.

Day 3
Maps: 33, 34.
Altitude difference, Distance and Walking time: 500 m ascent to Jabel Mas'uda, 500 m descent to the base of Ras 'Athud, 300 m ascent and descent to the summit of Ras 'Athud, 100 m descent to the camping site, 22 km, 10 hours.
Water: Salty but potable water in 'Ein Nukheileh about 4 hours from the trailhead. Fine water in 'Ein Mishazza.

Leaving 'Ein es-Sadeh follow the wadi bed downwards for 20 minutes to reach a dirt track, stretching along the south bank of the wadi. Follow the track, paralleling the wadi for 15 minutes to reach a major track connecting the Edom Plateau with the 'Araba Valley. This track links the village of Risha with the village of Dilagha and is mostly used by Bedouin from the Sa'idiyin tribe.

Turn left (south) along the track, cross a shoulder and ascend steeply on the north flank of Jabel Mas'uda. It takes about two hours from the junction to reach a col where the track slips over to the south flank of the mountain. The views from the col are breathtaking. To the east, sandstone massifs rise steeply above a colorful rolling area. The mountains of Petra can be seen to the north as well as the prominent summit of Jabel Harun.

Proceed southwards for another 500 m to reach a saddle. Leaving the track, turn southwest (right) to embark on a winding donkey path on the west bank of the descending wadi.

It takes about an hour from the saddle to reach the bed of Wadi Mishazza. Soon afterwards a badly worn track crosses the wadi. The spring of 'Ein Nukheileh is a few minutes ahead. Continue according to Route 57.

Day 4–6
Maps: 34, 35.

Follow Route 57.

62. Wadi Khubat
Map 38

Carved into colorful rock formations, Wadi Khubat offers a tiny stream and a string of potholes, which may provide sparkling pools during springtime. A small copper mine, probably from the Roman period, can be easily reached as a side trip from the wadi.

Type of route: One-way.
Altitude difference, Distance and Walking time: 900 m descent, 16 km to the outlet of the wadi, additional 5 km to the village of Rahma, 10 hours, including the side trip to the mining cave.
Rating: Moderate.
Special equipment: None.
Guides: Might help. Try asking for Hussein Abu Ruweis at the village of Quweira or Muhammad and Hassan Hamed en-Najadat.
Water: The little stream of Wadi Khubat is reached within an hour's walk. Seeps in the wadi bed can be found 7 hours away from the trailhead. Consider carrying 3 liters each.
Season: Spring, fall and winter. Be aware of flash flood risk, especially during winter!
Getting there and back: The trail starts about 13 km northwest of the village of Quweira. To reach the village from 'Aqaba take a taxi for about 8 JD, or use one of the local buses. Once in Quweira you have to organize a pickup truck. The track to the trailhead branches from the 'Aqaba-Amman highway about 3 km north of Quweira's last houses. Ask the driver to head towards Ras Naqb Nukheileh (the head of a well-known camel path). Two km south of Ras Naqb Nukheileh, a side track branches to the west. Within a few hundred metres the track ends above a steep escarpment which marks the head of this route.
On your west is an area of white sandstone domes, and a yellowish hogback can be seen to the south. Behind this hogback and unseen from the trailhead stretches a flat area with cultivated land, called es-Safra.
The trail ends at the outlet of Wadi Khubat whose lower reaches are called Wadi Turban. A 5 km dirt track connects the outlet of the wadi with the village of Rahma (50 km north of 'Aqaba).

Leaving the end of the track descend southwest into a white, rocky gully. There is no clear trail so pick a route along the bare rocks. Once in the gully, descend easily for 40 minutes to reach a deep east-to-west canyon.

Contour eastwards above the cliffs of the canyon, until it is possible to descend into its bed. Bouldering your way amidst red sandstone walls, ne-gotiate some tricky passages to reach Wadi Khubat within 40 minutes. Just before the confluence adhere to the left bank to skirt some giant boulders.

A brush of *Ficus* trees, tamarisk and sugarcane adorns the confluence where igneous rocks appear for the first time and a tiny stream issues. Turning east (left), walk upstream for a few minutes to reach a jungle of Euphrates poplar, oleander, reed and willow as well as some grapevines, pomegranates and figs — remnants of an abandoned orchard.

Backtracking to the confluence, continue down the wadi. Within minutes the stream dries out and a dry fall blocks your way. Bypass it on the left. Once back in the wadi bed ascend a short way to enjoy a dip in a pothole at the foot of the fall. After about an hour of many little potholes and dry falls the wadi widens.

Pass a major wadi joining from the right and continue towards a second confluence, reached within 90 minutes from the end of the pothole string. The wadi, which joins from the east (right), leads to an ancient copper mining cave, called by the Bedouin Mgharat el Ghula.

Should you decide to visit the cave, head eastwards amidst sheer red walls. 30 minutes away from the fork the canyon widens and a tiny gully joins from the right. The cave is located on the western wall of this gully, about 20 m above its bed. Chisel marks and specks of green copper ore are seen on its walls. Though the cave is only a few metres deep it is said to accommodate an evil monster, half-female, half-donkey, which feeds on human males. This feminine monster is aptly called by the Bedouin 'Ghula'.

Leaving the cave, backtrack to the confluence with Wadi Khubat. Soon the sandy character of the wadi changes and igneous rocks reappear. Descend a low dry fall to reach the head of a second higher fall. To bypass it, ascend a short way to the right towards a flat shoulder. Proceed southwards for 100 m to reach a cairned saddle. Short of descending through the saddle, go left (east) to the edge of the shoulder, where a steep gully of loose scree descends back into Wadi Khubat. The descent is rough but takes only minutes.

Turn left and ascend a short way, passing below two stone-built hunting shelters positioned on the south bank. Climb above a boulder to reach a small pothole with maidenhair fern, orchid, and elecampane (*Inula*) bushes.

Backtracking to the base of the scree proceed down the wadi, passing a clump of palm trees within 20 minutes. The narrows of Sid Mulesa ("the smooth gorge") are reached after another 40 minutes. At the head of the narrows are shallow water seeps, dug in the gravel by the Bedouin.

It takes several minutes to clear the narrows by sliding down on one's bottom. Soon afterwards, Wadi Sha'alan joins from the south.

The outlet of Wadi Khubat to the 'Araba Valley is 50 minutes ahead. If you have not arranged to be picked up, follow the dirt track southwards to reach Rahma village within an hour from the outlet.

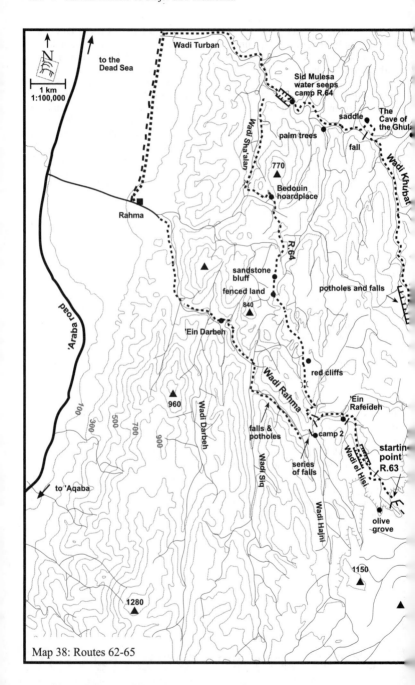

Map 38: Routes 62-65

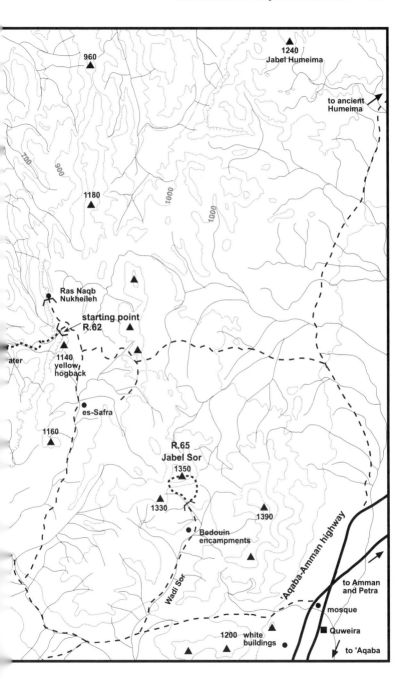

960

1240
Jabel Humeima

to ancient
Humeima

700

900

1180

1000

1000

Ras Naqb
Nukheileh

starting point
R.62

ater

1140
yellow
hogback

es-Safra

1160

R.65
Jabel Sor
1350

1330

1390

Bedouin
encampments

Wadi Sor

Aqaba-Amman highway

to Amman
and Petra

mosque

Quweira

1200 white
buildings

to 'Aqaba

63. Wadi Rahma
Map 38

Breaching a sheer wall of black rocks, Wadi Rahma descends through a spectacular serious of dry falls and giant potholes, often holding water long after the rains. Its major tributaries descend from south to north, directed by faults paralleling the Rift. The wadi terminates in a mud pan in the 'Araba Valley without reaching the Gulf of 'Aqaba. At its outlet is the village of Rahma.

Type of route: One-way.

Altitude difference, Distance and Walking time: 900 m descent, 14 km (10 km if you arrange to be picked up), 10 hours (3 hours to the first fall. 3 hours from the bottom of the third fall to the village of Rahma).

Rating: Moderate. **Abseiling is unavoidable.** The route may include swimming across water-filled potholes.

Falls: Three dry falls which require abseiling.

Special equipment: Two 50 m ropes and ordinary abseiling gear. A waterproof bag might be useful.

Guides: Might help. See Route 62.

Water: The tiny spring of 'Ein Rafeideh is about 90 minutes from the trailhead. Seasonal ponds in potholes. A little stream issues at the spring of 'Ein Darbeh, about 2 hours before the end of the trail. Consider carrying 3 liters each.

Season: Spring is the best period. Fall is also fine but the potholes may be dry or contain foul water.

Getting there and back: The trail starts about 11 km west of the village of Quweira. To reach the village from 'Aqaba take a taxi for about 8 JD, or use one of the local buses. Once in Quweira you have to organize a pickup truck.

The track to the trailhead branches from the 'Aqaba-Amman highway near Quweira's northern houses, just opposite the mosque. Leaving the highway, head west towards a prominent low hill, which rises amidst two high ranges. Proceed in the same direction before veering northwest about 8 km from the road, where the northern range ends. Proceed through a rolling area for an additional 4 km to reach the rim of the escarpment. The trail starts about 1 km northeast of a small olive grove (Umm ed-Dughara) located at the head of a tributary of Wadi Rahma, known as Wadi el Hisi (and also as the wadi of 'Ein Rafeideh).

The trail ends at the village of Rahma in the 'Araba Valley. High-clearance vehicles can drive up the lower part of the wadi and thus save you an unnecessary 4 km walk.

Leaving the elevated plateau, descend northwest into Wadi el Hisi upon a rocky slope with no obvious trail. The wadi floor is reached within 10 minutes. Bypass a dry fall from the left 10 minutes later and descend into a red sandstone canyon with *Ficus* trees and potholes. It takes about 6(

minutes to reach another fall, which plunges into a gorge.

Bypass the fall on the right and descend to a junction of wadis. Before proceeding further down turn left and back into the gorge, whose entrance is marked by a lone palm tree and a little spring called 'Ein Rafeideh. The gorge is an excellent place for rest, offering a sandy floor, pink vertical walls, plenty of shade and, in season, a large pond.

Leaving the spring you enter a granite environment and within 40 minutes the wadi is blocked by a dry fall.

Fall 1: 30 m high, with a 10 m pothole at its bottom. Crossing the pothole may require swimming.

Below the fall, the gorge runs north-south for a while before it changes direction dramatically and breaks through a narrow cleft. Below the cleft is a savage canyon with dry falls and potholes. For some superb views, climb to the narrow spur just left of the cleft.

Fall 2: 40 m.

Fall 3: 40 m. With a 15 m pothole at its bottom. Usually it holds water and must be crossed by swimming. The pond is surrounded by tamarisk, reeds and mint bushes. The only natural anchor is a tamarisk tree, 10 m back of the abseiling point.

Bypass a 4 m fall from the right, passing through a few more potholes before a side wadi joins from the left and the main wadi widens. Another series of easily negotiable dry falls and potholes begins 30 minutes later. Soon afterwards Wadi Siq joins from the left.

Some 40 minutes later, the granite walls of the wadi draw closer, and a small stream ('Ein Darbeh) appears, sparkling among mint bushes. Reaching a small dam and a cluster of palm trees the stream soon dries out. The confluence with Wadi Darbeh is a few minutes ahead.

If you have not arranged to be picked up from the confluence, continue for 75 minutes (4 km) to reach the village of Rahma.

64. From Wadi Khubat to Wadi Rahma
Map 38

A three-day route, linking the two canyons of Wadi Khubat and Wadi
Rahma through a mountainous trail with wide-open views.

> **Type of route:** One-way.
> **Route:**
>> **Day 1:** Wadi Khubat. Camping site above the narrows of Sid
>> Mulesa.
>> **Day 2:** Wadi Sha'alan to Wadi Rahma. Camping site above the
>> second fall of Wadi Rahma.
>> **Day 3:** Wadi Rahma to the village of Rahma.
>
> **Rating:** Strenuous. **Abseiling is unavoidable.** The route includes
> crossing water-filled potholes by swimming.
> **Special equipment:** Two 50 m ropes and ordinary abseiling gear. A
> waterproof bag might be useful.
> **Guides:** Might help. See Route 62.
> **Water:** Consider carrying 4.5 liters each. One of the suggested
> camping sites has no reliable nearby water source.
> **Season:** Spring is the best period. Fall is also fine but the potholes
> are usually dry.
> **Getting there and back:** The trail starts at the head of Wadi Khubat
> (see Route 62). The trail ends at the village Rahma (see Route 63).

Day 1
**Altitude difference, Distance and
Walking time:** 800 m descent, 12 km,
8 hours.
Falls: Abseiling is not required.
Water: The little stream of Wadi
Khubat is reached within 90 minutes
from the trailhead, but it soon dries
out. There are water seeps at the
suggested camping site.

Follow Route 62 through Wadi Khubat. Water is available above the narrows of Sid Mulesa.

Day 2
**Altitude difference, Distance and
Walking time:** 600 m ascent, 10 km, 5
hours.
Falls: None.
Water: No perennial water source. Fill
up before leaving Sid Mulesa! Potholes and a seasonal spring are found
near the camping site.

Leaving Sid Mulesa by sliding down
its narrows, you reach the confluence
with Wadi Sha'alan within 30 minutes. Turn south (left), ascending
through numerous acacia trees to
reach a saddle within an hour. Leaving the saddle, bear southwest, contouring along the contact between the
igneous rocks and the sandstone.
Skirt a side wadi which descends
from the north, to arrive at a rock-
built Bedouin hoardplace.

Ascend to the southeast through a
series of switchbacks to reach a wide
shoulder. Once on the shoulder, the
views open up. Proceeding along the
crest of the shoulder, cross a saddle
and ascend towards a prominent
sandstone bluff about 1 hour from
the saddle of Wadi Sha'alan. Continue past another saddle with fenced
agricultural land, now abandoned.
Leave the saddle, bearing southeast
along the crest towards an elongate

red sandstone cliff, stretching from north to south. Reaching the red cliffs in about half an hour, proceed south past a number of caves.

Another saddle is reached after 20 minutes along the red cliff. Descend south to a junction of three wadis which drain into Wadi Rahma. Once at the junction, climb a short way on the west bank, heading south towards a low col in order to bypass a dry fall. Slipping over the col, follow the stony gully back to the wadi bed. There is no trail but the scree is manageable. The proposed camping site is 200 m ahead, above a dry fall (see Route 63, Fall 2). There are two giant potholes nearby. If water is not available, abseil to the potholes below and camp there.

Day 3
Altitude difference, Distance and Walking time: 500 m descent, 10 km or 7 km if you have arranged to be picked up, 7 hours (3 hours from the bottom of the third fall to the village).
Falls: Three dry falls. The route starts below Fall 1. Falls 2 and 3 must be abseiled.
Water: Seasonal water-filled potholes. A small year-round stream called 'Ein Darbeh is located about 90 minutes from the end of the trail.

Follow Route 63.

The Ship of the Desert

No animal symbolizes the desert and its nomadic inhabitants more than the camel. Being highly adapted to desert conditions, the camel can go for more than a week without drinking and still carry loads!

Several physiological and behavioral traits help the camel to conserve its water. Its body temperature fluctuates between 35^0 and 41^0 degrees centigrade. By sustaining an elevated body temperature the camel reduces the need for perspiration and thus can save about 5 liters a day. Camel dung is very dry, and contains only 40% water, as compared to 80% in most other mammals. It is often used by Bedouin as fuel for fire. Camel urine is concentrated and in its stomach are bacteria, which can break down urea as a substitute for urination. Most of the camel's fat is concentrated in his hump (up to 40 kg). This leaves his body with only a thin layer of fat, which enables efficient cooling by radiation. Upon reaching a water source, a thirsty camel can drink more then 100 liters (20% percent of its body weight) in less than ten minutes!

65. Jabel Sor
Map 38

The table mountain of Jabel Sor (1,350 m) rises 400 m above the surrounding plains. It is focally positioned between the inselbergs of Wadi Rum, the flats of Humeima, and the rugged escarpment of the 'Araba Valley. The view from its summit is highly rewarding.

Type of route: One-way and back or circular.
Altitude difference, Distance and Walking time: 250 m ascent and descent, 2 km, 3 hours.
Rating: Easy, with a steep ascent and descent.
Guides: Not really needed. Ask the Bedouin at the encampment in Wadi Sor.
Special equipment: None.
Water: None. Consider carrying 1.5 liters each.
Season: Year-round.
Getting there and back: The trail starts west of the village of Quweira at the small Bedouin encampment of Wadi Sor. To reach Quweira from 'Aqaba take a taxi for about 8 JD or use one of the local buses. Once in Quweira you need to organize a pickup truck.
The track to the trailhead branches from the 'Aqaba-Amman highway near Quweira's northern houses, just opposite the mosque. Leaving the highway, head west towards a prominent low hill, which rises amidst two high ranges. Proceed in the same direction before turning north to Wadi Sor about 5 km from the road. Reaching the Bedouin encampment of Wadi Sor after 3 km, pass its northernmost tents and turn left into a side wadi where the track ends. The trail starts and ends here.

Leaving the end of the track, climb northeast to reach the crest of a wide spur. Veer northwest along the crest and continue straight all the way to the summit. The ascent takes about an hour.

The views from the top include vast expanses of rolling terrain to the north, ending abruptly beneath the escarpment of Ras en-Naqb. These flats drain southwards to an enormous sand pan. The 'Aqaba-Amman highway crosses the flats from south to north before scaling the escarpment of Ras en-Naqb. Along the road is the settlement of New Humeima and further to the north is the village of Dabet Hanut. The Nabataean ruins of Humeima are located a few km west of the modern village, on the eastern edge of the rocky uplands. West of ancient Humeima rises the prominent Jabel Humeima with its red cliffs (see Route 59). Further to the west is the table mountain of Jabel Umm Asawir. To the east and southeast stretches the colorful inselberg terrain of Wadi Rum where Jabel Rum and Jabel Umm 'Ishrin tower above the sand flats. To the south are numerous granite ranges. Among those is Jabel Baqer (see Route 66).

You can retrace your steps to the trailhead or take an alternative route to the foot of the mountain by heading southwest towards a prominent saddle. Reaching the saddle involves scrambling down a rocky slope with some vertical rock ledges and no real trail. From the saddle, the trail into the wadi and then onward to the end point is quite easy.

The mountains of 'Aqaba
From Wadi Rahma to the Gulf of 'Aqaba

Driving south along the 'Araba Valley from Rahma to 'Aqaba, lofty granite mountains rise up from the plains. Their jagged peaks reach almost 1,600 m, more than 1,000 m above the valley flats. Jabel Baqer is the highest peak in the region, (1,590 m) offering spectacular views towards the Gulf of 'Aqaba, the mountains of Eilat, the Sinai Peninsula and the 'Araba Valley.

The sandstone, so common north of Wadi Rahma, has totally disappeared, leaving the landscape to the hegemony of igneous rocks. As there is no sandstone cover above the igneous rocks, the seepage of rainwater is scarce and as a result springs are very rare. The topography of this granite massif combined with the lack of water sources makes long explorations through this region quite difficult.

The chief town in the region is 'Aqaba, with more than 80,000 inhabitants and many tourist facilities. The city is Jordan's only port and a resort for Jordanians and foreigners alike. The rich tropical marine life of the Red Sea attracts divers from all over the world.

Only one route is suggested in this region, but many of its prominent peaks look promising.

Route	Days	Rating	Season	Description
66. Jabel Baqer	1 (6 hours)	moderate	all-year	Splendid views over the Gulf of Aqaba, granite croppings.

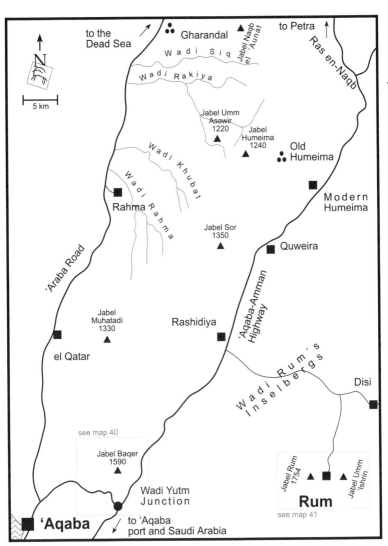

Map 39: The mountains of 'Aqaba — from Wadi Rahma to the Gulf of 'Aqaba, and Wadi Rum

66. Jabel Baqer
Map 40

"Nothing could be more beautiful than the Gulf of 'Aqaba, gleaming through its fringe of palm-trees, as we left the fort, like a placid lake - an eye, rather, of the deepest blue, eye-lashed with palms, and eye-lidded with the Arabian mountains." (Lord Lindsay, 1837)

For magnificent views over the Gulf of 'Aqaba and the 'Araba Valley, no other peak in the area can compete with Jabel Baqer. Towering to 1590 m, this lofty granite mountain overlooks Jordan, Egypt, Saudi Arabia and Israel.

Type of route: One-way and back.
Altitude difference, Distance and Walking time: 700 m ascent and descent, 6 km, 6 hours.
Rating: Moderate.
Special equipment: None.
Guides: Might help. Try the Bedouin who encamp at the entrance to Wadi Mizfar.
Water: None. Consider carrying 3 liters each.
Season: Year-round. Avoid hot summer days. Visibility is usually at its best straight after a rainy day.
Getting there and back: A high-clearance vehicle is needed in order to approach the mountain. You can find a pickup truck in 'Aqaba (in the fruit market), Quweira or Rashidiya depending on the direction you are coming from. The approach to the mountain starts at Wadi Mizfar, which is crossed by the Amman-'Aqaba road 8 km north of Wadi Yutm junction and 19 km south of the junction to Wadi Rum. (About 1 km south of Wadi Mizfar is the resthouse el Istiraha el Faranciya, used mostly by truck drivers)
Turn west toward white buildings on the north bank of Wadi Mizfar. Passing the buildings, descend into the actual bed and continue west to reach a fork, 4 km from the road. Take left at the fork towards a tin hut built on a concrete base. Make arrangements to be picked up from the same place.

Leaving the tin hut climb south along a side wadi, which leads towards the obvious saddle of Jabel Baqer. Within about 30 minutes, a cluster of palm trees is seen to the left. Above the palms is a deserted agricultural terrace, where pomegranate and grapevine were once cultivated. Another 40 minutes will take you to the saddle (1,280 m), from where you see the railroad to 'Aqaba winding through Wadi Yutm. The pile of stones is probably a ruined leopard trap.

To reach the summit, adhere to the north face of the mountain, slogging over granite croppings without a clear trail. Along the way are many resting patches of ibex, as well as a few juniper trees, which manage to thrive between the pink boulders. The summit is reached within about 45 minutes from the saddle. Should you fancy spending the night at the mountain top, it offers a few level patches, beside a spectacular panorama of views.

Three neighboring countries are seen from the summit: Saudi Arabia far to the south, Egypt to the southwest and Israel to the west. The 'Araba Valley and the Gulf of 'Aqaba yawn at your feet. 'Aqaba and its twin city Eilat share the northern tip of the Gulf. The most prominent among the mountains of Eilat is Mount Solomon, which rises darkly just behind the city. Further to the north is the flat-topped Mount Timna', similarly hued, looming above its ancient copper valley. The equivalent mines in Jordan are located 105 km to the north at Feinan (Route 38). The difference in latitudes is the result of the tectonic displacement along the Dead Sea Rift.

Toward the southwest, one can follow the coastline of the Sinai Peninsula, with a string of world-famous diving resorts. The mountains of Sinai rise almost straight from the shore, towering to the highest altitudes at the southwestern horizon. Visibility permitting, it may be possible to identify Jabel Katharina (2,644 m) the highest peak in Sinai, and in the entire region.

The landscape to the south is dominated by countless granite peaks, veined through by dykes. On the east, behind a dark ridge, rise Jabel Rum (1,754 m) and Jabel Umm 'Ishrin (1,753 m). These summits are the second highest in Jordan. North of these stretches a vast flat area, which ends at the escarpment of Ras en-Naqb.

Retrace your steps to the foot of the mountain. The way back takes about two hours.

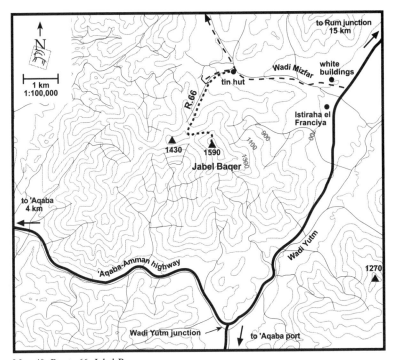

Map 40: Route 66. Jabel Baqer

Wadi Rum

"Our little caravan grew self-conscious and fell dead quiet, afraid and ashamed to flaunt its smallness in the presence of the stupendous hills. Landscapes, in childhood's dream, were so vast and silent." (T. E. Lawrence, The Seven Pillars of Wisdom)

Set back and eastward from the margins of the Dead Sea Rift, this majestic region is dominated by Jordan's loftiest sandstone mountains. Its inselbergs rise 800 m above the surrounding sand flats with vertical cliffs of more than 200 m and an enchanting array of colors. The wide valleys between the inselbergs are a terrain for 4-wheel-drive vehicles, while trekking, wandering, climbing or scrambling on the inselbergs themselves offer rock labyrinths and breathtaking views.

Rum is the name of a wide valley, and a small village of the Howeitat Bedouin, lying at the foot of Jabel Rum and Jabel Umm 'Ishrin. Nowadays the name is widely used to describe the whole inselberg region.

The vast pasturelands of Rum, combined with its several tiny perennial springs, have drawn human attention through the ages. Ancient rock inscriptions, mostly attributed to Thamudic tribes from the deserts of Arabia, are seen on many rock outcrops, with drawings of camels, ibex and hunting scenes. Caravan routes from northern Arabia to the interior of Jordan and Syria passed through the area of Rum, and the Nabataean goddess Allat had her temple hereabouts.

Rum came into latter-day fame as the setting for the movie "Lawrence of Arabia". T. E. Lawrence passed through the region in 1916, the time of the "Great Arab Revolt", and was deeply impressed by its natural beauty. Today, the area draws increasing attention ever since its climbing and trekking possibilities were explored and described by the British climber Tony Howard (see recommended guidebooks).

A small resthouse with a restaurant, as well as a camping compound equipped with tents, showers and a souvenir shop, operate in the village of Rum. The local Bedouin provide jeep tours and guides. The village has a few basic grocery stores. Entrance to the area of Rum costs 1 JD.

Several other Bedouin-operated campsites can be found in the region of Rum, not to mention the excellent option of sleeping under the stars.

Getting there and back: There is an early morning bus (6:30) from Petra to Rum and sometimes also a second bus around noon. Two daily buses depart from 'Aqaba at similar hours. A taxi from 'Aqaba to Rum costs around 12 JD. It takes about 90 minutes to reach Rum from Petra as well as from 'Aqaba.

The following routes are suggested in Wadi Rum:

Route	Days	Rating	Season	Description
67. Across Jabel Umm 'Ishrin	1 (3 hours)	moderate	all-year	Gallery of red sandstone, sand dunes.
68. To the summit of Jabel Rum	1 (10 hours)	strenuous	all-year	Majestic summit, spectacular views.

67. Across Jabel Umm 'Ishrin
through Raqabat Umm Ejil
Map 41

This short route crosses Jabel Umm 'Ishrin from west to east through an amazing gallery of red sandstone. Be prepared to scramble upon rock slopes as well as to traverse an exposed rock ledge. At the outlet of the canyon of Raqabat Umm Ejil you may see some of the most impressive sand dunes of the Rum region.

Type of route: One-way, One-way and back or Circular.
Altitude difference, Distance and Walking time: 200 m ascent and descent, 3 km, 3 hours for one-way.
Rating: Moderate. Route-finding may be difficult!
Special equipment: None.
Guides: Might help. Inquire at the resthouse.
Water: None. Consider carrying 3 liters each.
Season: Year-round.
Getting there and back: The trail starts at the Rum resthouse and ends at the outlet of Wadi Raqabat Umm Ejil towards Wadi Umm 'Ishrin. You can easily arrange to be picked up at the end of the route. Alternatively, you can backtrack to the resthouse or skirt the southern tip of Jabel Umm 'Ishrin, reaching the resthouse in 2 hours of unhurried walk.

Leaving the resthouse, head straight east towards a cluster of vegetation at the mouth of a prominent canyon. Just south of this cluster pick out a goat trail, which climbs on stable scree towards a cleft in a 2 m sandstone cliff within 30 minutes from the resthouse. Relatively flat terrain is reached just above the cleft. Continue a short way (100 m) southeastward before descending into the wadi on your left. Proceed in the actual wadi bed for 100 m, keeping an eye out for cairns which mark a bypass on the left (east) bank. Should you miss the bypass your way will soon be barred anyway by a dry fall.

Climb some steep rock slabs, following several marked arrows. About 30 m above the wadi bed follow an exposed rock ledge and descend back into the wadi shortly afterwards.

Once in the wadi, climb through a 2 m dry fall to reach a junction immediately afterwards. Go left arriving at a T-junction where you should bear right. Veer left 5 m later, ascending a short way upon a talus slope, which leads to a col within 90 minutes from the resthouse.

Descend the scree, crossing a steep rock ledge to reach a junction of wadis. Turn right adhering to the left side of the wadi bed until a prominent cairn marks a 2 m ascent on your right and then an easy descent through a graded dry fall. Go under a giant boulder and within minutes, magnificent red dunes come into sight. The vehicle should be waiting beyond the dunes. Otherwise backtrack or skirt the southern tip of Jabel Umm 'Ishrin to reach the resthouse within 2 hours.

68. To the summit of Jabel Rum
Map 41

If you could climb only one summit in Jordan, Jabel Rum should be it! Rising to 1,754 m it majestically overlooks a sea of sand, dotted by colorful inselbergs. Climbing up through a red gorge you gain altitude on an exposed rock ledge among awe-inspiring junipers. This narrow ledge finally emerges into a spectacular kingdom of white sandstone knolls, not before it makes you negotiate a few perched chimneys. Be prepared for steep gradients as well as for route-finding difficulties. Scaling the summit is a demanding trek, which can almost be considered a technical climb. **Do not attempt it without a professional guide, unless you have well-tried mountaineering experience!**

Type of route: One-way and back.
Altitude difference, Distance and Walking time: 600 m ascent and descent, 6 km, 10 hours (4 hours up, 4 hours down and 2 hours at the summit).
Rating: Strenuous. Exposed rock ledges and chimneys.
Special equipment: Two 30 m ropes and climbing gear are recommended.
Guides: Recommended. Inquire at the resthouse.
Water: During springtime water-filled potholes may be found beneath the summit.
Season: Year-round. Consider carrying 3 liters each. Do not climb the mountain on hot summer days. Be aware of flash flood risk, especially during winter!
Getting there and back: The trail starts and ends at the foot of Jabel Rumman, 9 km away from Rum resthouse. To reach the place, skirt the southern tip of the Jabel Rum massif using a 4 WD vehicle. The starting point is marked by a not-so-obvious boulder with an arrow mark, at the north bank of a vegetated wadi. Make arrangements to be picked up at the end of the day.

Follow the cairns and a few marked arrows up stable scree with no obvious trail. Reaching the contact between the igneous rocks and the red sandstone within 50 minutes, veer right (east) to reach the head of a wadi, which descends southwards.

Straight ahead (east) is the mouth of an impressive gorge leading toward the summit. To reach it, cross the wadi below and contour on its opposite bank adhering to the level of a prominent cave. Once in the gorge, advance among giant boulders with occasional cairns marking the way.

Within 40 minutes the grades diminish and a sandy section covered with desert broom commences. The way is soon barred by a graded, red dry fall.

To reach the head of the fall climb steeply through its right side. Looking south and upwards you have to spot a narrow ledge perched some 70 m above the wadi bed and gradually ascending towards the head of the gorge.

Reaching the ledge involves climbing over steep rock slabs. The trick is to bear up and west, backtracking horizontally about 50 m as you gain

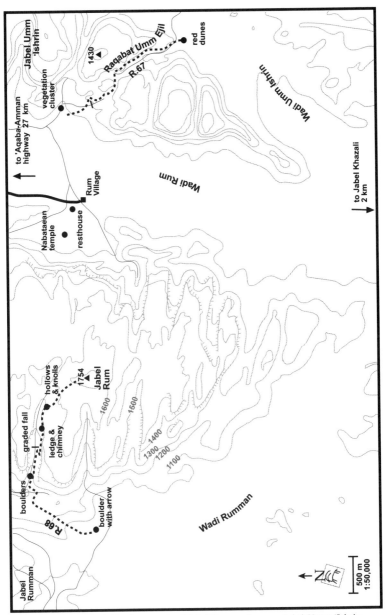

Map 41: Routes 67, 68. To the summit of Jabel Rum and across Jabel Umm 'Ishrin

altitude. Once on the ledge, head eastwards with extra caution — the ledge is narrow and exposed! Advancing among ancient junipers, which erupt from the red cliffs, your first serious barrier is a 5 m chimney. Ropes and climbing gear might be needed to negotiate it.

Reaching a second chimney you go under some boulders before climbing another rock slab leading to the last juniper on the ledge. Within minutes you emerge into a little white hollow which marks the beginning of a kingdom of white sandstone knolls. To your left is a small, hidden pothole. A small party may take about an hour to reach this spot from the graded fall.

Go straight (east) through a tiny gully with a juniper tree before veering 180^0 (west) to acquire a narrow ledge leading to a second higher hollow. Proceeding east through an impressive cleft, which is less than 1 m wide, you soon reach a third hollow.

Slog up the steep slope, which ascends eastwards. Its grades might look impossible, but the friction between the sandstone and your shoes makes the ascent easier than it seems. Proceeding along this shoulder you arrive at another chimney. Bearing south (right) at its head you are still facing a few steep ups and downs to and from hollows and knolls. Though the real summit is still obscured, the general direction is due south. Follow the cairns carefully to save frustrating encounters with impossible clefts! The whole climb from the head of the ledge to the summit takes about 90 minutes.

Once at the summit you are encircled by extraordinary spectacles of sands and cliffs. To the east is Jabel Umm 'Ishrin. To the south lies the Khazali Massif, and numerous ranges near the border with Saudi Arabia. To the west are the flats of Quweira, and further away, across the Rift Valley, the Mountains of Eilat. The north is dominated by the escarpment of Ras en-Naqb and the mountains of Humeima.

Retracing your steps to the foot of the mountain takes about 4 hours.

Glossary

Abseiling moving down along a vertical rock face with the aid of ropes and special equipment. Also called rappelling.

Bluff a cliff or hill with a broad steep face.

Cascades rapids and waterfalls lower than 2 m.

Canyon a steep-sided valley.

Col a narrow depression or pass in the crest of a ridge.

Dyke a narrow, elongate body of igneous rock.

Exposed a trail which passes very close to a vertical drop, as on a narrow ledge.

Falls a fall is a vertical drop in the wadi bed. There are dry falls and waterfalls.

Gorge an especially narrow section along a canyon.

Gully a small valley down a slope.

Hoardplace a cave, niche or overhang, closed by masonry to serve as a hoarding place for Bedouin belongings which are not needed during wandering.

Igneous rock a rock which solidified from magma, for example granite or basalt.

Inselberg an insular mountain rising from a plain.

Knoll a small rounded hill.

Ledge a rock shelf edged by a vertical drop.

Leopard trap a shallow elongate chamber of stones usually positioned at a saddle, designed to hold bait and to pin down big predators such as wolf or leopard (see page 36).

Narrows a short narrow section along a canyon.

Pan a low-lying undrained area containing mud, sand, water or mineral salts.

Perennial year-round, all-year.

Potable water water which is suitable for drinking.

Pothole a rounded depression scoured out in a rocky wadi bed especially beneath waterfalls and dry falls. Potholes may contain seasonal ponds in winter and spring. In the summer they are either dry or contain foul water. Flash floods may fill a pothole with gravel.

Ravine a little steep-sided valley.

Saddle a wide depression on the crest of a ridge between two higher elevations.

Scree stones and rocks draped steeply against a slope. Also called talus slope.

Shoulder 1. a step-like change in the contour.
2. a low spur.

Slabs small stair-like rock shelves which can be used to negotiate steep or even vertical sections.

Spur a ridge projecting from the main body of a mountain.

Talus slope a slope consisting of stones and gravel. Also called scree.

Travertine porous limestone precipitated from natural waters, mostly by springs and waterfalls.

Wadi Arabic name for any sort of valley.

Index

Map Legend

——	main road	⌇	contour
—	secondary road	300	elevation (m)
- - - - ·	track	~	wadi (flowing or dry)
⌐⌐→	end of road or track	✕	waterfall or dry fall
⨯	bridge	⫱	narrows, gorge
·······.	trek route	⟿	canyon with a fall at its head
•	point of interest	ʃᵣ	col, saddle
▲	summit, hill	◇	lake, sea
■ ■	settlement	⁖	nature reserve
∴	archeological site		